IMAGES
*of America*

# RICHWOOD

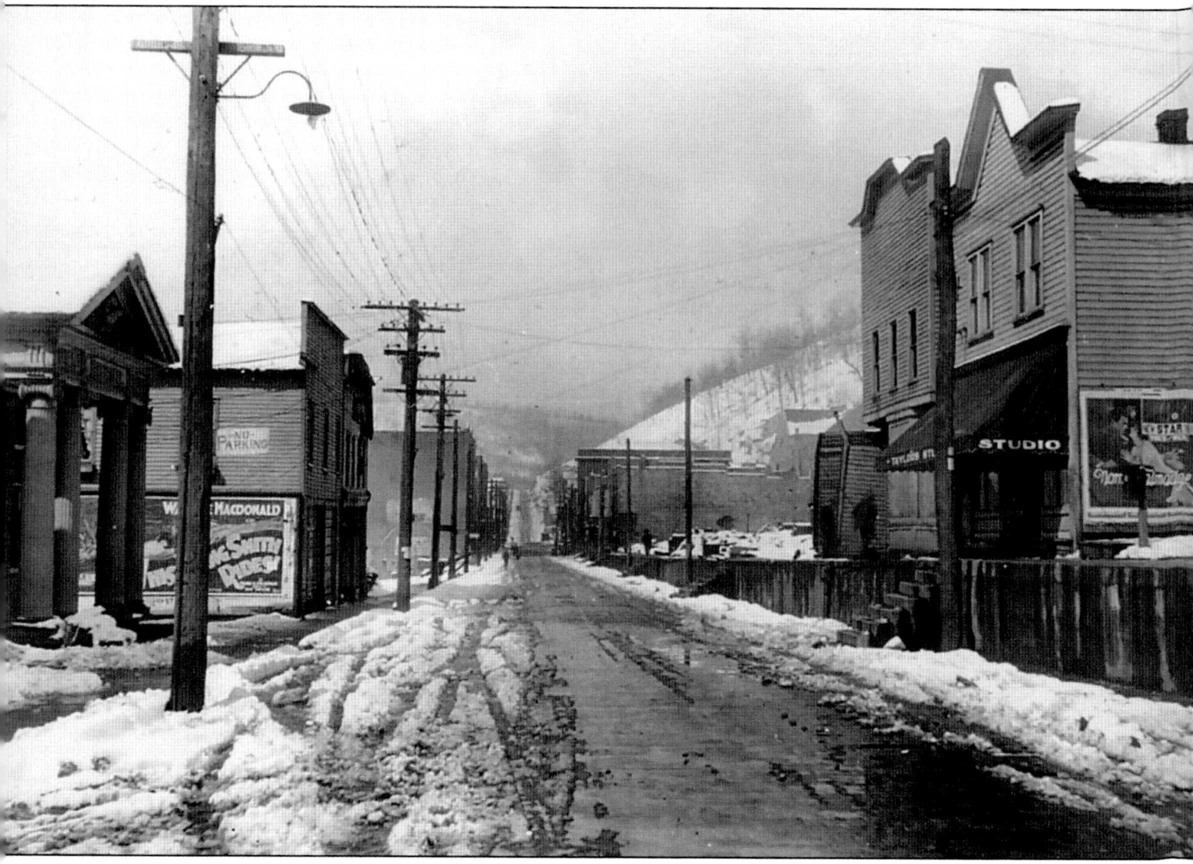


The images that make up this pictorial regional history of the heyday of Richwood, West Virginia, constitute a somewhat unique *Images of America* volume in that nearly all of the images are the work of one photographer, Finley Taylor. Taylor was a studio photographer for approximately 50 years of the town's first century of existence, and there is hardly any aspect of the town's early life that he didn't record. The photograph above of his studio on East Main Street shows how close we may have come to losing his early work. The catastrophic fire of 1921 came within one building of burning his studio and all of its precious contents. Firemen dynamited the building two doors up the street from his studio to make a firebrake to stop the advance of the fire. This photograph was taken *c.* 1925. A few buildings on both sides of Main Street nearest the corner of Oakford Avenue and Main Street have been rebuilt, but large gaps still remain where businesses once stood.

IMAGES
*of America*

# RICHWOOD

Luther D. Baker

ARCADIA
PUBLISHING

ISBN 978-0-7385-1518-2

Published by Arcadia Publishing
Charleston, South Carolina

Printed in the United States of America

Library of Congress Catalog Card Number: 2003101431

For all general information contact Arcadia Publishing at:
Telephone 843-853-2070
Fax 843-853-0044
E-Mail sales@arcadiapublishing.com
For customer service and orders:
Toll-Free 1-888-313-2665

Visit us on the Internet at www.arcadiapublishing.com

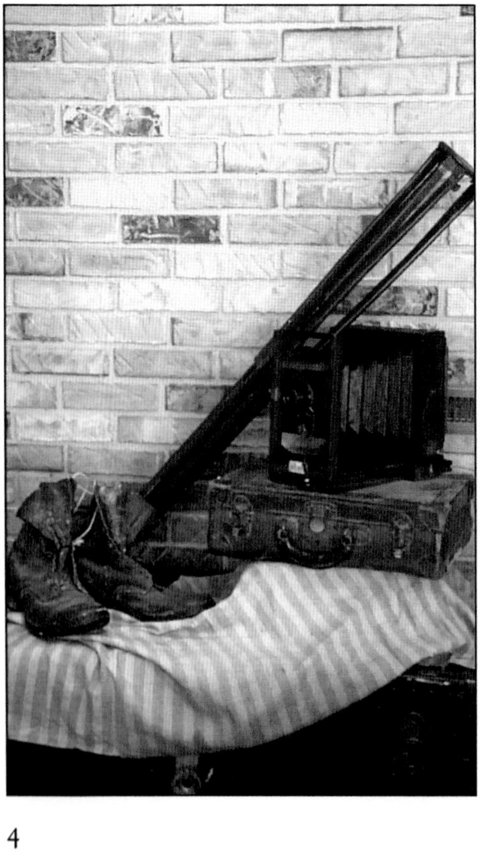

The half-century's worth of negatives Finley Taylor left behind reveal that he, like many studio photographers, earned most of his income from studio portraits. In addition to taking portraits of nearly every person in Richwood, many individuals from nearby communities and towns traveled to his studio to have their portraits made. To our great fortune, he also traveled outside his studio to photograph special events, people in their home and work environments, and especially, people in logging camps. Judging from the large number of photographs he took of individuals, work crews, and families working in logging operations in the area, the logging industry must have been his favorite subject. Most of his work outside of the studio was 5-by-7 inch format. He sometimes used 3-by-5 inch format when he intended for the image to be printed onto a postcard. With this size format he could make a contact print directly from the negative and eliminate the need to use a photographic enlarger in the printing process. In the photograph to the left are Finley's "1000 Mile Wolverine" coon hunting boots, his Rochester Optical Company 5-by-7 view camera, head cloth, camera case, and tripod.

# Contents

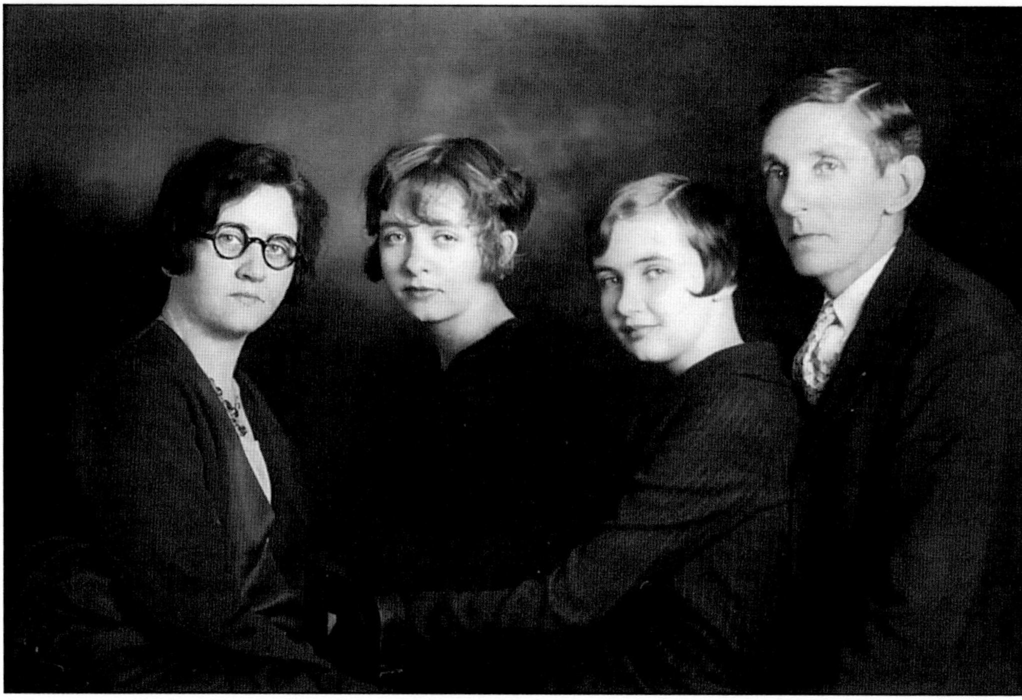

Above is a Finley Taylor family portrait. From left to right are his wife Ethel, his daughters Marie and Maureen, and Finley himself. All are deceased. Finley died on February 13, 1976 at the age of 89. It was Maureen who passed her father's negative collection to me after his death. At the time, I was the closest person living in the town who was filling his shoes as the town photographer. I did professional freelance work form my home on Oakford Avenue during the nearly 10 years I taught at Richwood High School. I photographed many of the town's weddings during this period. I also took high school year book photographs, passport photographs, and commercial photographs. Ironically, I never met Finley although he lived only a couple of blocks from me. Although I had no connection with him, the countless hours I have spent in going through his negatives, making prints from them, and searching for information about the subjects in the prints, I feel like I have worked for him. At the very least, I have come to view him as a kindred spirit.

# INTRODUCTION

Before 1900, Cherry Tree Bottoms at the forks of Cherry River in Nicholas County, West Virginia, was as isolated as Cades Cove in the Great Smoky Mountains of Tennessee. The roads leading to this river bottom from the east and west more closely resembled animal paths than wagon roads. Both routes approached along the mountain ridges forming the narrow river valley. To get to the forks, travelers had to cross numerous rivers and small streams. There were no bridges, so travelers had to ford the places where the road crossed shallow water or utilize one of the few river ferries for deep-river crossings.

Cherry Tree Bottoms was at the edge of a virgin wilderness lying to the north and to the east. Land speculators had gobbled up most of the land in the 1880s, aware of the potential value of the timber and underground minerals. Commercial logging operations began before 1900 in Nicholas and surrounding counties. Land close to the main rivers was timbered and logs floated down the streams to mills and markets during times of high water. Sometimes splash dams were built to raise water levels and were then released to float the logs. The timber in the upper reaches of the streams' water sheds could not be harvested economically because the distance to streams large enough to float the logs was too great.

In 1900, only three small farms populated by 24 individuals existed in Cherry Tree Bottoms. That same year, the Baltimore and Ohio Railroad reached the forks. In return for this investment, Cherry River Boom & Lumber Company had signed an agreement to construct a band saw mill, which was completed in 1901. The number of individuals living at the forks after the mill started up was sufficient enough to warrant the incorporation of a new town appropriately named Richwood. The town grew rapidly, boasting a population of 3,061 citizens in 1910. This number would more than double at the town's population peak in the 1930s.

Harvesting this vast expanse of virgin timber was expedited by a machine, an invention of Ephriam Shay of Lima, Ohio. Shay's invention was a steam-powered locomotive with a drive-gear mechanism that applied direct traction on the rails from all of the engine's wheels. The shay engine, as it was called after its inventor, had the power and traction to pull heavy loads along steep grades of up to 14 percent. Cherry River built many miles of railroads from the end of the Baltimore and Ohio main line into its timber holdings. The company bought and leased more timber property, eventually owning more than 200,000 acres of timberland covering portions of five counties.

The vast amount of timber the company owned and its facilities for delivering it to Richwood attracted other industries based on wood processing. In 1901, the Dodge Clothes Pin factory (later called the Steele-Wallace Corporation) constructed in Richwood the largest wooden clothes pin factory in the world. Cherry River Boom and Lumber Company supplied the factory with beech and maple logs for the manufacture of their clothes pins. Later the factory expanded production to include butter trays. In 1902, the Cherry River Tanning Company (later the Mosser Company) built what was, for a period of time, the largest shoe-sole tannery in the world. It utilized large quantities of hemlock bark the lumber company provided to tan its leather. In 1903, the Sherwood Manufacturing Company built a plant to make wagon hubs from birch logs the lumber company furnished. In 1904, the same corporation in Philadelphia that owned the lumber company built a large paper mill to utilize spruce, hemlock pulpwood, and slabwood from the lumber mill that would otherwise have been wasted. Finally, in 1913, the J.D. Westcott & Sons Company built a plant to manufacture broom handles, dowels, and chair rounds from the beech and maple supplied by the lumber company.

The large mills and plants and the people they employed spawned a thriving small business community. Main Street, the primary east-west avenue, and Oakford Avenue, the main north-south artery, were humming with activity. Yet the roads leading into town were as bad as ever. Only two passenger trains arriving and departing daily were the town's connection to the outside world.. It was possible to take a train excursion trip to Washington, D.C. and back in less time than it took to drive to towns in neighboring counties.

Among the small businesses that operated in Richwood between the two great wars were several photography studios. These included the Palace Studio, Elite Studio, Clarke Studio, and Taylor Studio (later The Art Studio). Seldom did the studios include their name on the prints they made and seldom were they given credit when their photographs were published. It was also rare for them to advertise their businesses in local newspapers. Consequently, it has been difficult to establish the exact years these studios were operating. I have established that Finley Taylor was working as early as 1912 and as late as 1949 when he took a portrait of me as a four-year-old in his studio on East Main Street.

Finley Taylor died in 1976 at the age of 89. After his death, his daughter Maureen Taylor Justice called me and offered to sell what was left of the contents of his studio. I could not afford to pay her what the material was worth, and so I referred her to other individuals who could. The next summer, Mrs. Justice called me again and informed me that she still had the material and insisted that I come to her home and look at it. When I arrived, she directed me to the basement where there were several boxes of negatives and old cameras. It was clear that she wanted me to have the material and getting top-dollar for the items was not her main concern. I believe she felt I would appreciate her father's work and hoped that I would preserve the images for posterity and bring them into public view so others might appreciate his work.

This book is one of a number of past and future projects that I hope fulfill Mrs. Justice's expectations. It is a view of Richwood during its lumbering heyday through the eyes of a fine small-town photographer who plied his trade for a generation. It is not intended to be a comprehensive pictorial history of Richwood for the period. I have tried to take a selection of the images from Finley Taylor's negatives and tell as much of the story as can be told with them. The real story lies in the people portrayed in the photographs. They were, are, and always will be some of the kindest, most hospitable people you could ever meet . . . these Richwooders. This book is for you, Maureen.

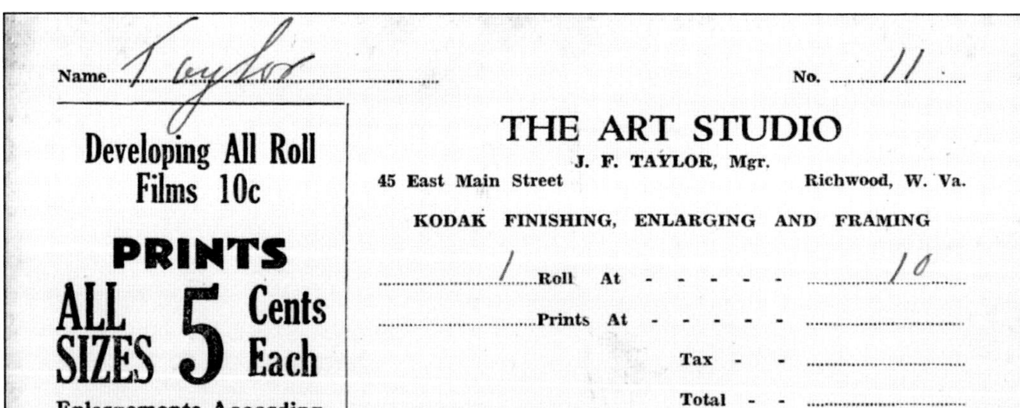
Name Taylor

No. 11

Developing All Roll Films 10c

PRINTS

ALL SIZES 5 Cents Each

Enlargements According to Size. All Prints With White Borders.

Our Motto: Service Plus Courtesy

THE ART STUDIO

J. F. TAYLOR, Mgr.

45 East Main Street Richwood, W. Va.

KODAK FINISHING, ENLARGING AND FRAMING

1 Roll At - - - - - - 10

Prints At - - - - -

Tax - -

Total - -

WE MAKE ENLARGEMENTS FROM YOUR FAVORITE NEGATIVES

Order No. 1

# One

# Richwood's Thriving Industries

*"The Shay was the total logging transportation machine: typically weighing between 50 and 100 tons, it could go anywhere, pull almost anything, and was perfectly at ease on the rudes of tracks. In Fact, it is said a Shaly engineer driving his engine at night could always tell if the engine derailed—the ride suddenly got smoother!" William E. Warden,* West Virginia Logging Railroads, *Walsworth Publishing Company, 1993.*

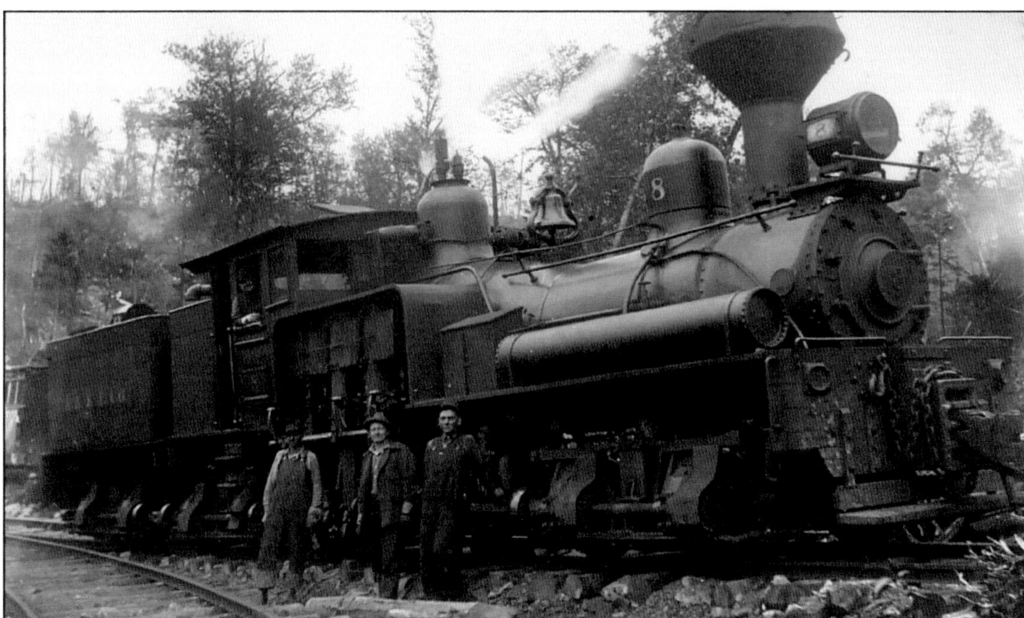

Above is Cherry River Boom & Lumber Company shay engine No. 8 taken at the company's logging operations near Jerryville on Gauley River. The engineer in the train cab is "Big" Jim Conner. Standing in front of the engine, in the middle, is Jimmy Aken. The shay engine is characterized by vertical cylinders on the side of the engine in front of the cab. These drive a horizontal shaft running the length of the engine, providing power directly to all of the wheels. This allowed for the traction to pull heavy loads up very steep railroad grades. The shay made it economical to timber the most remote reaches of the company's vast timber holdings.

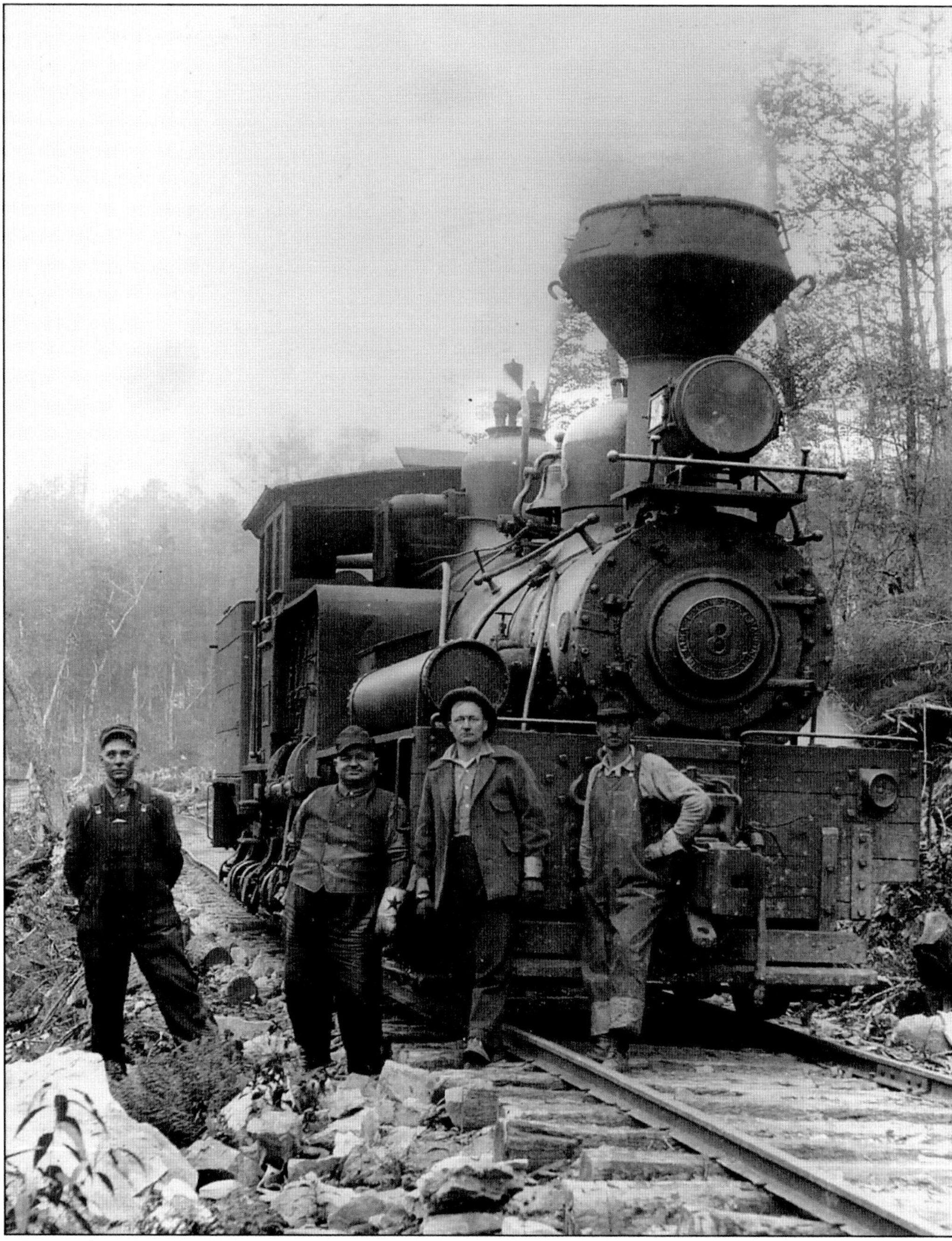

This is the front view of Cherry River Boom & Lumber Company shay engine No. 8. Jimmy Aken, third from the left, is the only man identified. At its peak of operations, the company had nearly 140 miles of railroads extending from the end of the Baltimore & Ohio Railroad mainline in Richwood to the far reaches of its timberlands. It operated nearly a score of steam locomotives including rod engines that were used around the mill yard and on the relatively level grades of its railroads.

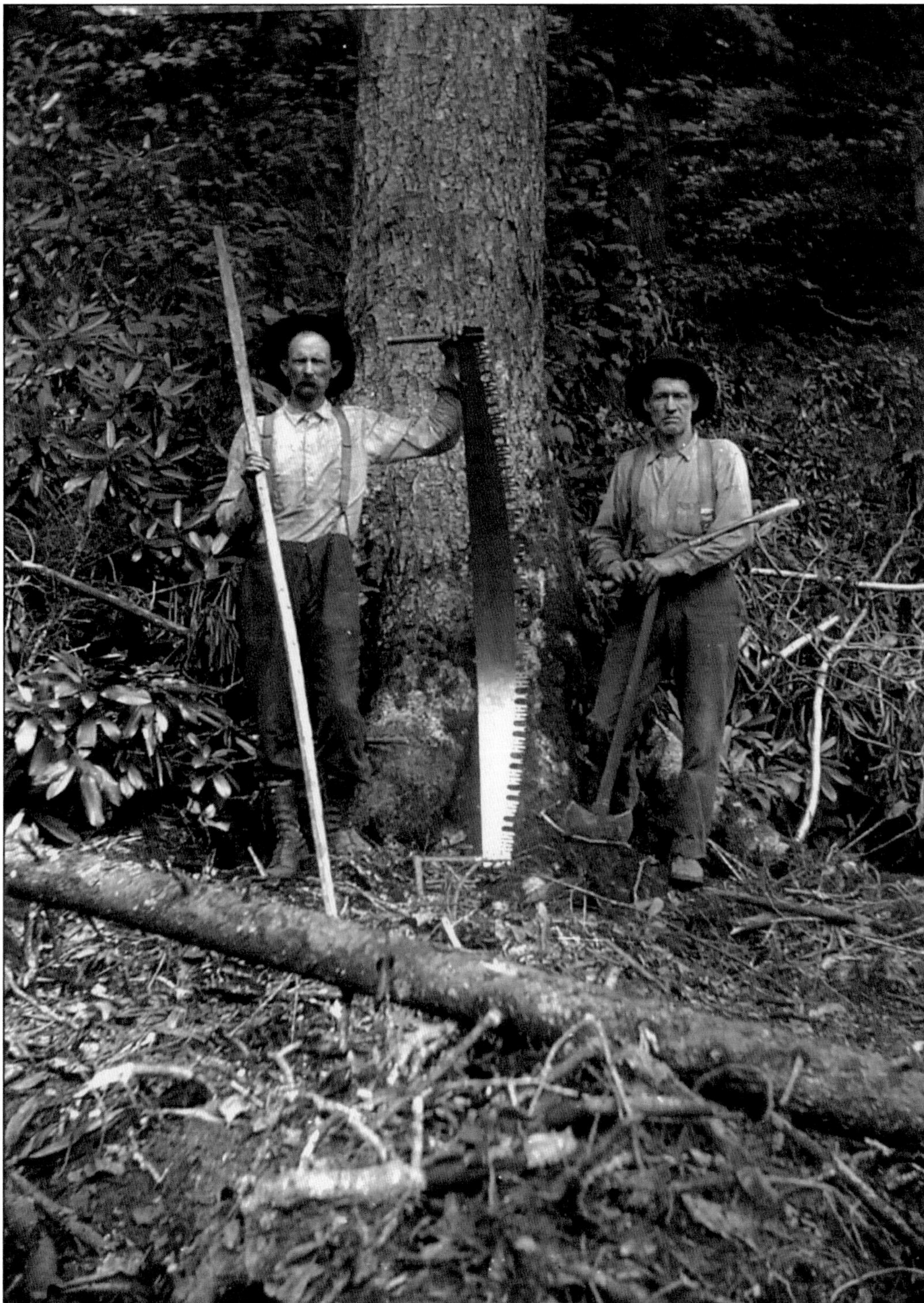

Before the invention of the gasoline-powered chain saw, trees were felled by two-man teams using a cross cut saw, as pictured here. Properly sharpened, two men using a cross cut saw could fell an average-size tree in a remarkably short time.

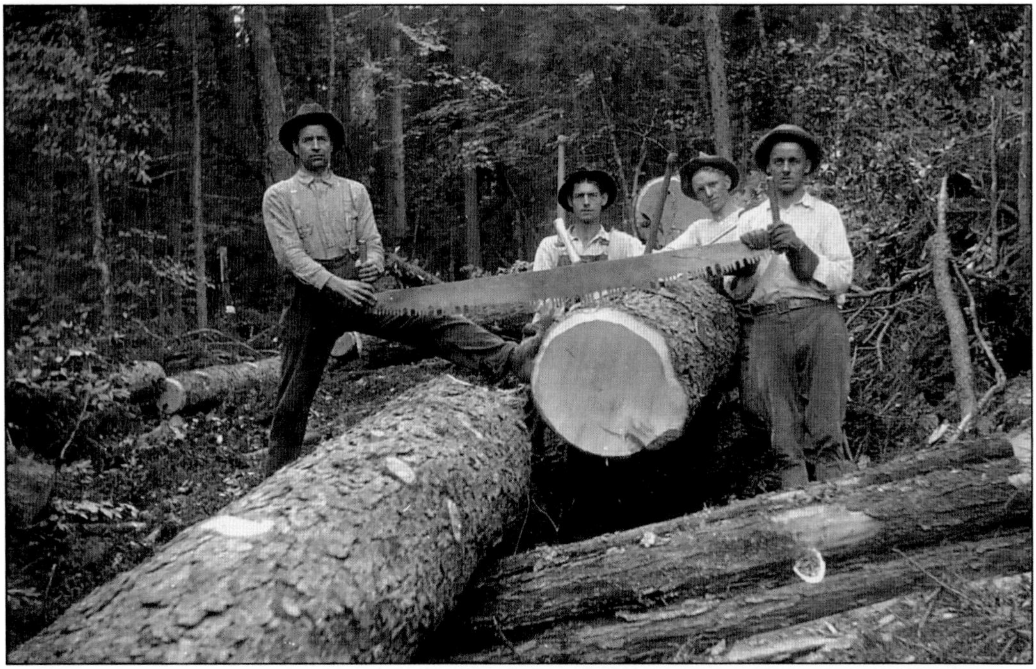

Timber crews were specialized. The men that cut the trees did not trim them of their limbs or cut them into shorter logs. This was the work of the timber buckers pictured here.

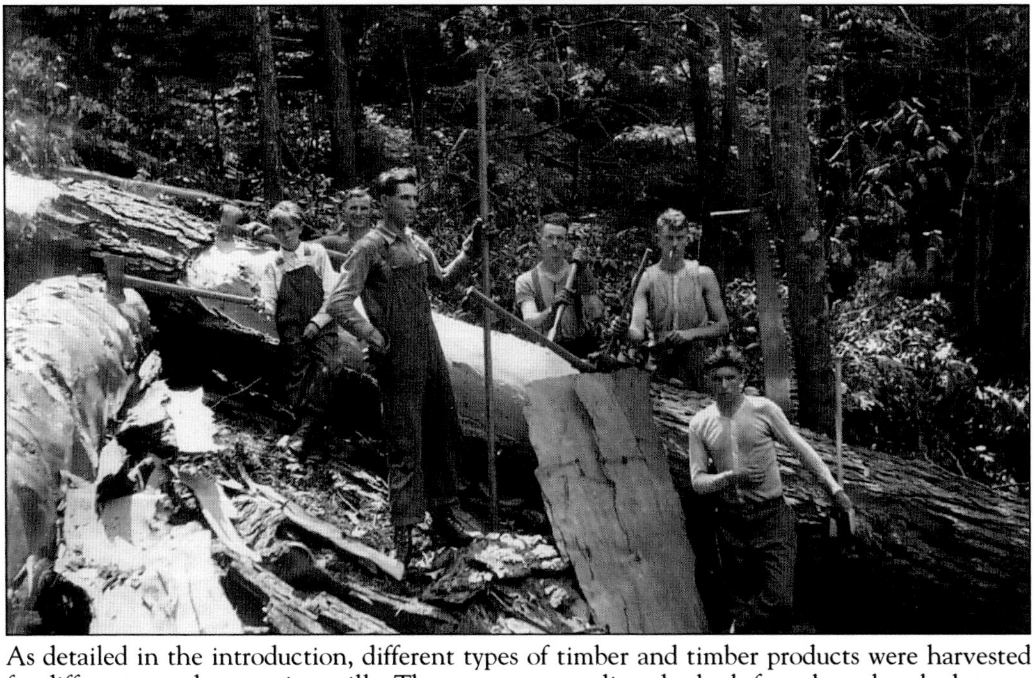

As detailed in the introduction, different types of timber and timber products were harvested for different wood processing mills. These men are peeling the bark from large hemlock trees. The bark will be delivered to the tannery in Richwood for use in turning the raw cowhides into leather. Some of the hemlock trees were left in the woods after the bark was removed. Notice the young boy in the photograph. It wasn't uncommon for children to do some of the lighter work around the woods, such as carrying water to the men.

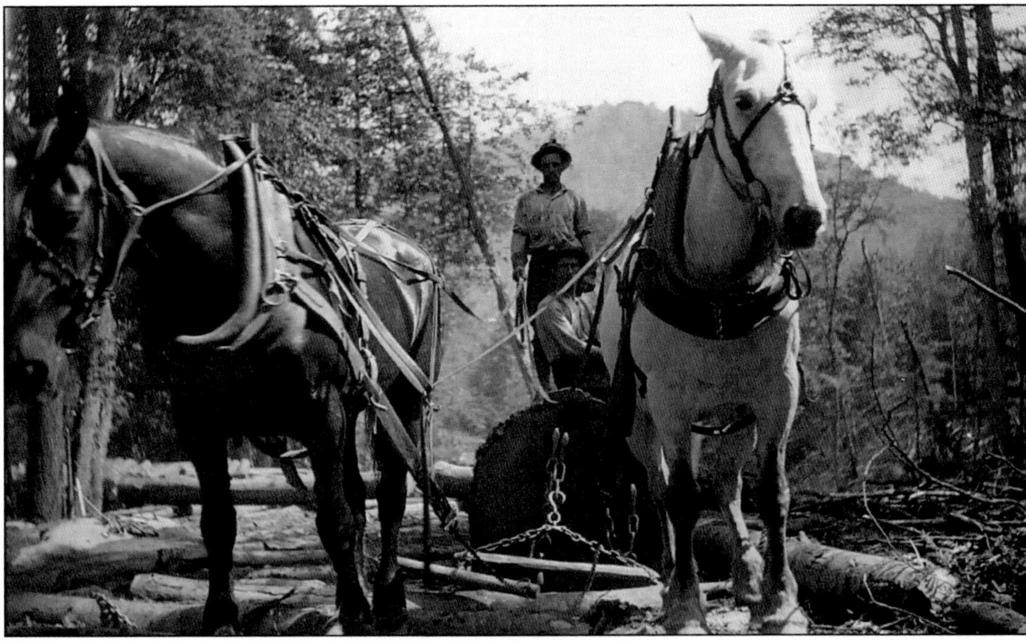

This *c.* 1930 image depicts a horse team and teamster skidding logs to a "rough and tumble" log landing where they will be loaded onto railroad flat cars for their trip to the mill. Skidding logs and working around the log landing was dangerous work. A careless moment could quickly kill or seriously injure a logger.

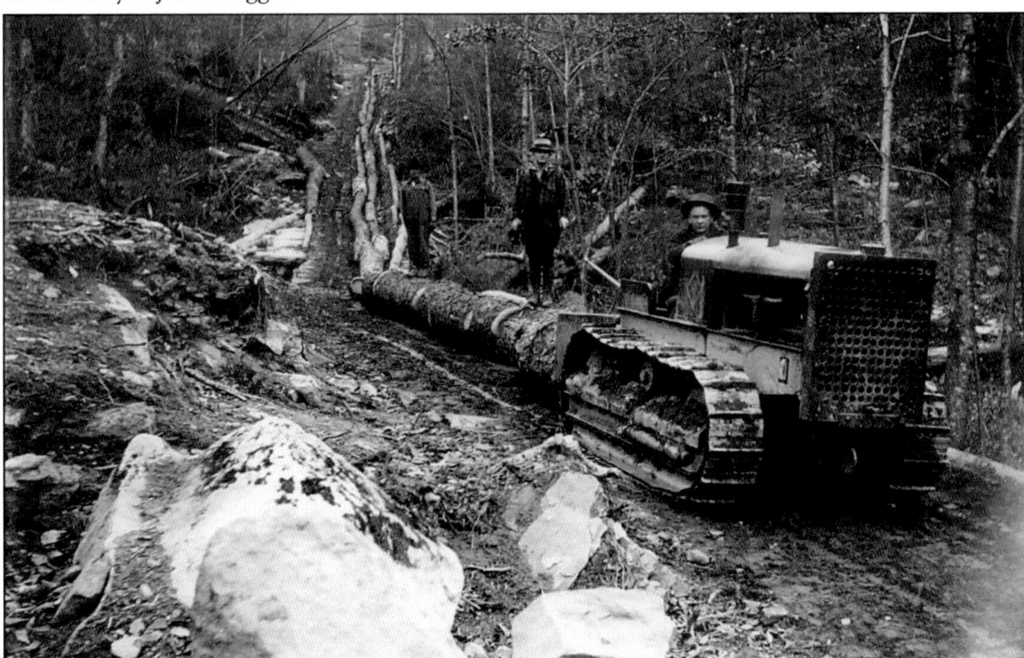

In the later years of its logging operations, Cherry River Boom & Lumber Company and others began using diesel-powered dozers to skid logs to the log landings. Here is a long string of logs being pulled down a skidding road to a log landing. Horse teams were not totally replaced by the dozers—horses continued to be utilized by logging companies well into the 1950s.

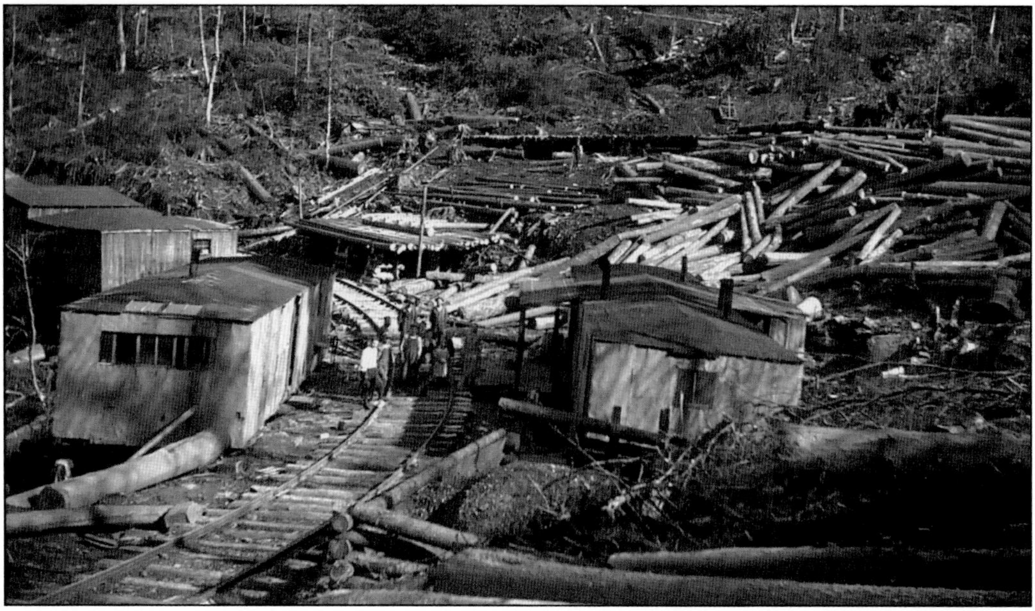

Pictured here is a rough-and-tumble landing containing enough logs to yield many thousands of board feet of lumber when the logs are milled in Richwood. Lumber quantity is measured by board foot units, which is a board 12-inches square and 1-inch in thickness or other dimension with the same 12-cubic-inch volume equivalent. The log shanties are mobile structures brought to the site on flat cars by the shay engines. When the immediate area was timbered and the logs removed to the mill, the shanties were loaded back onto flat cars and moved to the next site. Shanties were rented to men who wanted to have their families with them for $2 per month. For $4 per month, they could have two shanties placed together to accommodate larger families. Families paid the company 50¢ per month for access to the company doctor.

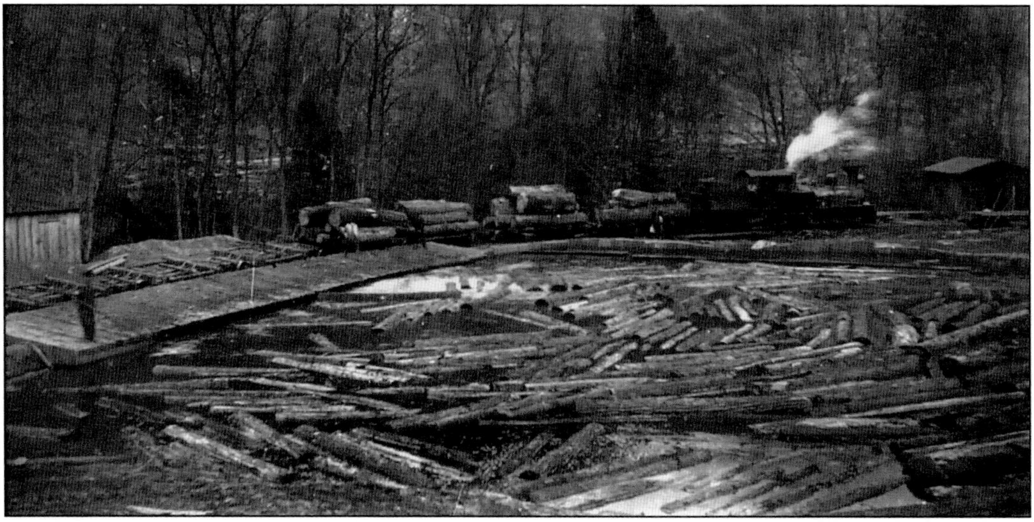

Here is a view of a shay engine nearing the mill with a load of logs destined to be dumped into the mill pond for easy access. Men working on the mill pond pulled the logs to a spiked chain called the jackslip that pulled the logs up an inclined ramp into the second story where the logs were sawed into lumber. Much of the first floor of a steam saw mill was taken up by the drive wheels that powered the many saws that operated on the floor above.

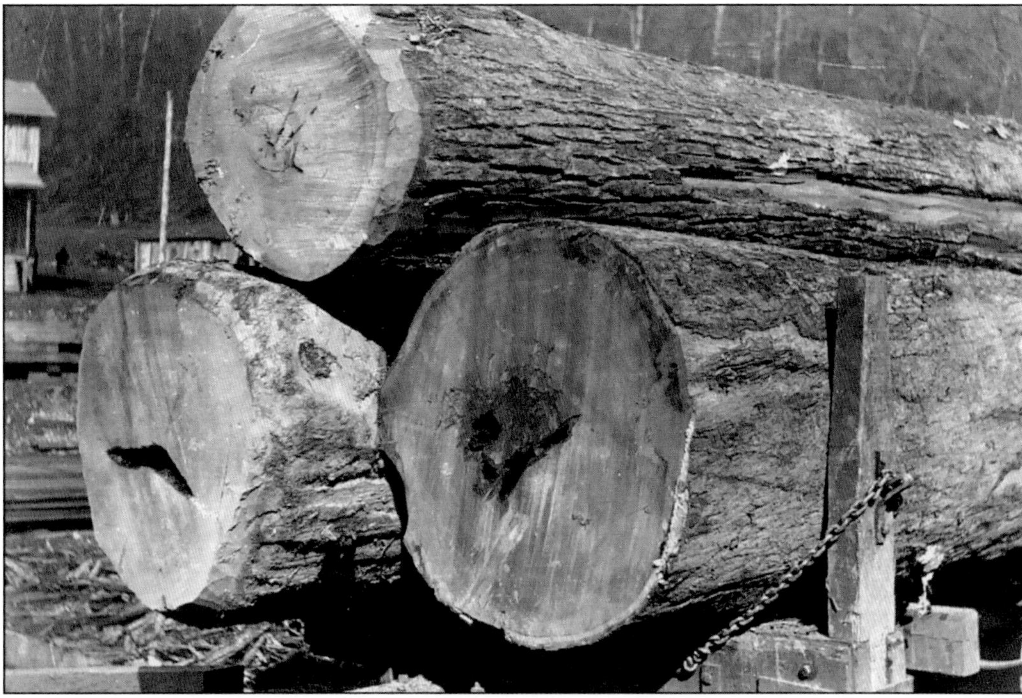

This photograph could almost be mistaken for a logging photograph from the West. Many of the trees harvested in the virgin timber stands were huge. The forests harvested by Cherry River and other companies in the region during the first three decades of the 20th century contained the finest hardwood timber in the world. These were the last virgin hardwood forests east of the Mississippi River. This image is a close-up of one of the log cars shown below.

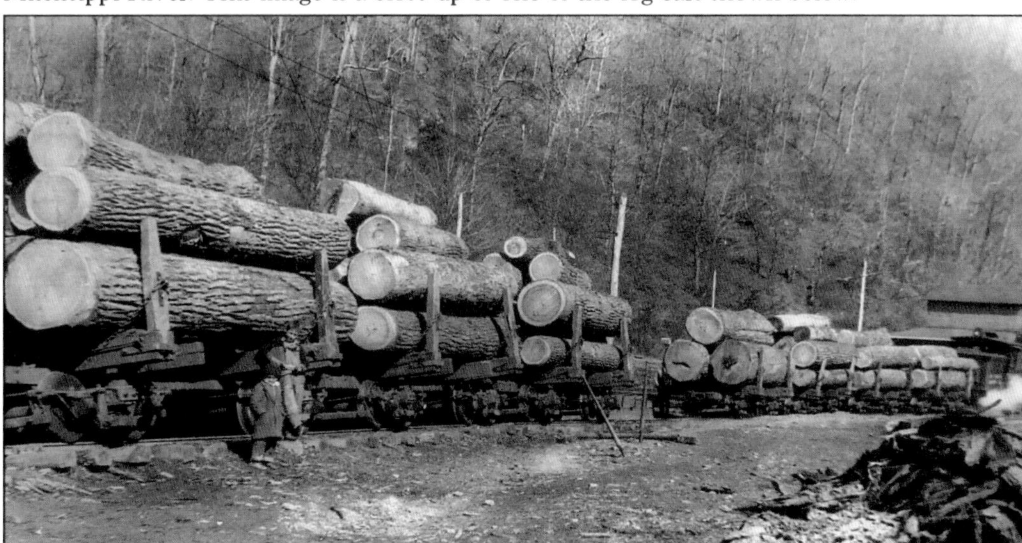

There is some controversy among those who have attempted to identify these two photographs. One theory is that this is a Cherry River Boom & Lumber Company photograph of a train at its Gauley Mills operation, 20 miles west of Richwood in Webster County. Another opinion is that it is an Ely Thomas Lumber Company photograph taken at its mill at Werth in Nicholas County.

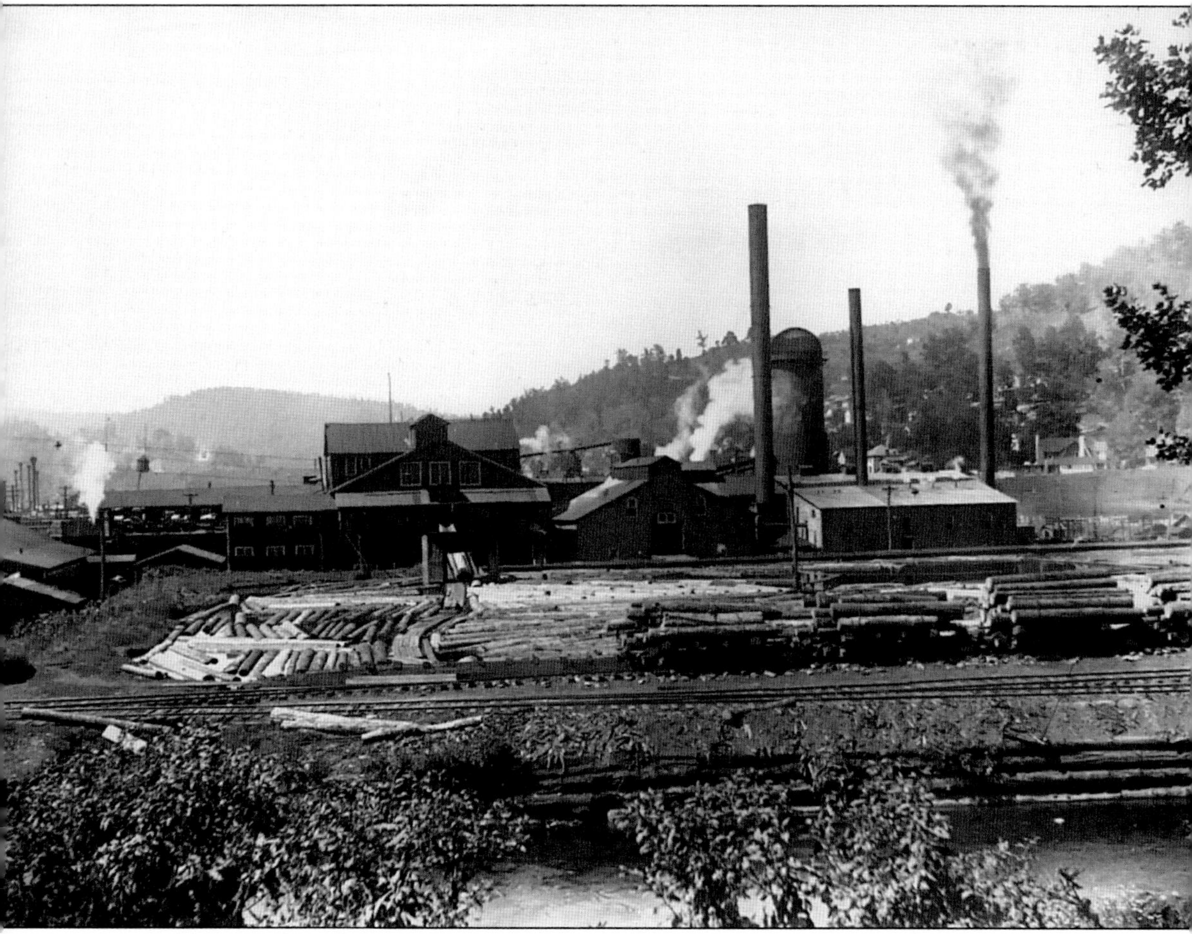

Pictured here is the Cherry River Boom & Lumber Company mill in Richwood, commonly called the "Big Mill" by town residents. While the original 1901 mill was destroyed in a 1924 fire, this photograph was taken after the mill was rebuilt. The mill was reconstructed better than before and was sawing lumber again by May of the following year. The Big Mill and the company's smaller mill at Gauley Mills (20 miles away) together cut 100 million board feet of lumber from the trees on 10,000 acres of land in 1929. This was enough wood to build all of the residences in the state's capital at Charleston!

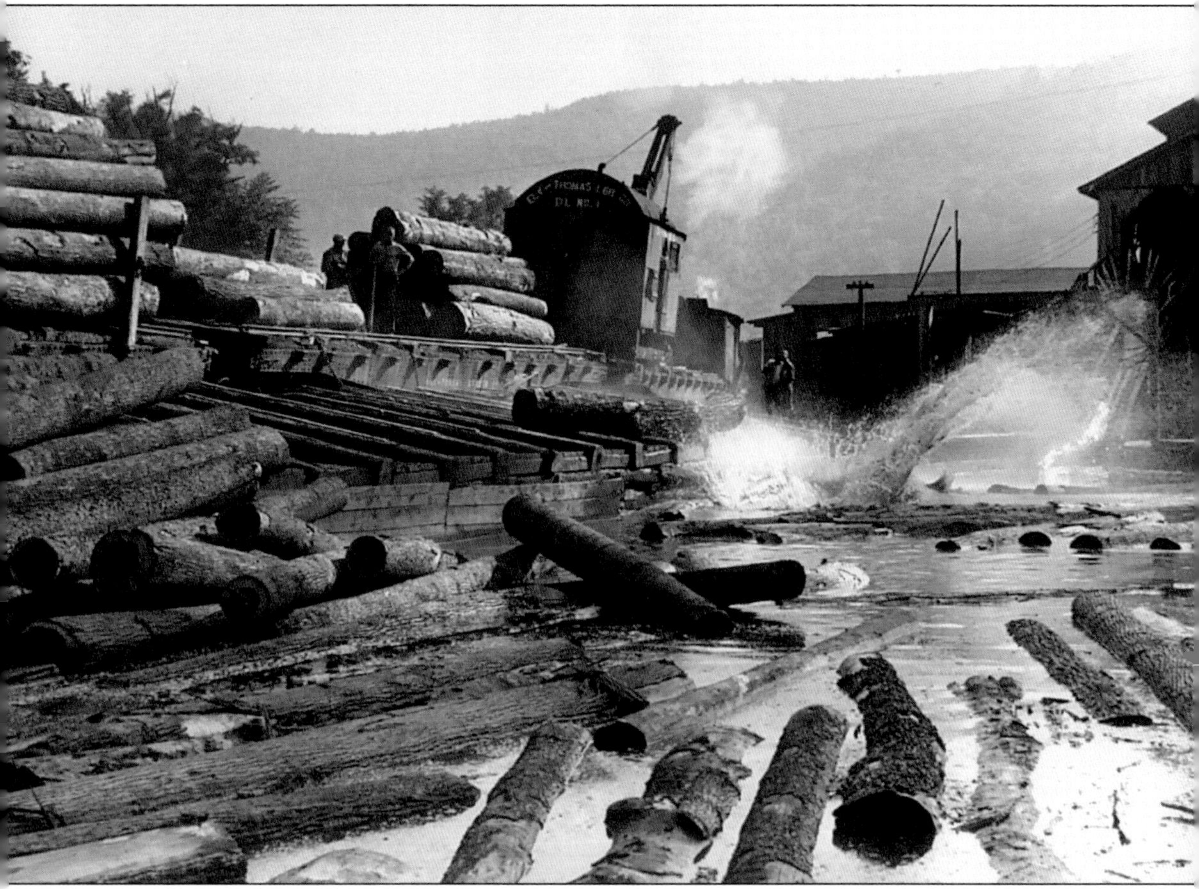

This great photograph captures a moment in time when logs are being dumped into a log pond from a log car. This is one of the very few photographs in chapters one through seven not taken by Finley Taylor. This photograph was taken by James Bradley of Harrisburg, Pennsylvania. The site is the mill pond of Ely-Thomas Lumber Company at Fenwick, three miles west of Richwood. The "pond man" pulled the logs up to the base of the jackslip visible beneath the spray at the extreme right side of the photograph. The jackslip was a wooden inline plane that acted as a ramp up which logs were pulled to the second floor-level of the mill where they were sawed into boards. A heavy chain with metal cleats moved along the bottom of the trough to pull the logs up the incline. The pond man used a 15-foot-long pike with a sharp metal point to pull the logs to the base of the jackslip. Depending on the density of the logs, some floated on top of the mill pond and some sank to the bottom. The pond man could pull even submerged logs to the jackslip with his pike because they were buoyant beneath the water.

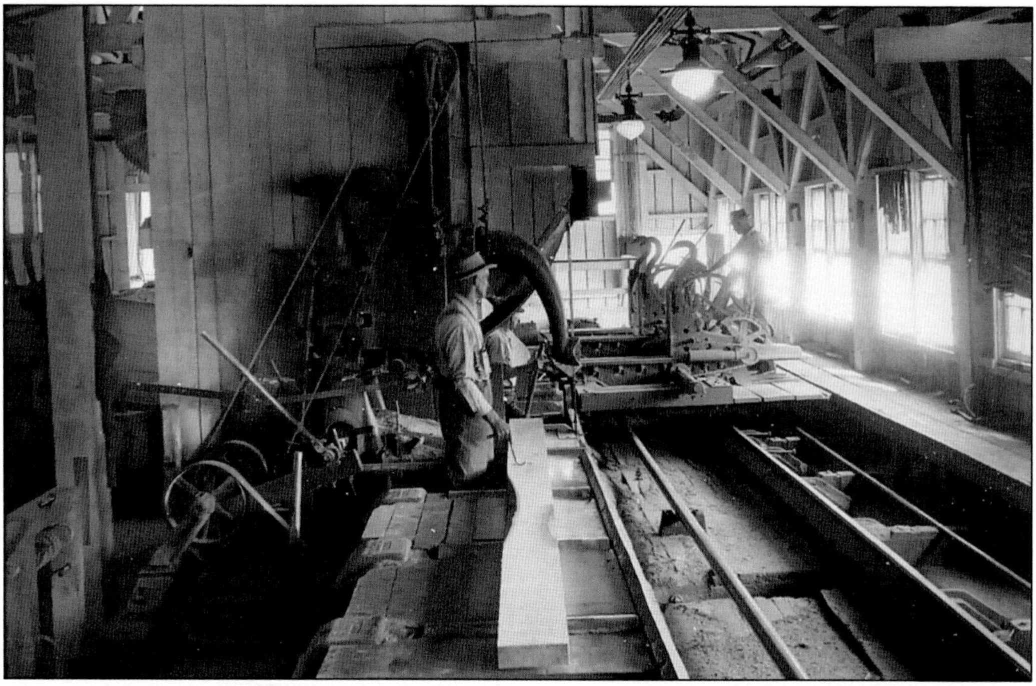

This is the business end of a band saw mill. The logs are anchored on the log carriage like a loaf of bologna on a meat slicer. Two men ride the carriage back and forth as the band saw cuts the boards from the log. They rotate the log back and forth according to the directions given to them by the sawyer standing beside the band saw blade. The sawyer was one of the most skilled jobs in the milling operation. The quality of the lumber being sawed was largely determined by how the log is oriented as it moves through the band saw. His knowledge of lumber and the directions he gave to the carriage men maximized the quality of the lumber. This scene may have been taken at the handle factory rather than the Big Mill.

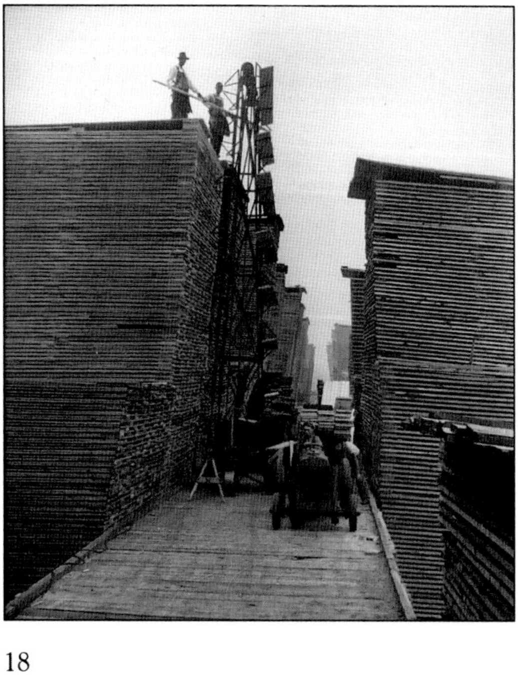

After the lumber was sawed into boards, the boards were taken to the lumber yard where they were stacked to air dry. Lumber was sold in several ways. It was sold as "green" lumber with no processing. It was sold after being kiln dried to low moisture content, planed smooth or unplanned. The company also processed kiln dried lumber into flooring, exterior siding, and interior paneling. The company's advertising slogan was "The Best Lumber."

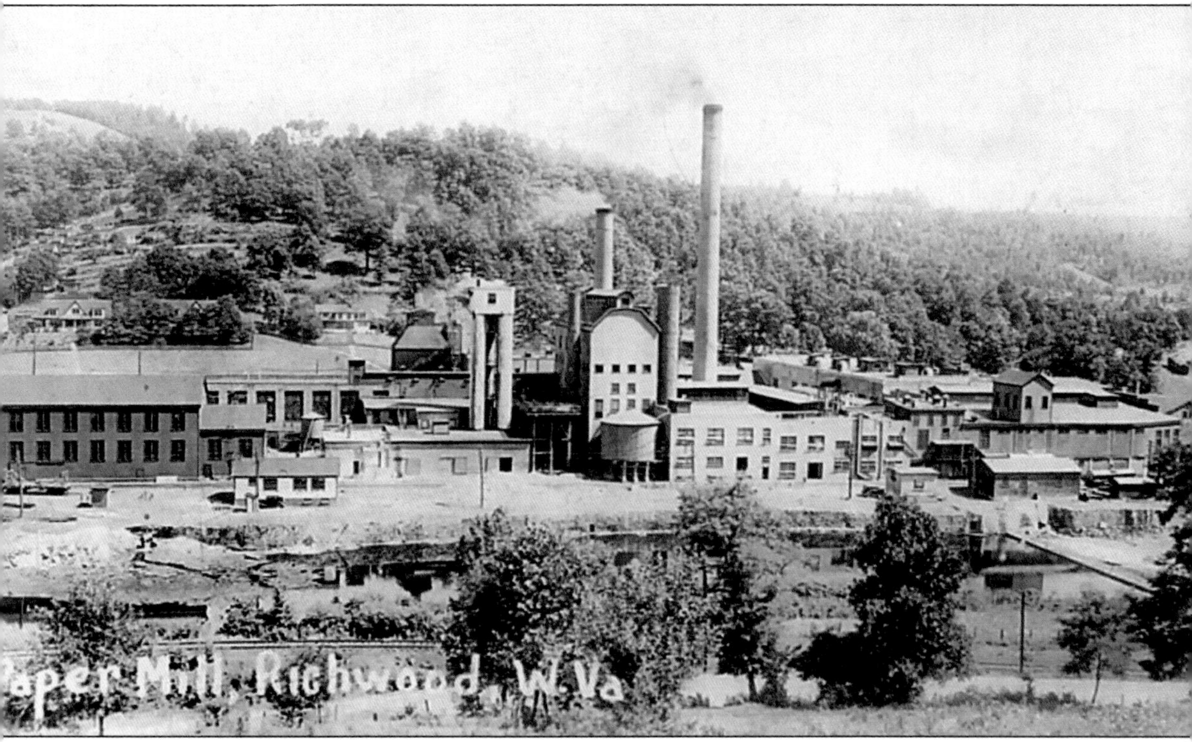


Pictured here is the Cherry River Paper Company mill owned by the same corporation in Scranton, Pennsylvania, that owned Cherry River Boom & Lumber Company. The mill processed hemlock and other low-grade pulpwood not suitable for lumber. It also used the logs slabs from the Big Mill that otherwise would have been wasted. Slabs are the first cuts from a log as the log is being squared in cross section to saw boards.

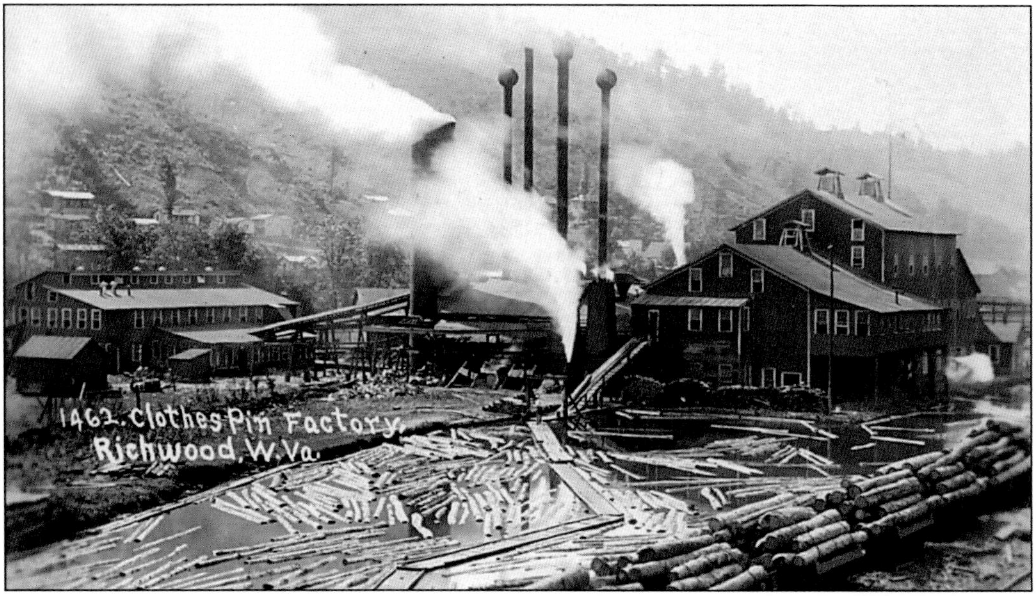


On this page are two views of the largest wooden clothes pin factory in the world during its years of operation through much of the first half of the 20th century. This is the Steele-Wallace Corporation mill. The milling operation started with large logs, which eventually were milled into the relatively tiny clothes pins. Although clothes pins are still used today, the invention of the clothes drier and plastic as a substitute for wood caused the "pin factory," as it was called, to close. The photograph below show the mill pond drained for its annual cleaning of bark from the many logs dumped into it.

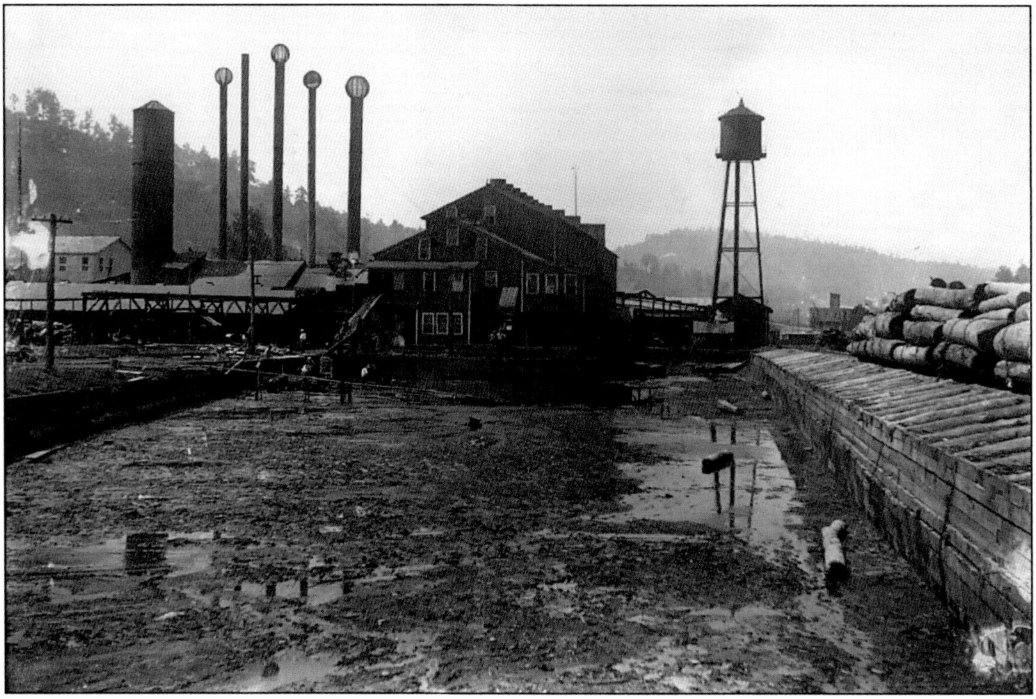

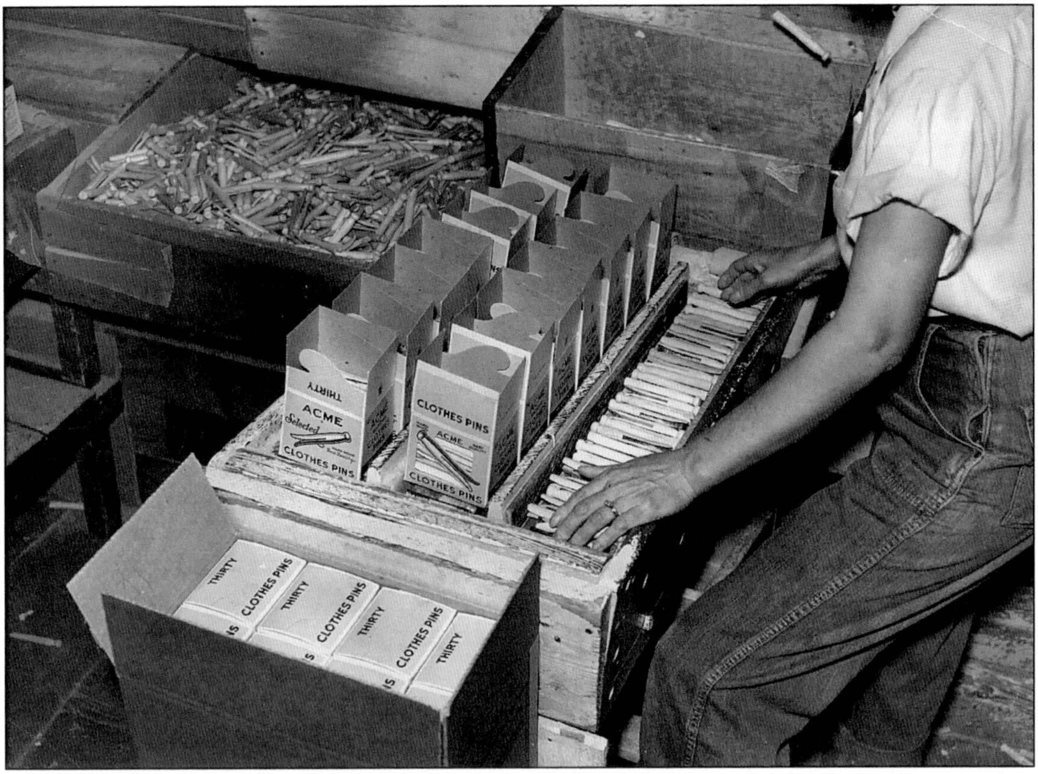


Pictured above is a photograph of the end products of the pin factory wood processing operation. Below is a photograph of some of the machinery located on the first floor that drove the milling machines.

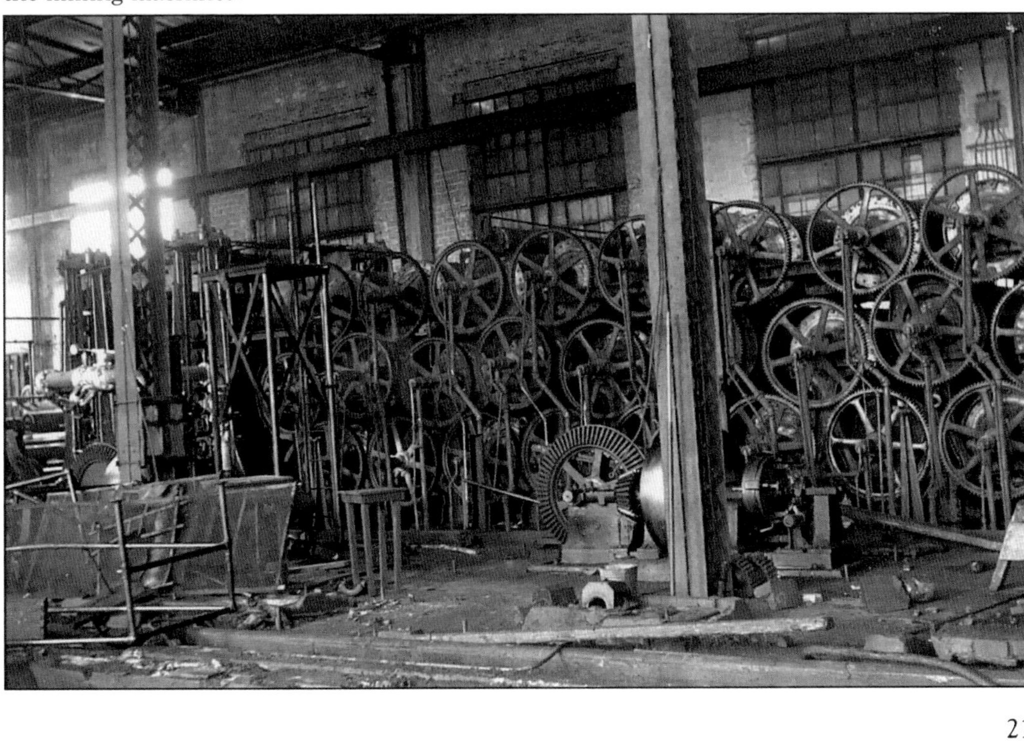

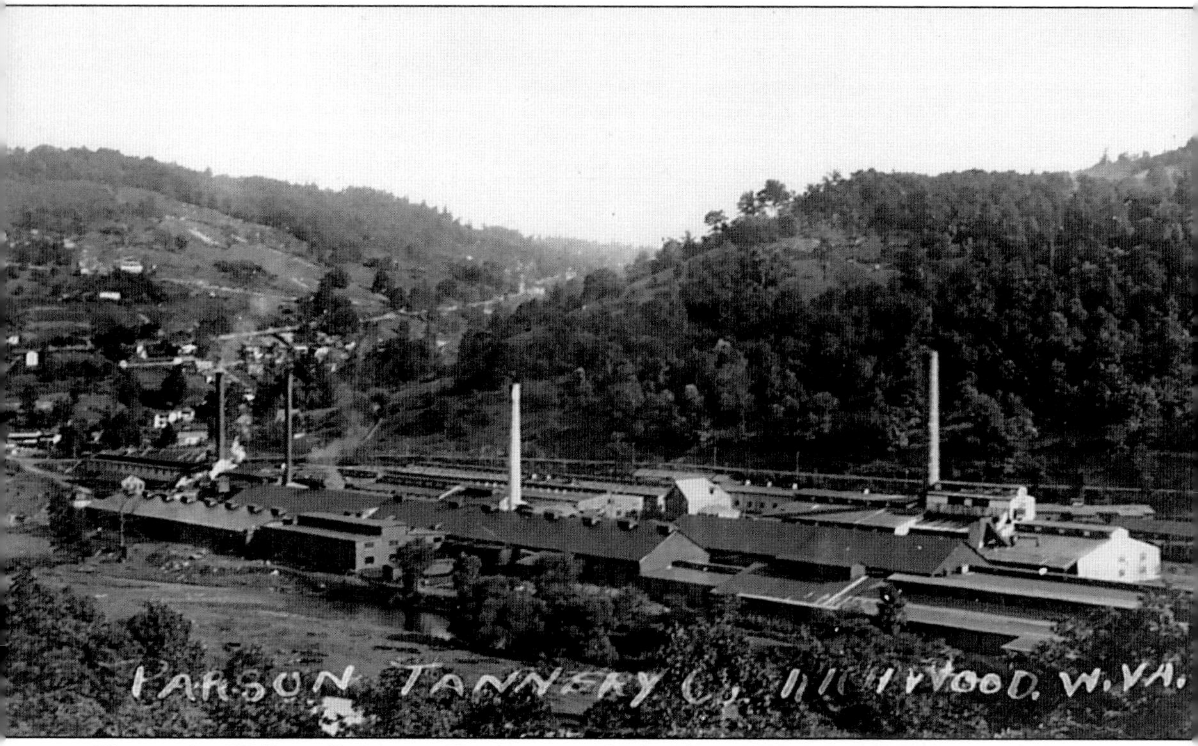


This is the William E. Mosser Tannery to which Cherry River supplied large amounts of hemlock for use in tanning raw cow hides into shoe leather and other products. At its peak, the tannery received many railroad carloads of cowhides per day and shipped out carloads of tanned leather products. It operated with the most advanced equipment available at the time and had two identical production lines. During one period of its production life, this was the largest shoe sole tannery in the world. The tannery was initially built in 1902. It was seriously damaged by a fire in 1906 and rebuilt better than before. It closed after the Depression years when the market was weak and the vast hemlock stands were depleted.

# *Two*

# Bridge and Road Construction

*"Well, do I remember 37 years ago I heard there was some work starting up at Cherry Tree Bottoms so I set out to find the place. I came [to] the road to Macedonia Church in New Hope. I inquired the way and I was told there was a bridle path or hog path around the mountain side that by close watch I might find the way." (Letter to C. Done Cook, editor,* Nicholas Republican, *dated January 2, 1933, from J.S. O'Dell.)*

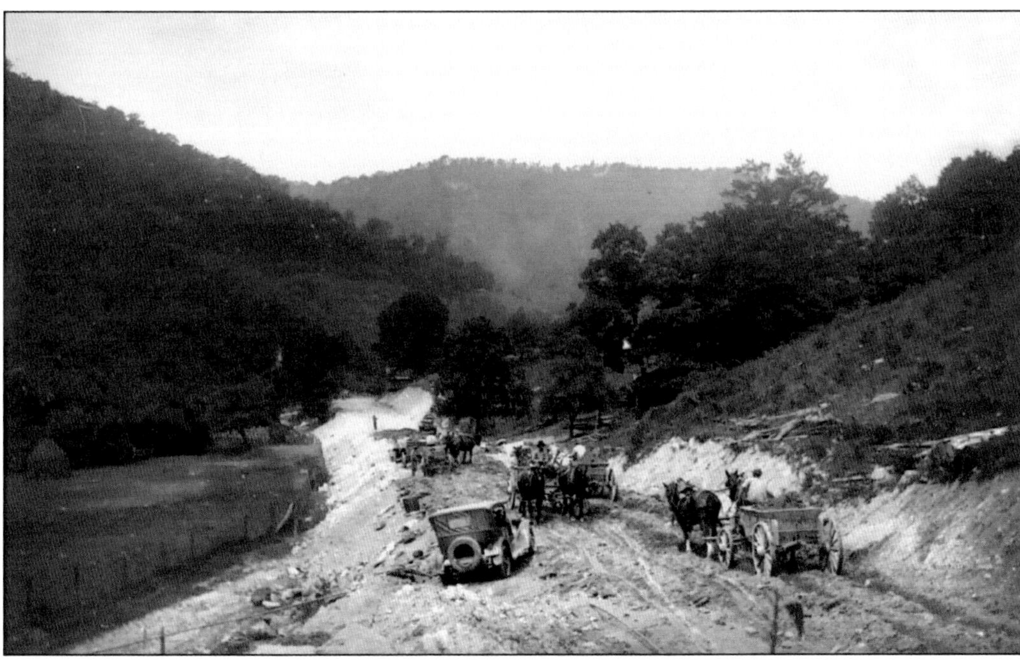

Pictured here is an image of early road building west of the town of Richwood. Notice the dump wagons that were used prior to the availability of dump trucks. The first roads followed animal paths or were laid out to skirt the farms as opposed to taking direct routes that crossed good farmland. Early roads followed the natural contour of the land to avoid the expense of excavating. As the district became more populous and more prosperous, county taxes and local bonds were levied to fund road improvements.

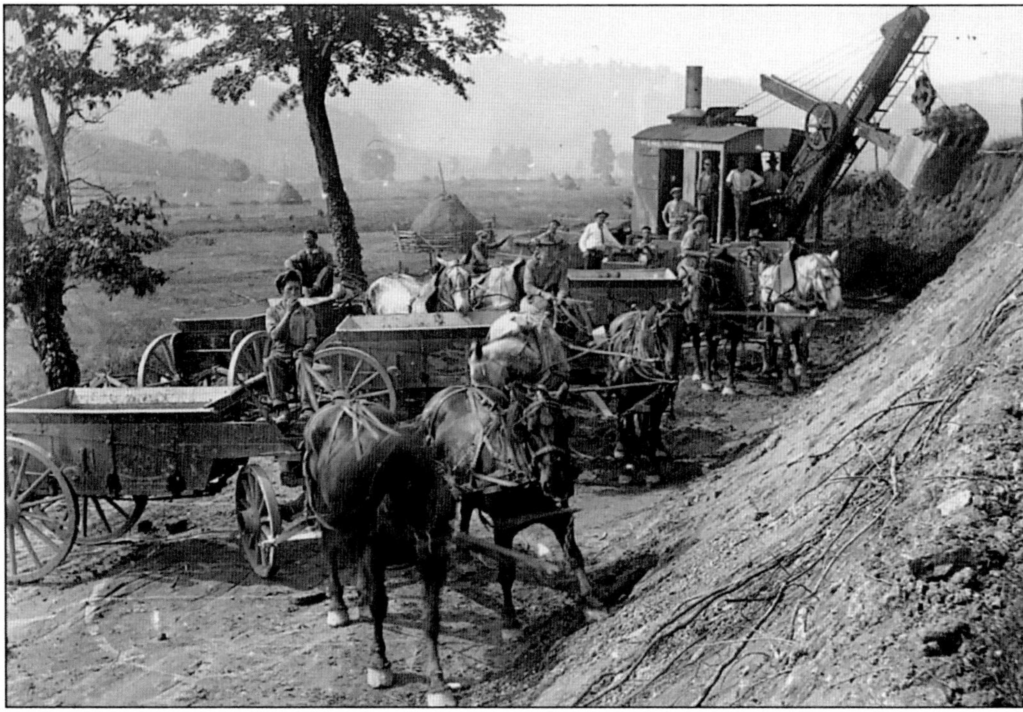

On this page are two images of road construction in the county. This was not the improvement of the existing road; rather, it is believed by the author to be the building of a new section between Persinger Hill to where it connected with old Route 19 four miles north of Summersville. Even the straight portion of this road was costly because the roadway had to be built up above the level of the fields through which it coursed.

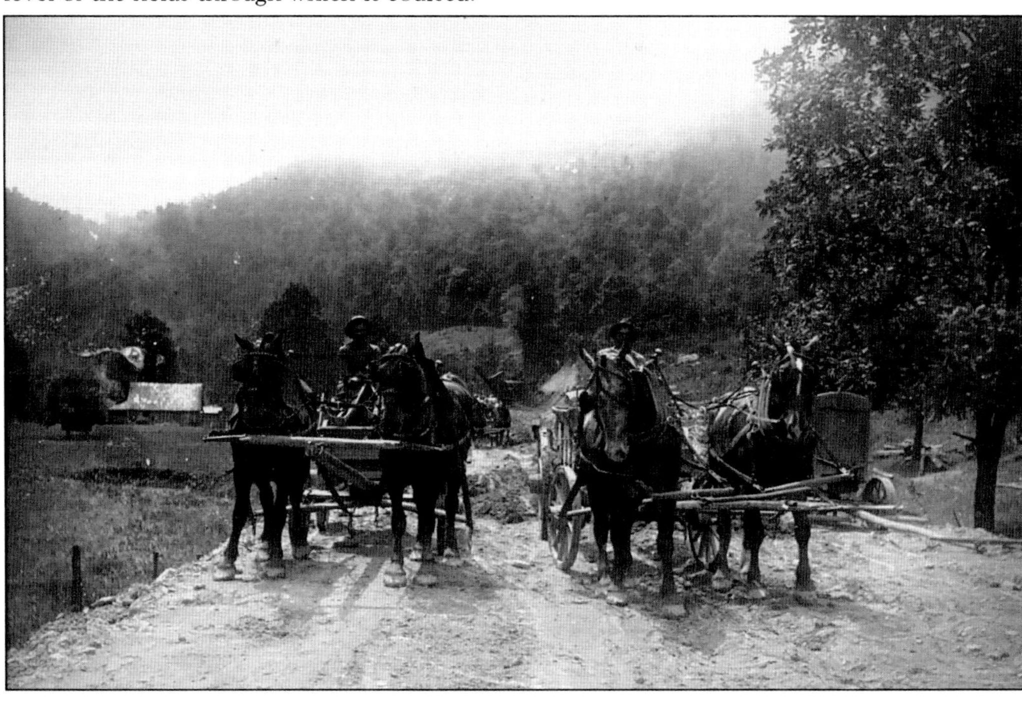

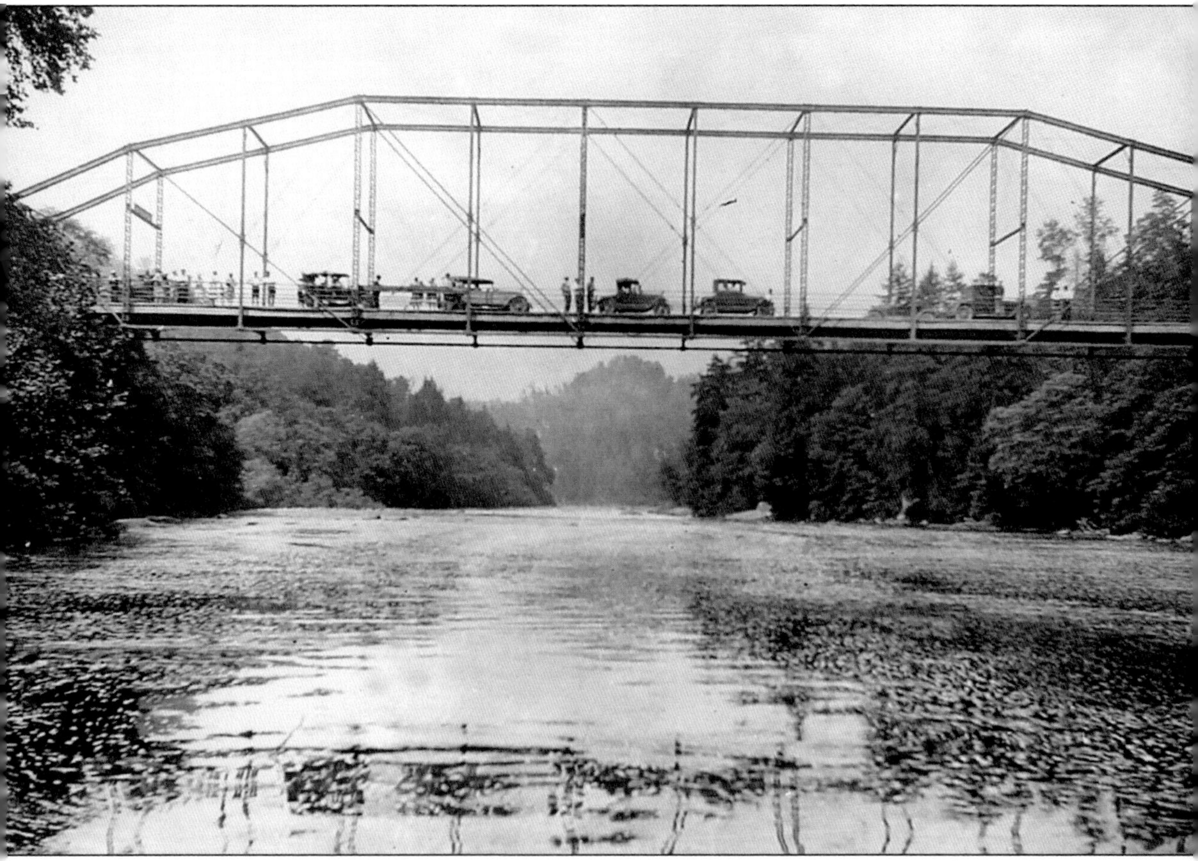

This is a photograph of Brock's Bridge, which was named after the Brock family that operated the river ferry it replaced. Brock's Ferry was one of five river ferries that crossed the Gauley River before bridges replaced them. The other ferries were Carnifax Ferry (of Civil War fame), Hughes' Ferry, Cranberry Ferry (at the mouth of Cranberry River), and Curtin Ferry. Brock's Bridge was torn down and replaced by a new, higher bridge when Summersville Dam was completed.

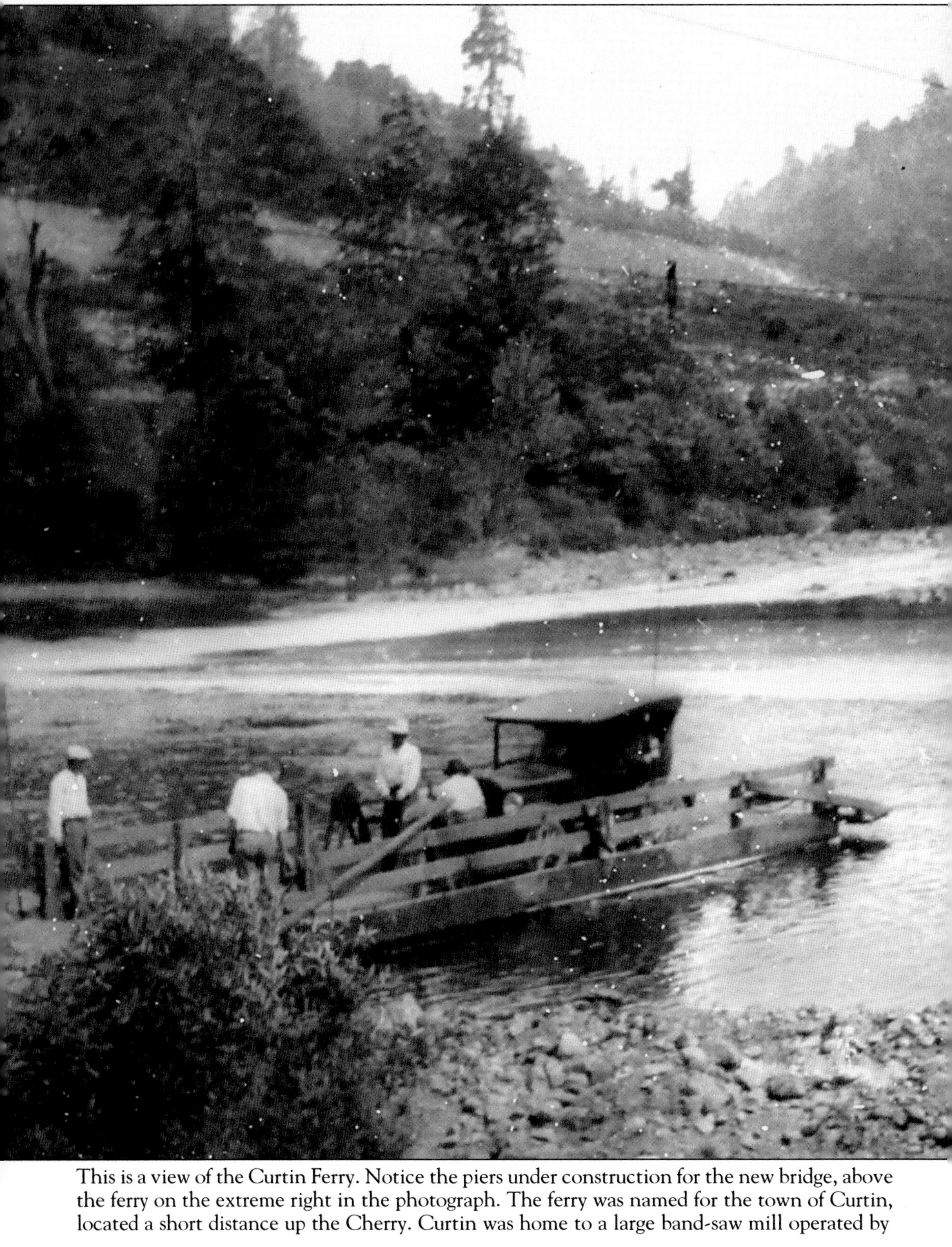

This is a view of the Curtin Ferry. Notice the piers under construction for the new bridge, above the ferry on the extreme right in the photograph. The ferry was named for the town of Curtin, located a short distance up the Cherry. Curtin was home to a large band-saw mill operated by

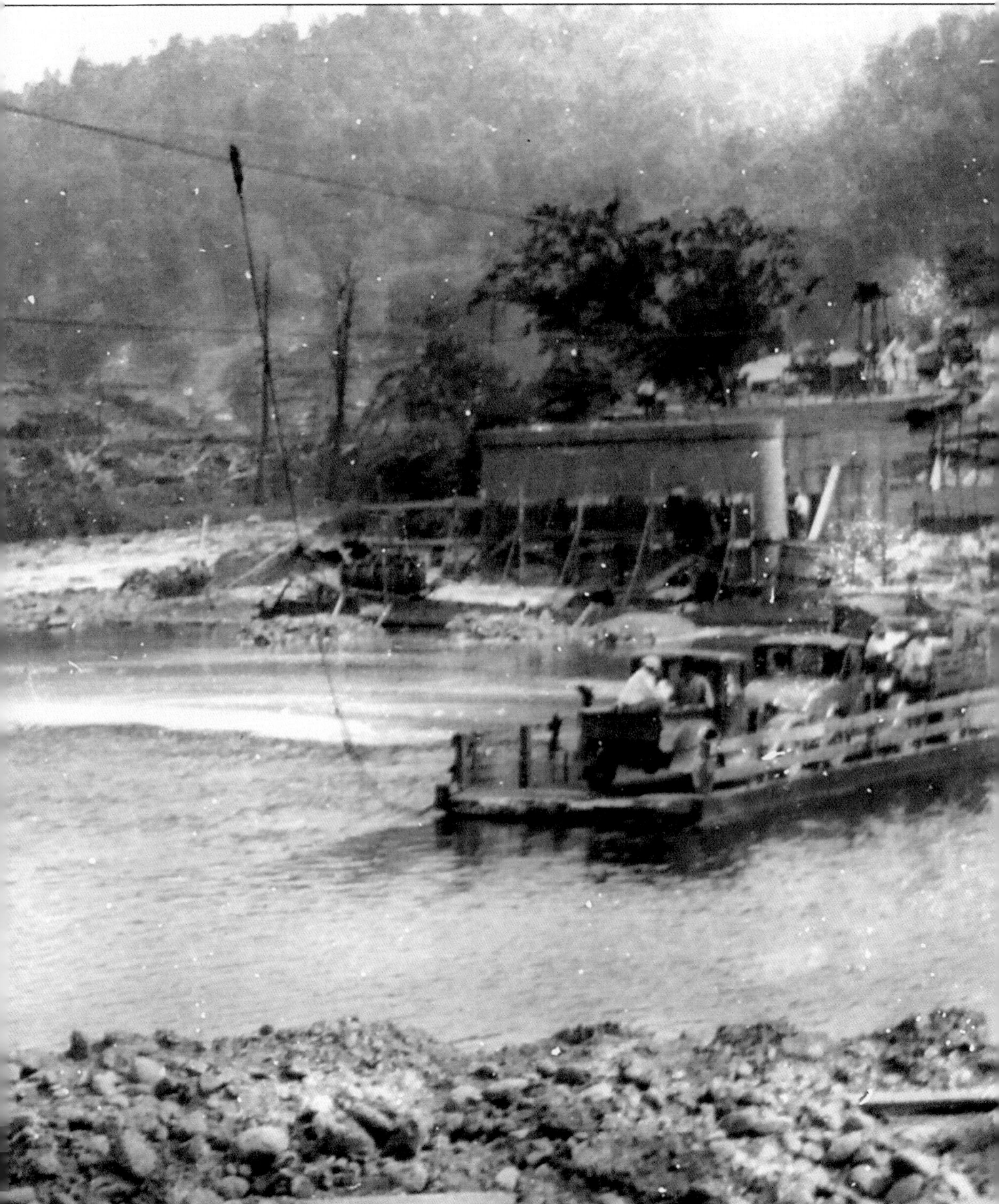

Pardee and Curtin Lumber Company. A second bridge was being constructed concurrently four miles to the east across Cherry River.

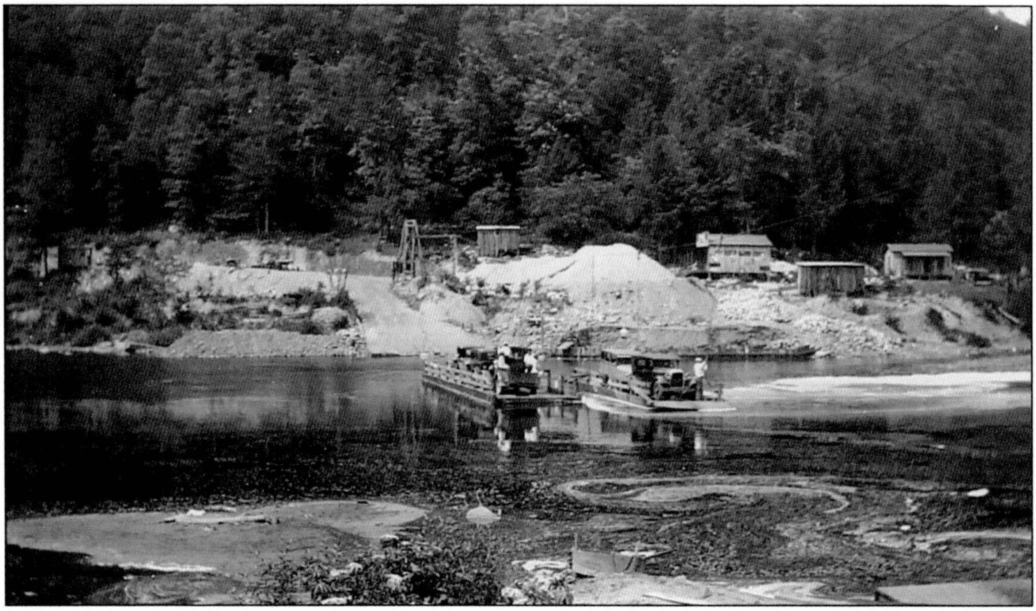

The images on this page are two views of the old Curtin Ferry that carried travelers across Gauley River at the mouth of Cherry River until 1934, when Curtin Bridge was built to replace it. The water level of the river was quite low at the time these photographs were made, probably in late summer. Ferry crossings could be quite dangerous. There were two fatalities recorded at this ferry site. A young man and young woman were drowned when the car they were riding in came onto the ferry at too great a speed and crashed through the boat's railing, sinking to the bottom of the river.

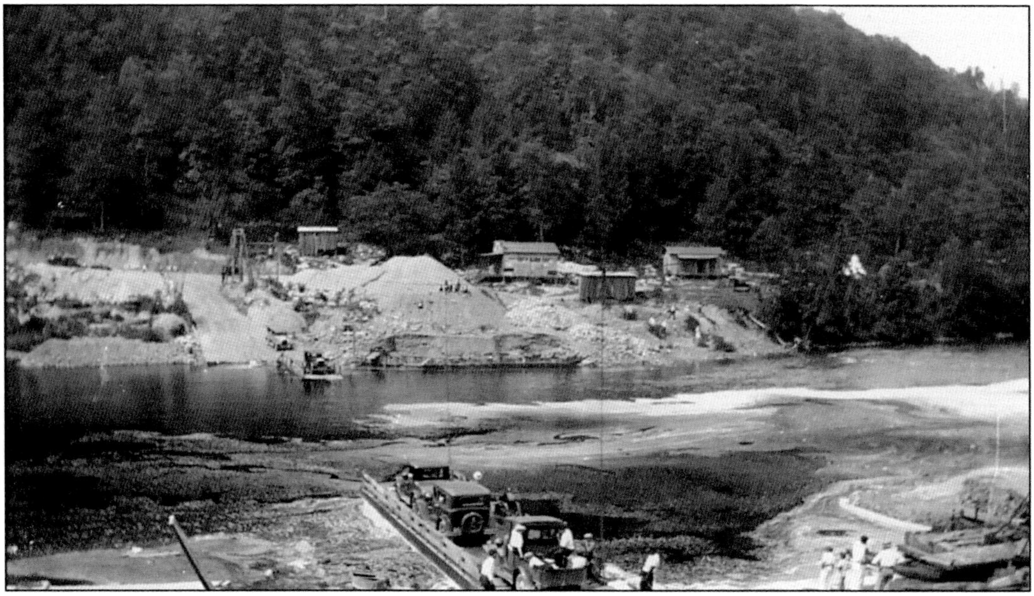

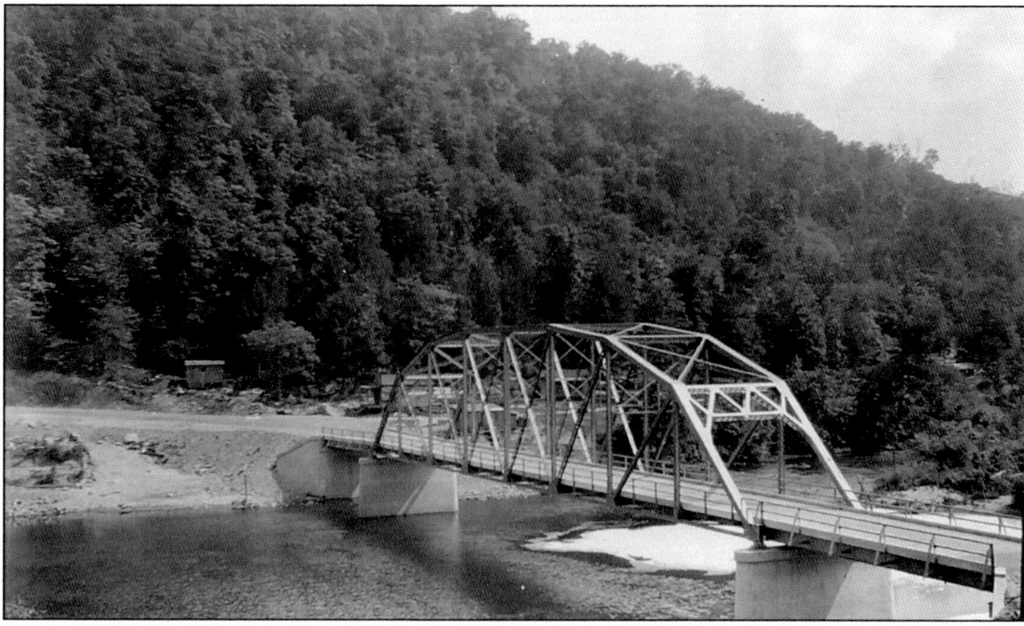

Curtin Bridge is shown in this photograph taken soon after its completion in 1934. A contest was held by the town of Richwood to find the best name for the bridge. The winning name was submitted by Mrs. T.L. Spaur of Southside in Richwood—"Mountain Trail Bridge"—but it didn't stick.

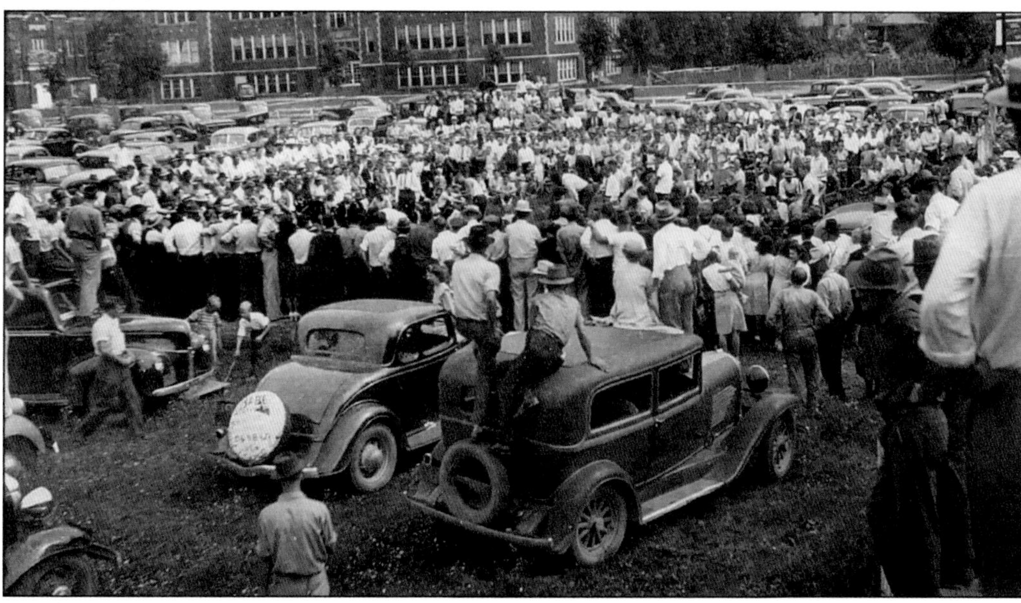

Until this space in front of the high school was developed, town festivals and celebrations were held there. The photographs above and below are believed to be the crowd gathered for the speeches and other activities celebrating the opening of Curtin and Holcomb bridges on June 20, 1934. The next major road project the town needed (to help shed its "end of the hollow" reputation) was a road connecting with Marlinton in neighboring Pocahontas County to the east. Until this link could be realized, citizens were forced to take one of two circuitous routes over very difficult terrain.

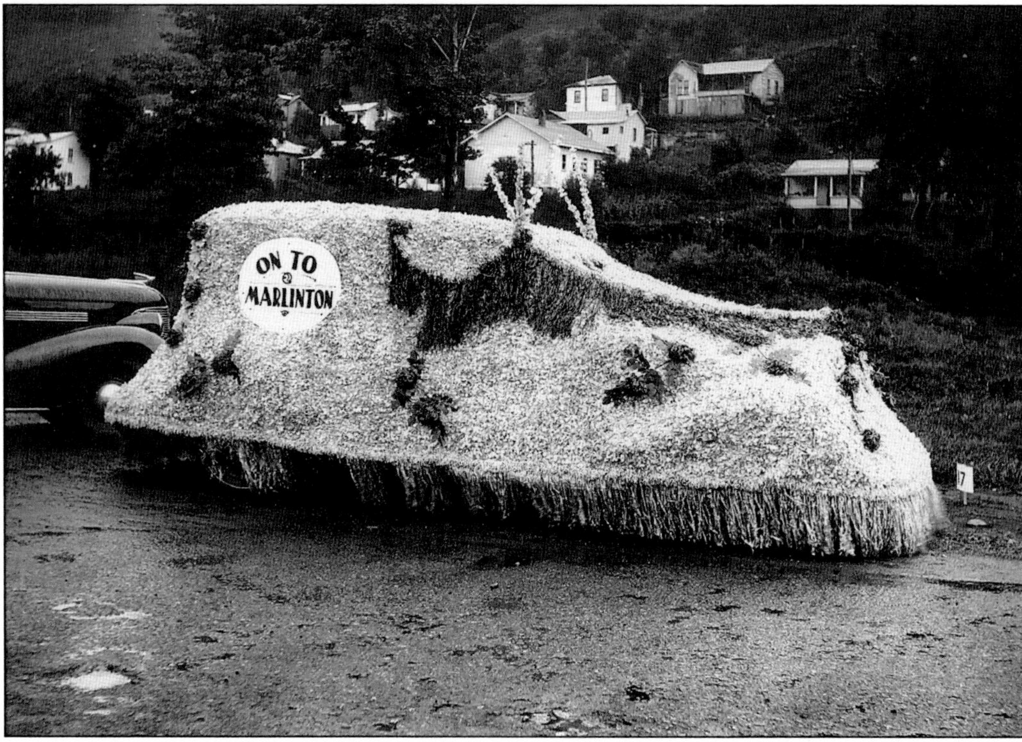


Pictured above and below are two floats bearing the slogan "On to Marlinton," which became the rallying cry in Richwood's efforts to obtain help from the state to construct the road to Marlinton. In 1937, the Cherry River Navy was chartered as a very clever initiative to draw attention to the need for state support. The road would not be completed until 1944. The project had several false starts and work was actually halted once because the governor at the time did not like the way the election went in Richwood.

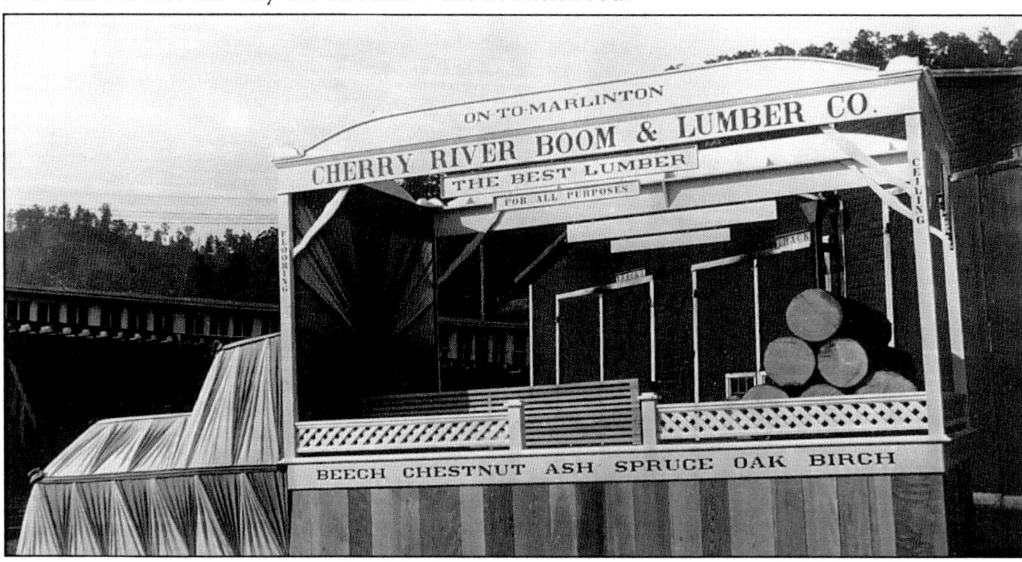

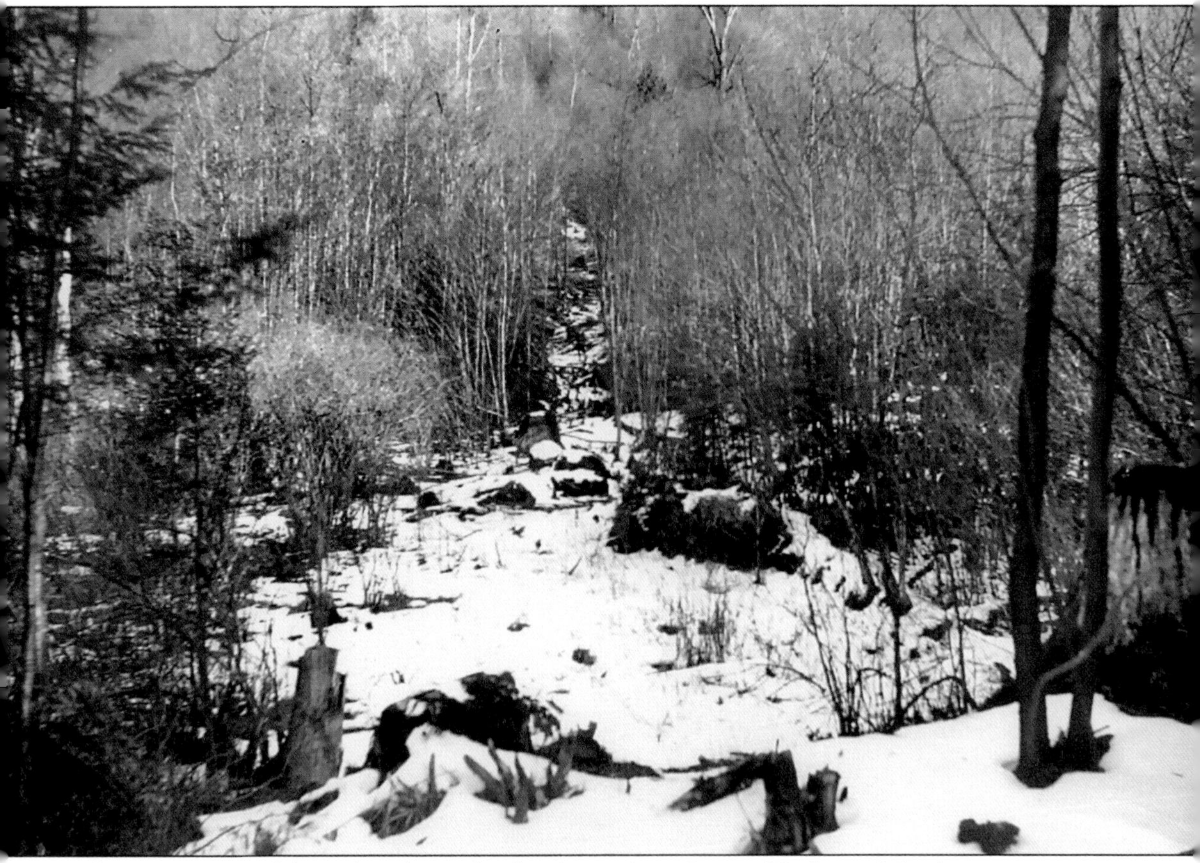

This is a picture of the right-of-way that has been cleared east of Richwood for the construction of what the townspeople came to call Marlinton Road (Route 39). Cherry River Boom & Lumber Company was the patron saint of the town, donating an 18-mile right-of-way through its timber lands for the construction of the new road. The company also donated tools to equip a crew of 90 men. Earlier, the company had donated the property to build the Richwood High School and the Presbyterian Church. When the schools became crowded, the company donated its employee recreation hall for use as an elementary school, which was appropriately named Milltown Elementary School. Almost 12 years elapsed from the time construction began on the road until it officially opened on September 28, 1944. The celebration for the road's opening was held at North Bend. The Richwood High School and Nicholas County High School bands both participated in the ceremony.

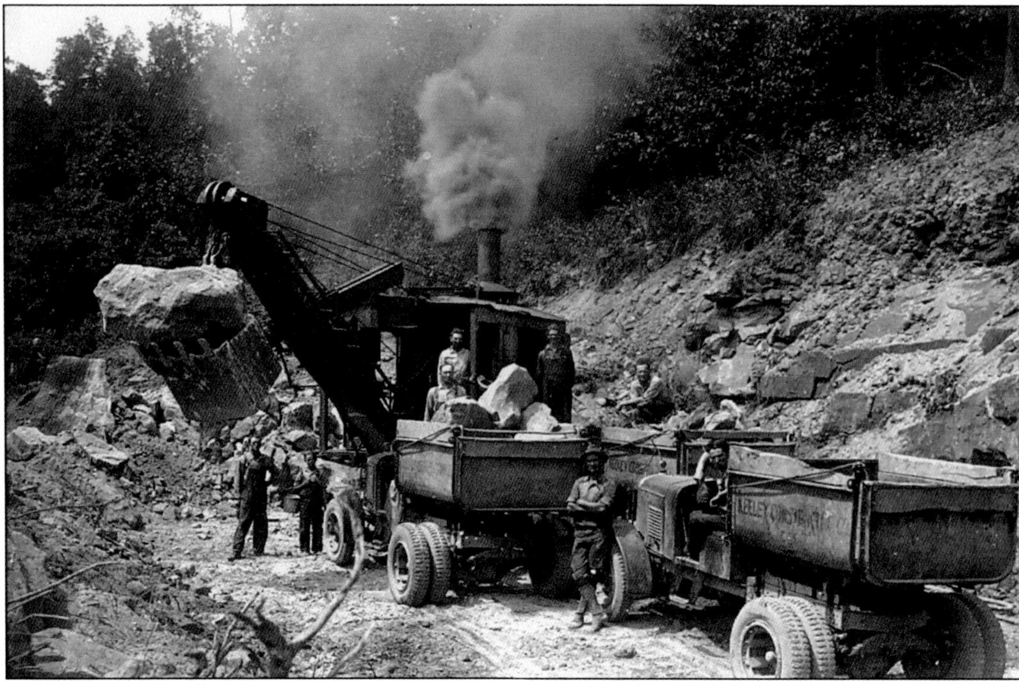

Pictured on this page are two images of the Marlinton Road construction and the two steam shovels utilized for the excavations. Fortunately, dump trucks had replaced dump wagons by 1937 when the work was begun. Unfortunately, there was nothing available to replace the barricades imposed on construction progress by state politics. The road was finally completed by Ma Staples, a woman contractor, a rarity at the time.

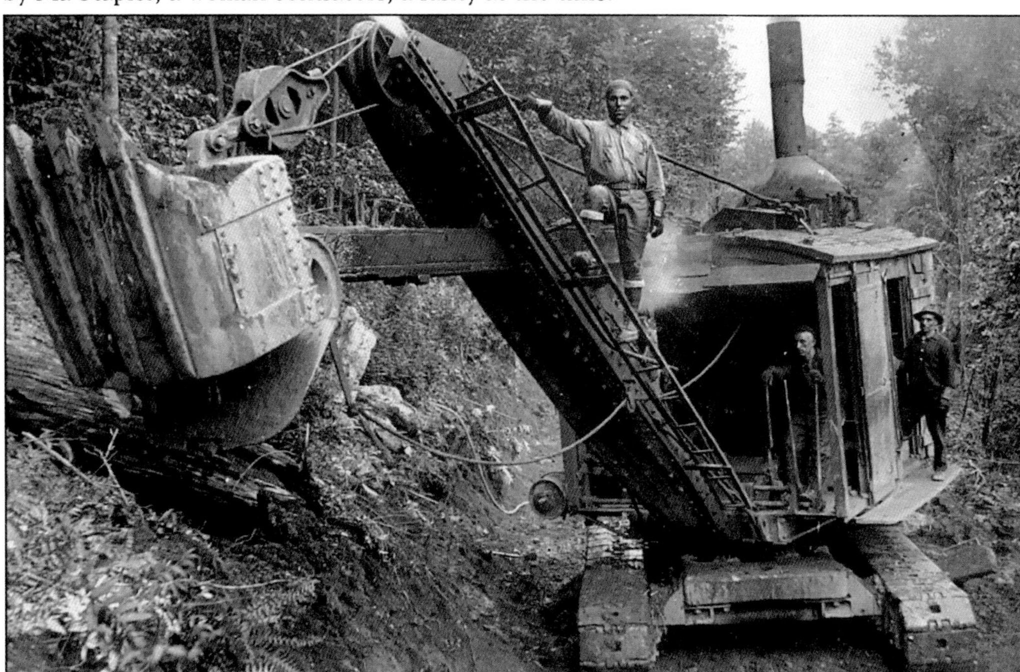

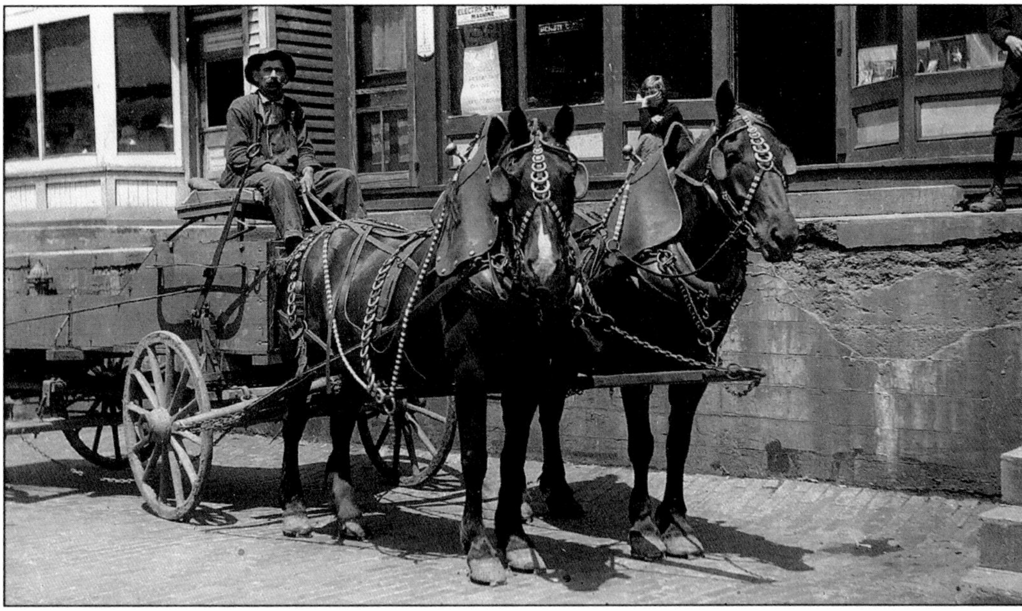

Pictured here is James Orville Kelly, who is thought to have picked up scrap wood from the pin factory to sell to individuals in town. It was common in the 1920s and 1930s to see wagons and automobiles on Richwood's streets at the same time. The town's doctors continued to attend to their patients in the area on horseback for many years. Although the main roads in and out of town were much improved, the roads to many people's homes still were still very poor.

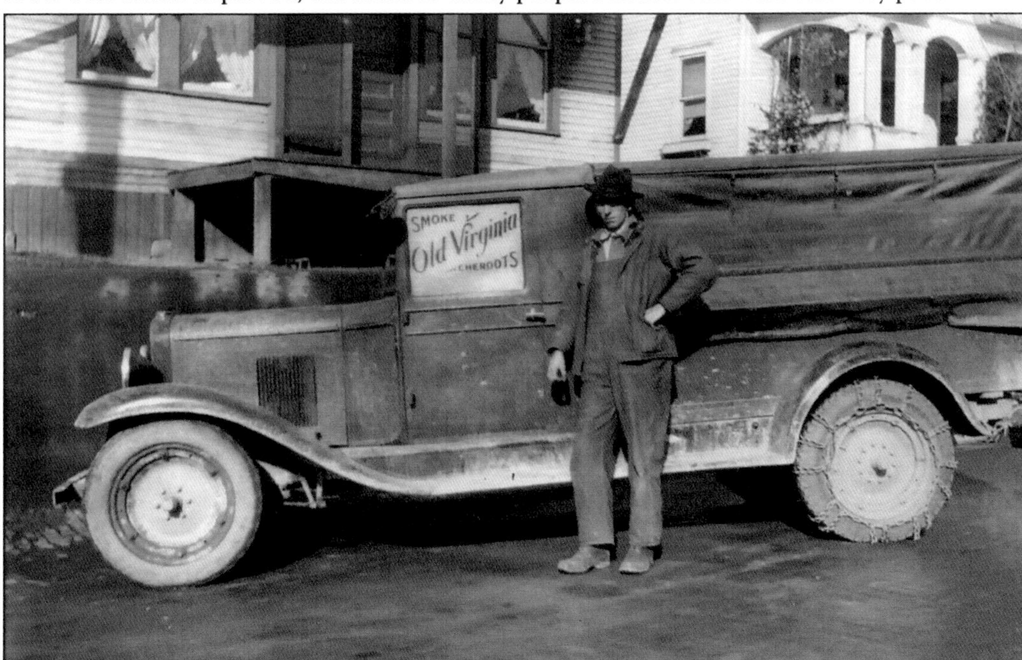


Above is Raleigh Umbarger, a farmer who lived on Horse Ridge above town. He made frequent trips to town to sell fresh vegetables to the townspeople. Note the chains on the rear wheels of his truck. Chains were necessary not only in wintertime, but in spring or even summertime when the rains made the roads muddy and almost impassable.

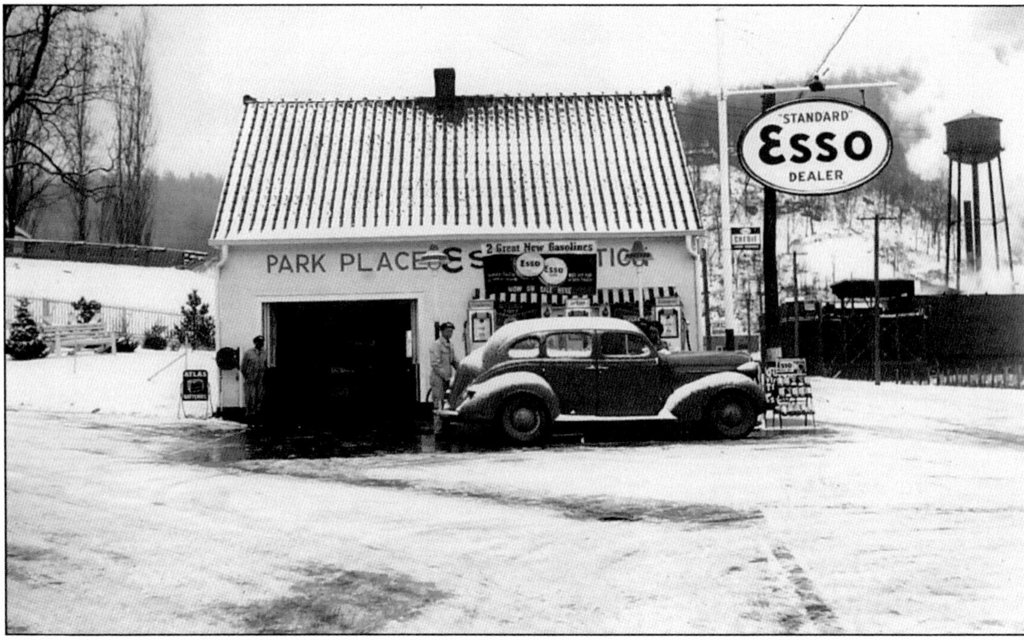


With the coming of better roads, people began to rely more on the automobile and less on the passenger train. Consequently, more cars meant more supportive services in the form of gasoline stations, garages, and car dealerships. Pictured here is Park Place Esso in its original state before it was enlarged to include an addition on the left side.

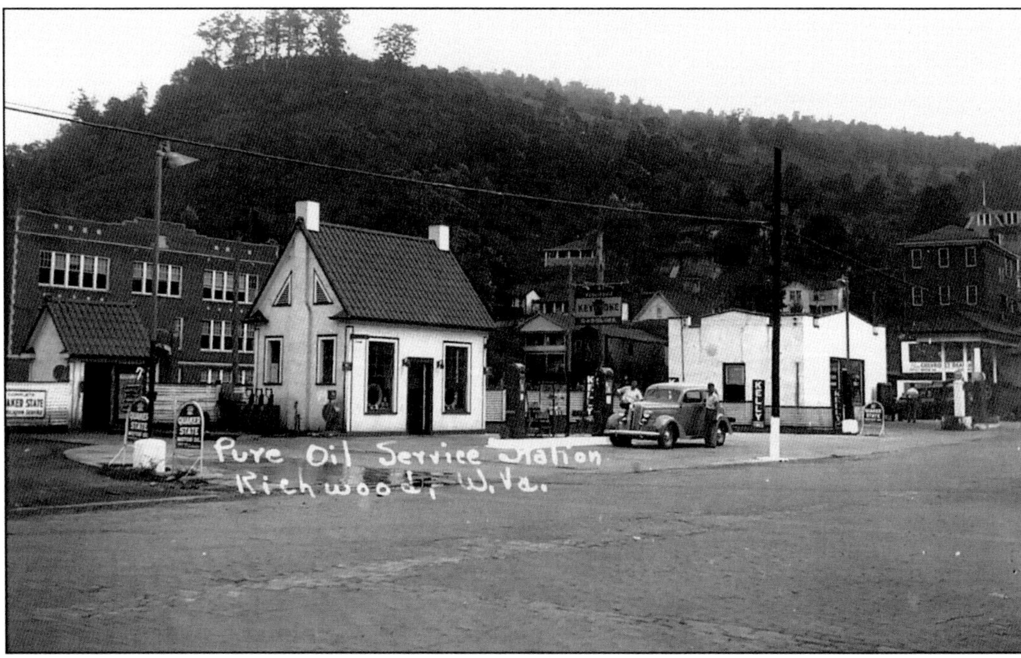


Pictured here is the Esso station at the end of Oakford Avenue. This station was later replaced by a car dealership. Finley Taylor took this photograph in 1937.

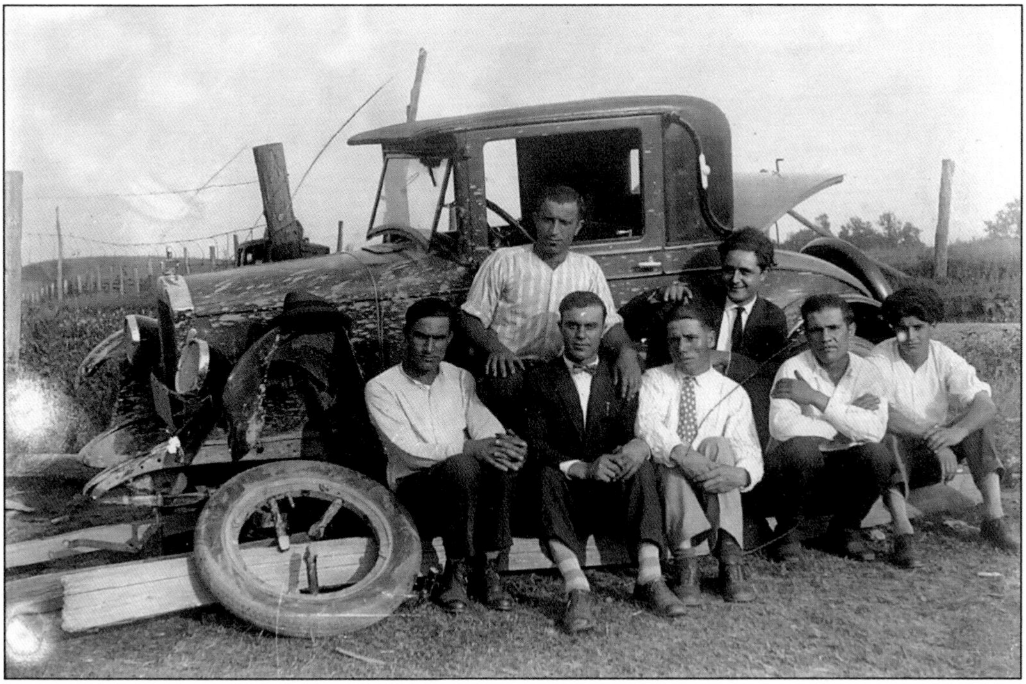

This is the wreck of a 1924 Chevy Star Coupe on Fenwick Mountain. The car failed to make a curve and ran into a rail fence. Pictured from left to right are Louis Darco, Patsy Mazella (behind Louis), Sam Leone, Sam Pacifco, Louis Conti, Frank Frontino, and Armando Conti.

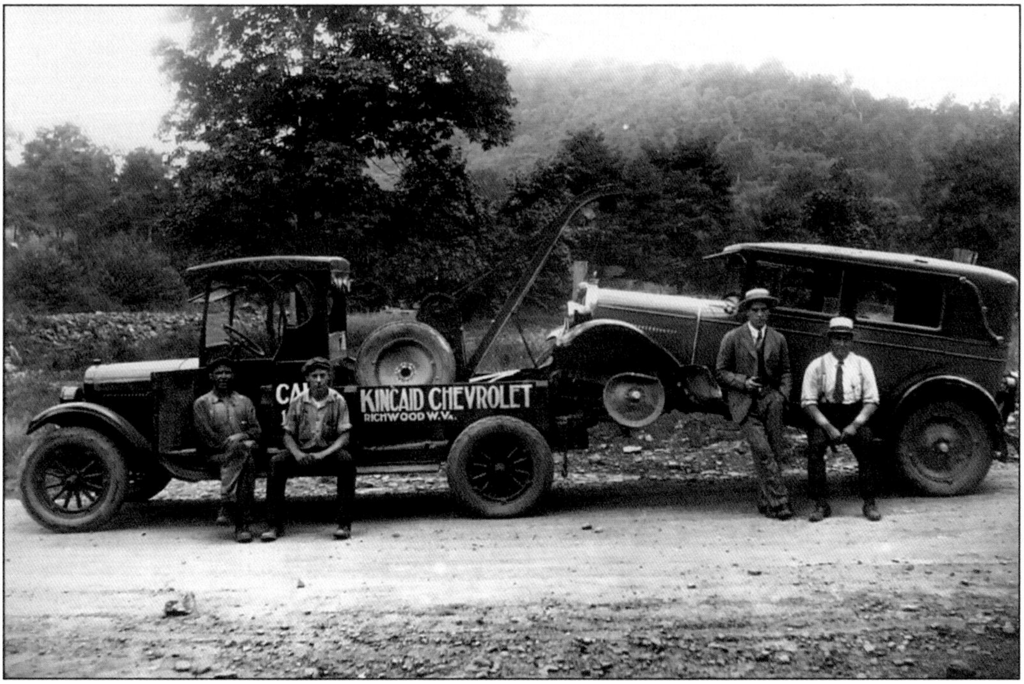


Pictured here is a truck being brought into town by a wrecker. Based on the frequent accounts of accidents given in the area's weekly newspapers during the early days of the automobile, percentage-wise there seemed to be as many accidents then as there are today.

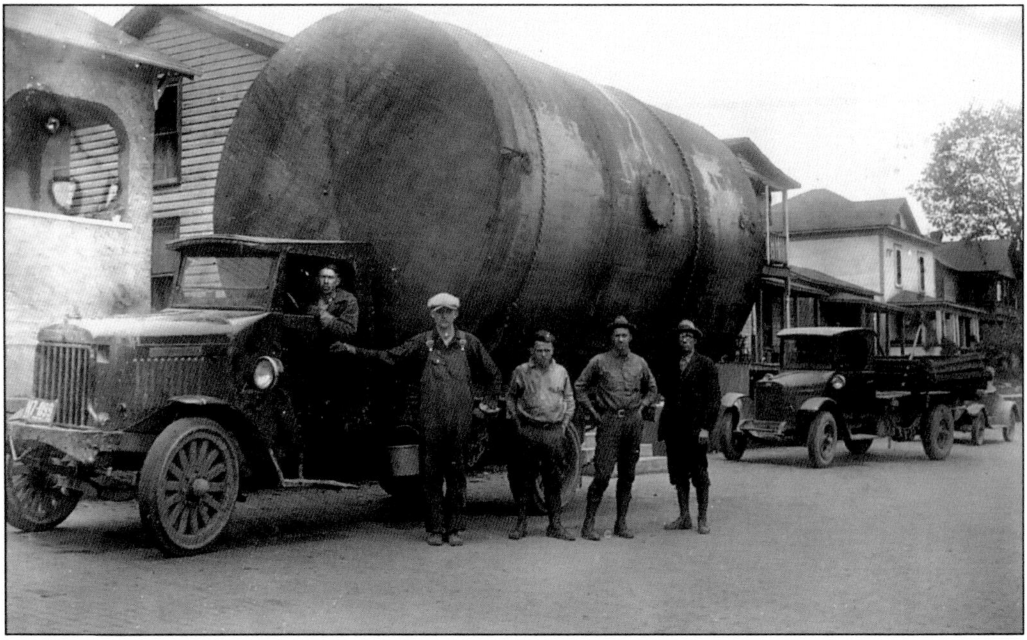

Not only did the railroad lose passengers to better highways, it also lost freight business. Small jobs like the ones pictured above and below did not pose a problem, however. As long as there were timber products rolling out of the mills and coals rolling out of the mines, the freight trains would continue to roll.

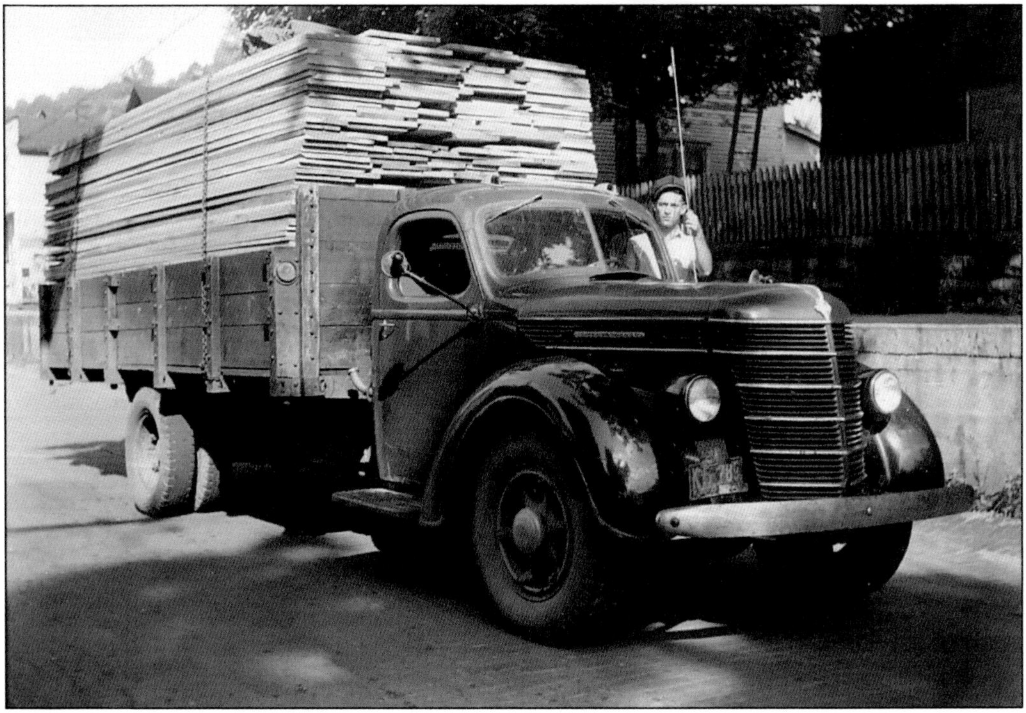

# *Three*

# FIRES, FLOODS, AND OTHER DISASTERS

*Richwood, West Virginia, August 15th, 4 a.m.: Fire of unknown origin started in the Busy Bee Restaurant Monday morning at 2:40 a.m. It spread rapidly...A great deal of the business section was destroyed as well as some of the best residences. The larger part of two blocks was totally destroyed... Our people have the proper spirit, not a coward among the whole list of those who suffered in the holocaust this morning. Even now, while the ruins are still smoldering, plans are being laid for the construction of new buildings from the ashes of the old. That's the spirit...! The stroke was a great one but the Richwood people are great in adversity." (By C. Donee Cook, editor, Nicholas Republican Special Edition, Monday, August 15, 1921.)*

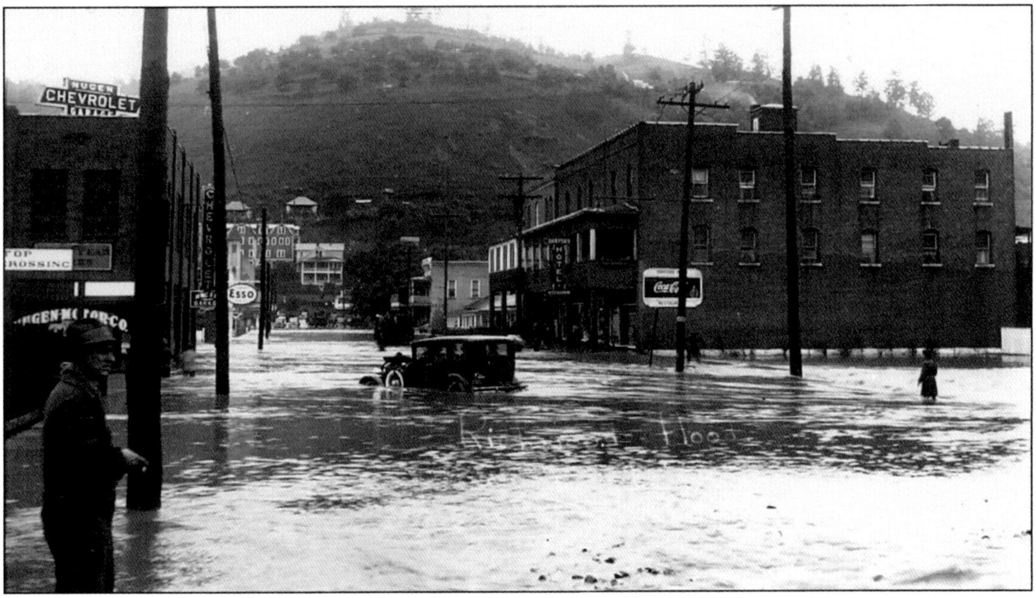


This image is one of the many floods that visited Richwood during its young life. This scene is of lower Oakford Avenue in the summer of 1940. Most of the level land in the flood plain was occupied by company mills and small businesses. Cleanup after the floods was difficult but rarely were there fatalities or buildings actually destroyed; more damage was done to outlying areas along the river. For example, seven homes were carried downriver to be torn apart on the car bridge at Fenwick in 1954. Fenwick is three miles downriver from Richwood.

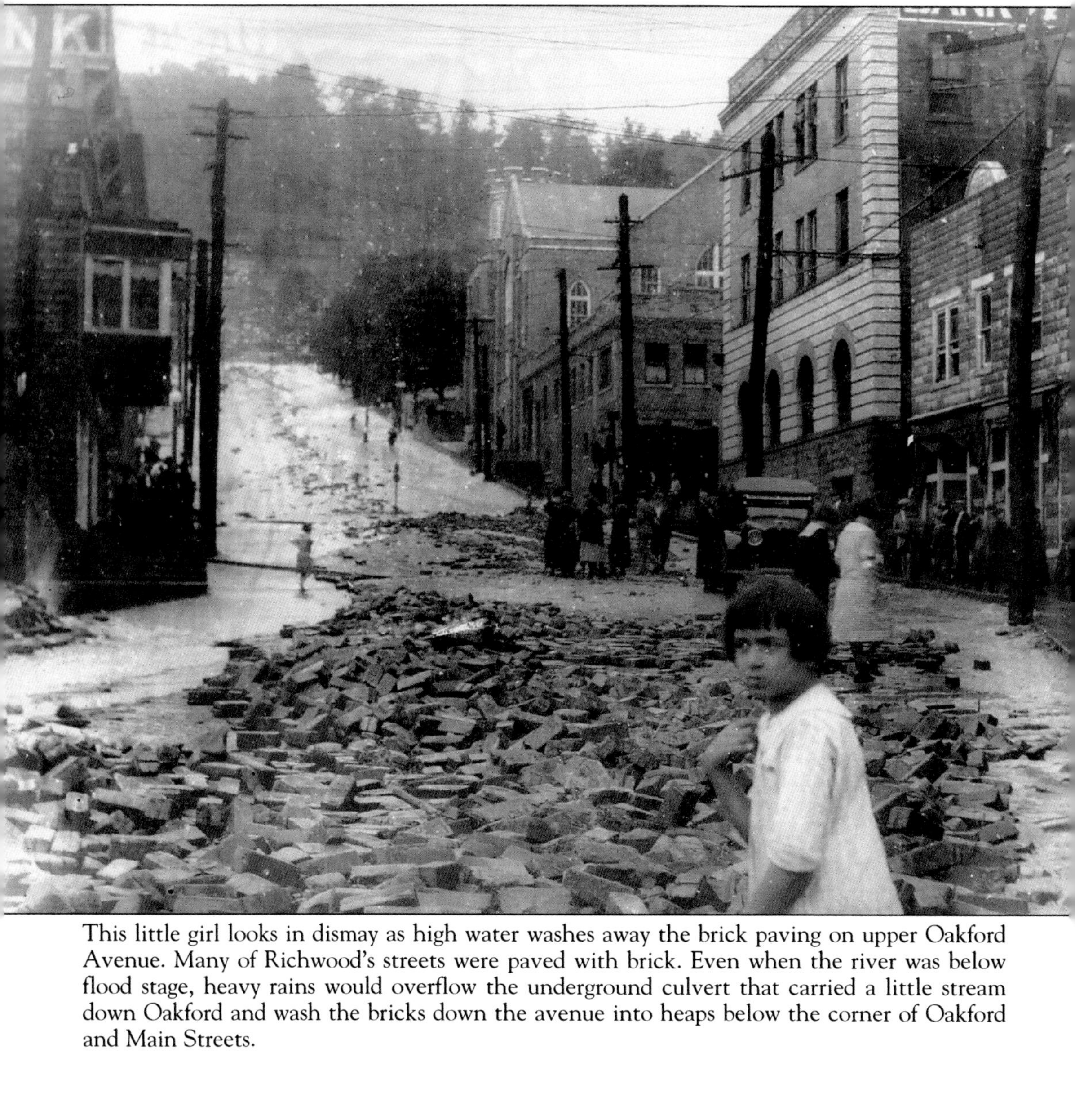

This little girl looks in dismay as high water washes away the brick paving on upper Oakford Avenue. Many of Richwood's streets were paved with brick. Even when the river was below flood stage, heavy rains would overflow the underground culvert that carried a little stream down Oakford and wash the bricks down the avenue into heaps below the corner of Oakford and Main Streets.

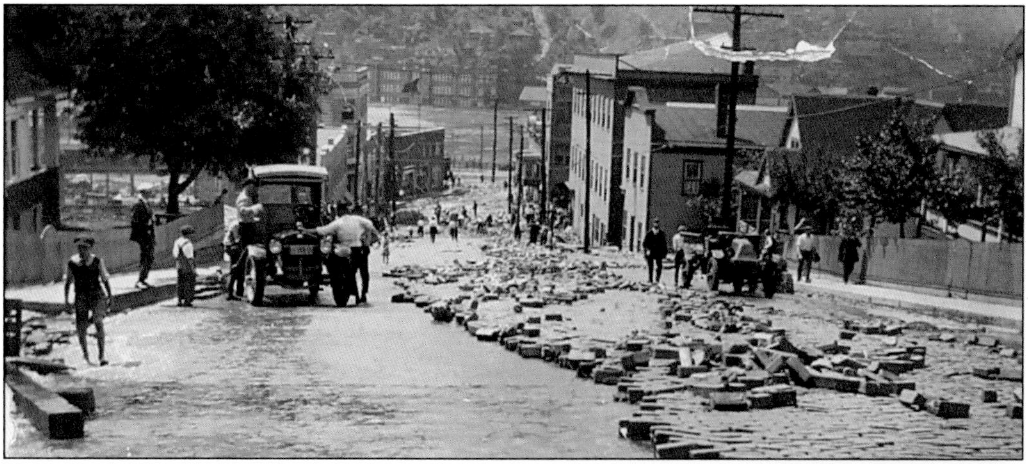

On this page are two additional images of the havoc heavy rains played upon Oakford Avenue. The bricks were returned to their places each time they were washed away.

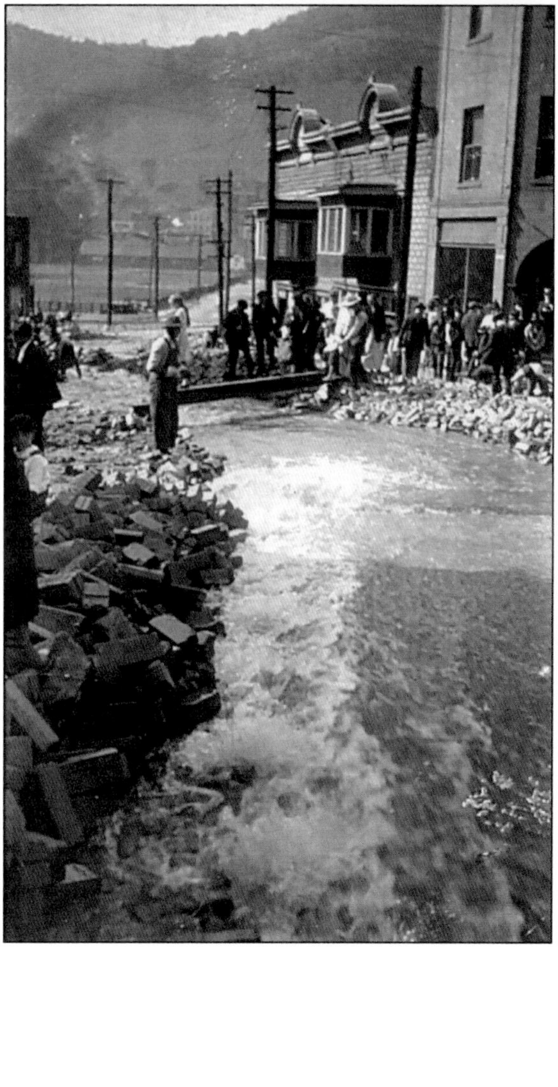

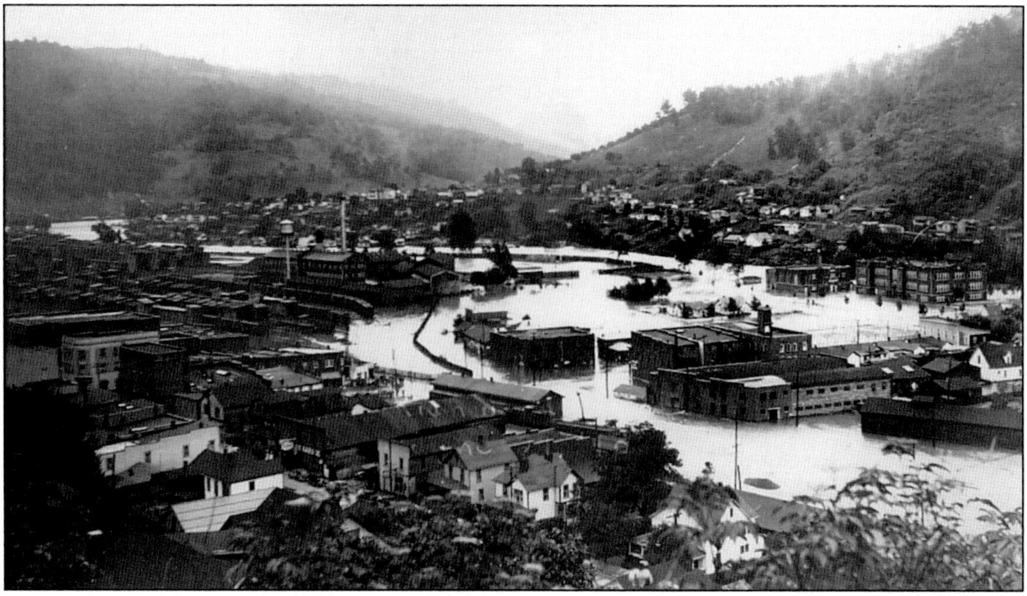

This is a wide view of the flood of 1940. You can see in these photographs that most of the town's residences are high and dry because the mills and businesses have been built on the level land in the flood plain along the river.

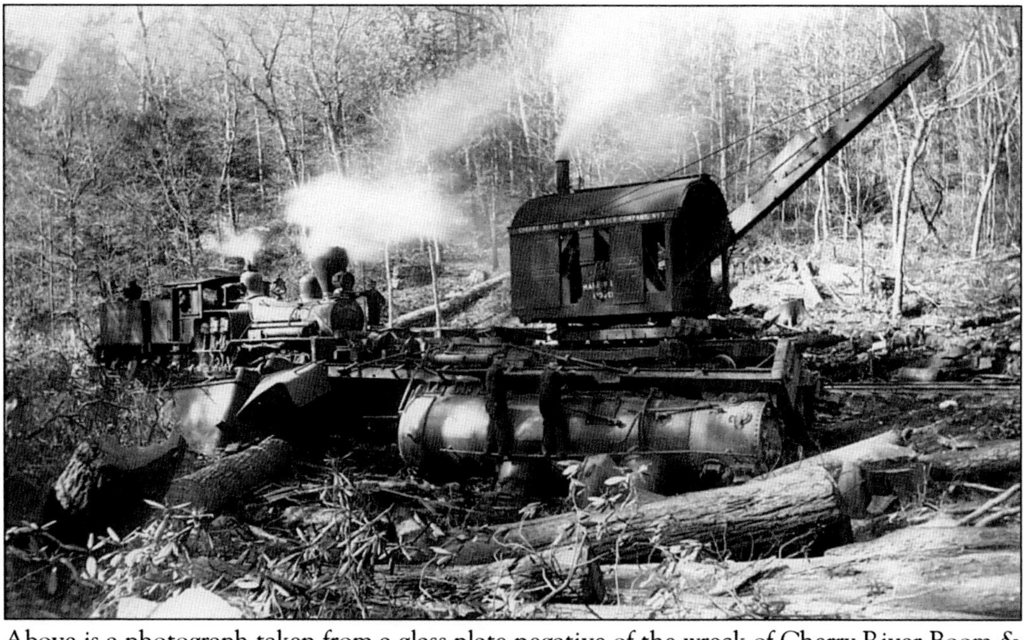

Above is a photograph taken from a glass plate negative of the wreck of Cherry River Boom & Lumber Company engine No. 7. The scene depicts the aftermath of the runaway shay engine that resulted in the death of three crewmen. The wreck occurred on April 16, 1912, at the headwaters of Barrenshe Run, a tributary of Cranberry River, close to the present-day site of Cherry River Country Club. Engineer Frazier Adams was killed when he tried to jump from the moving train. Brakeman Russell Berry and conductor Joe Taylor tried to ride it out but were killed when the engine turned over. Adams and Taylor were buried at Richwood Cemetery and the photograph on page 50 depicts the funeral procession to their grave sites.

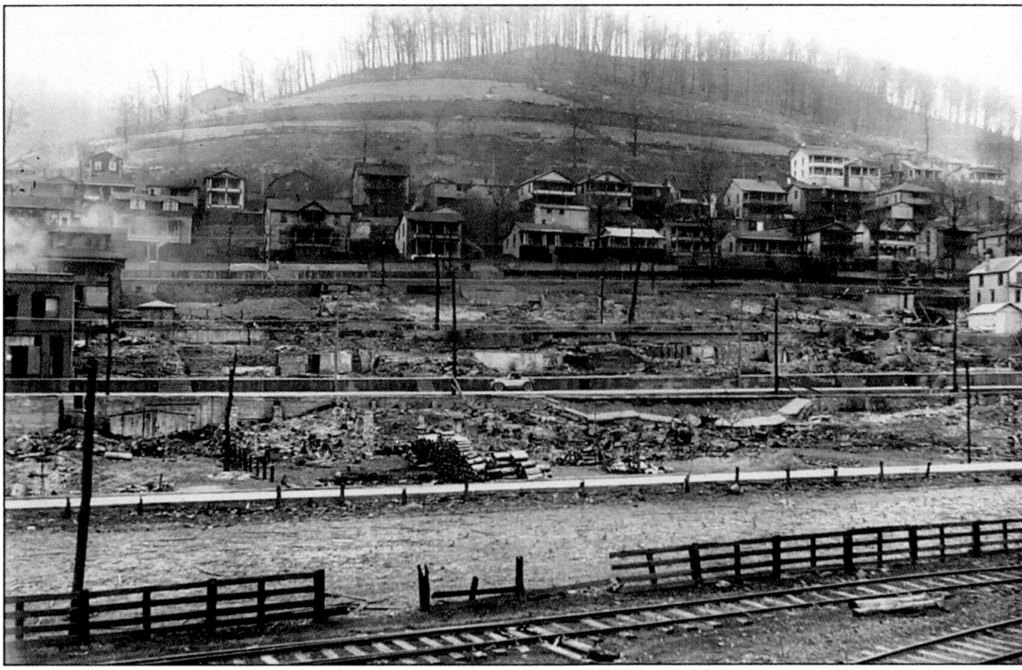

On this page are two views of the aftermath of the devastating fire that nearly destroyed the town on August 15, 1921. The fire destroyed buildings on both sides of Main Street and a smaller number of buildings on both sides of Walnut Street. While having residences built on high ground protected them from flood damage, it did not save them from being leveled by fire. Within 24 hours of the complete destruction of a score of businesses, many of the owners announced plans to rebuild.

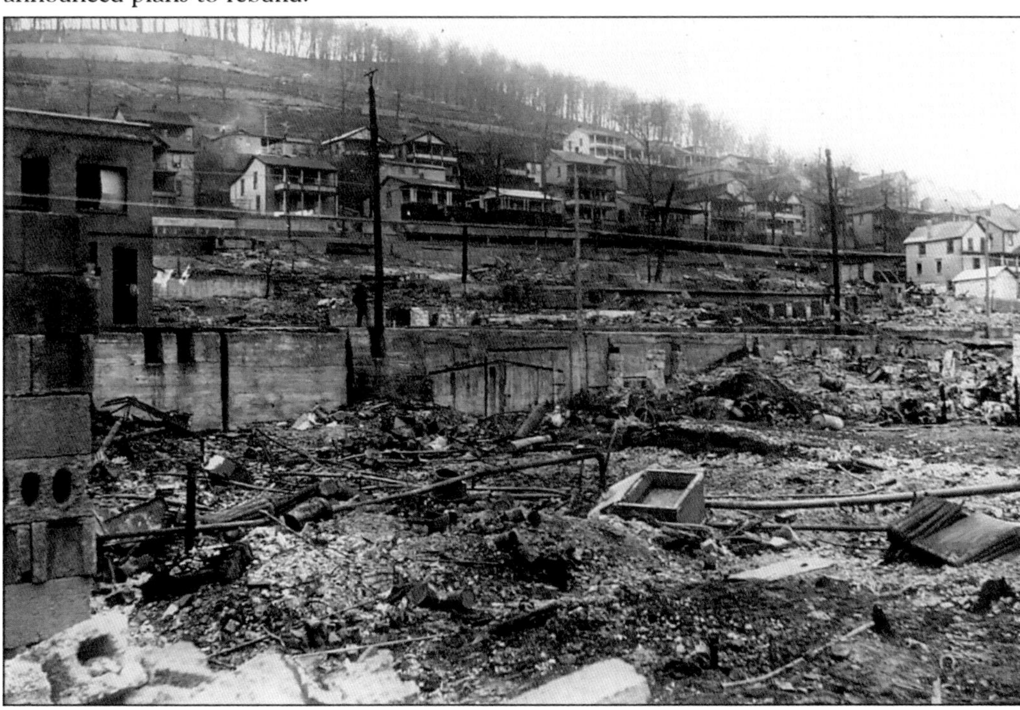

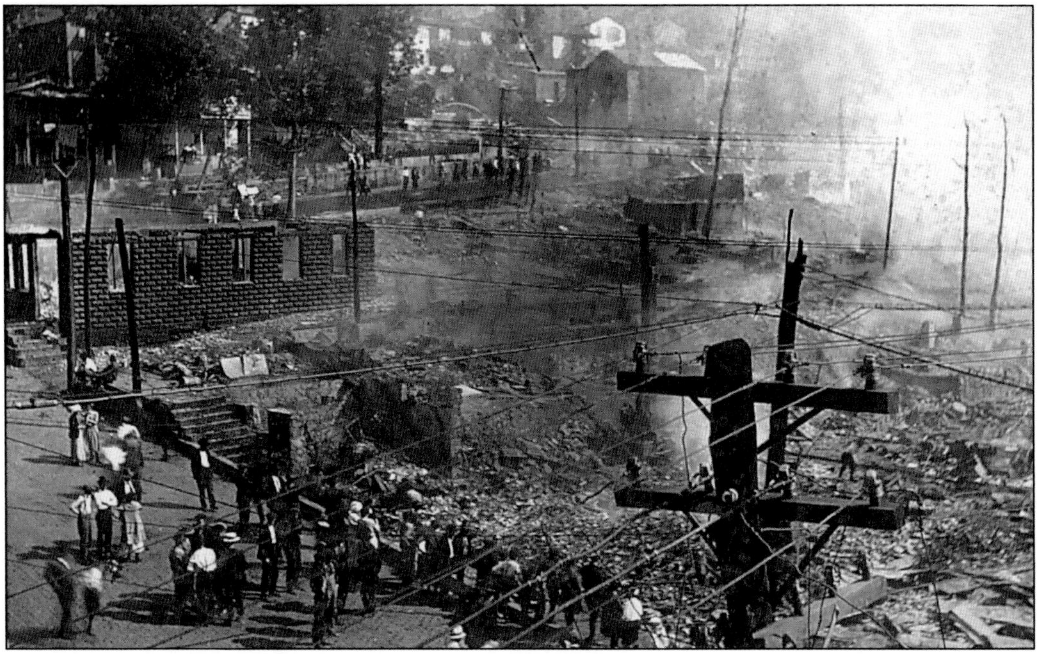

Here are two additional views of fire damage. Above is damage to lower Main Street from the fire of 1921. The picture below shows the damage done to the Big Mill when it was almost destroyed by fire in 1924. The tannery was heavily damaged by a fire in 1906. Both mills were rebuilt bigger and better, as was the case for the small businesses on Main Street that were lost to the 1921 fire.

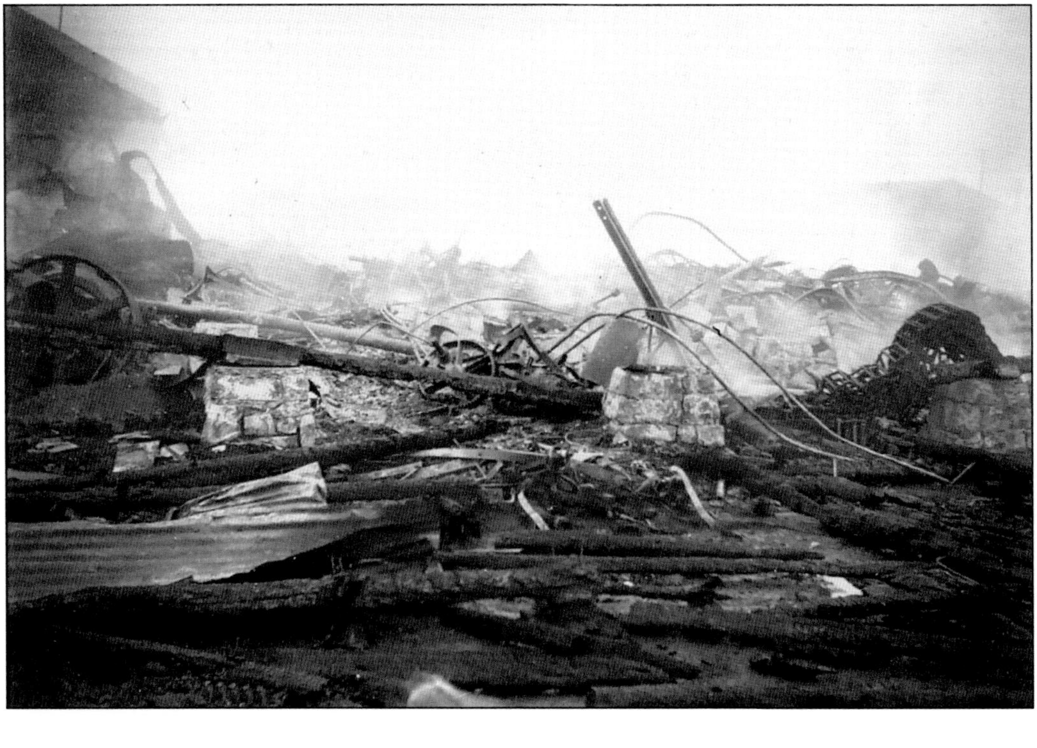

This is a photograph of the First Methodist Church on the corner of Walnut Street and Oakford Avenue. The Presbyterian Church on Main Street was the first church built in the town in 1902. It was badly damaged by fire in 1906 and completely rebuilt. It was one of very few buildings that was rebuilt as a wooden frame structure as opposed to brick.

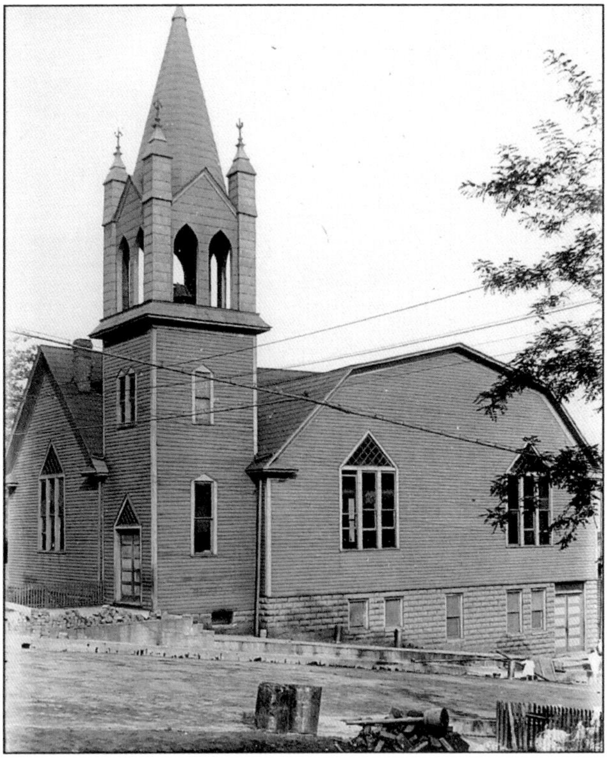

Below is the rebuilt First Methodist Church, which is still in use today. It was initially called the Northern Methodist Church. Only a couple of blocks away was the Southern Methodist Church, now called Faith United Methodist Church. Over time, the reduced membership of the town's churches became a greater threat than fire, and was primarily the result of a decline in the town's population. Both photographs on this page are taken from glass-plate negatives.

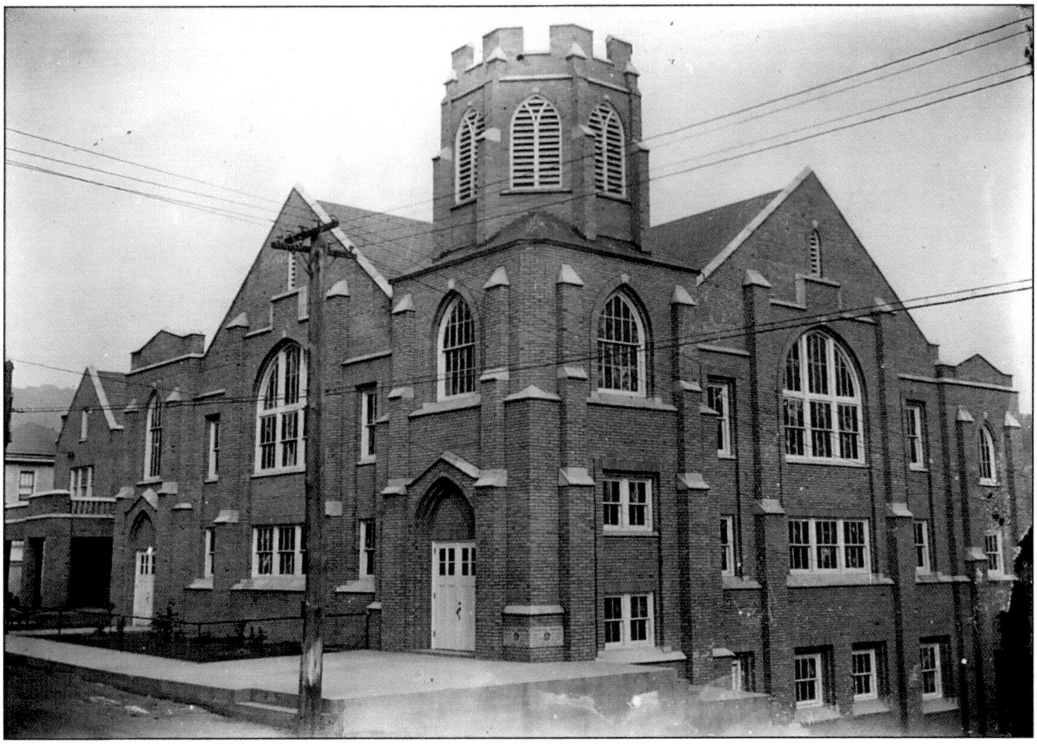

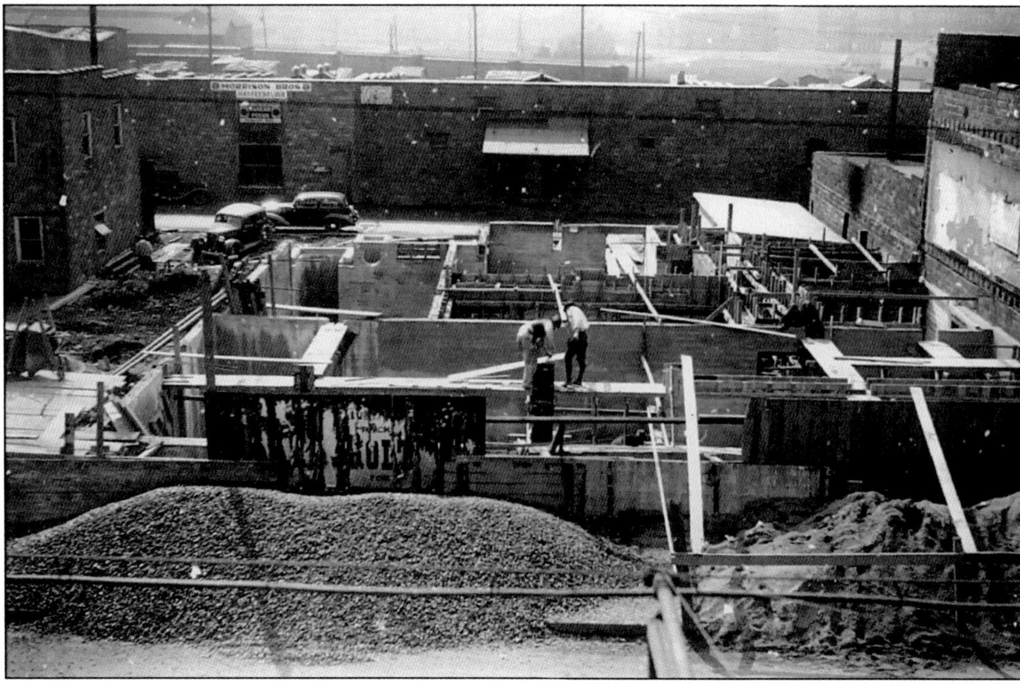

On this page are two views of the building of the present Richwood Post Office. Over time, most of the empty street frontage caused by fires was filled in by new buildings, usually made from brick. The post office was completed in 1937. Finley Taylor was contracted by the federal government to take periodic photographs of the different stages in the construction of the building. Letters he left in his studio indicated that he had to employ an attorney to get the government to pay him for his excellent work.

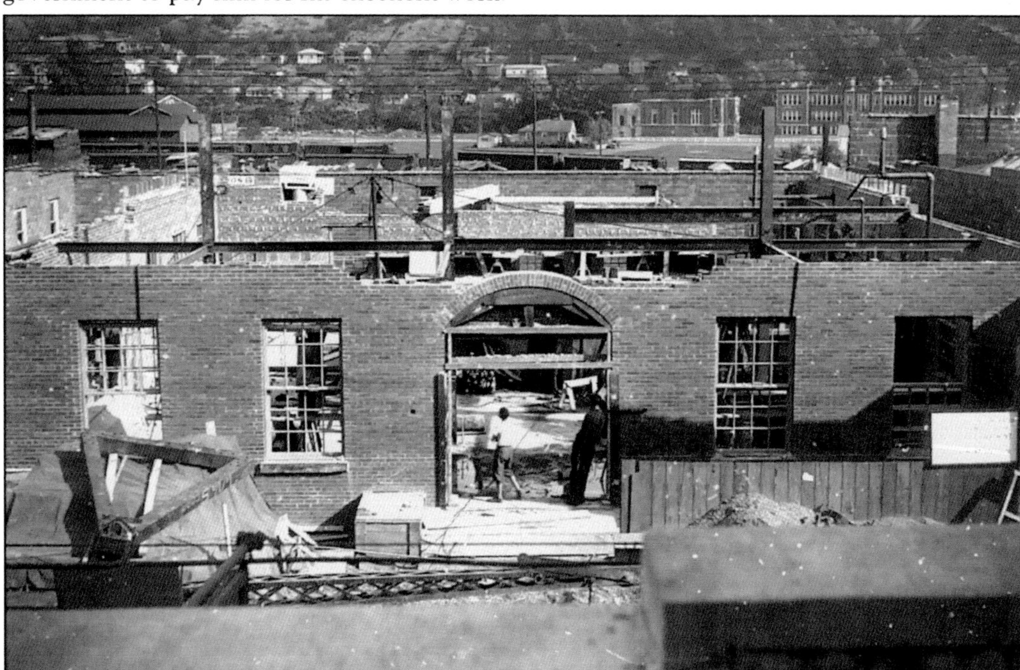

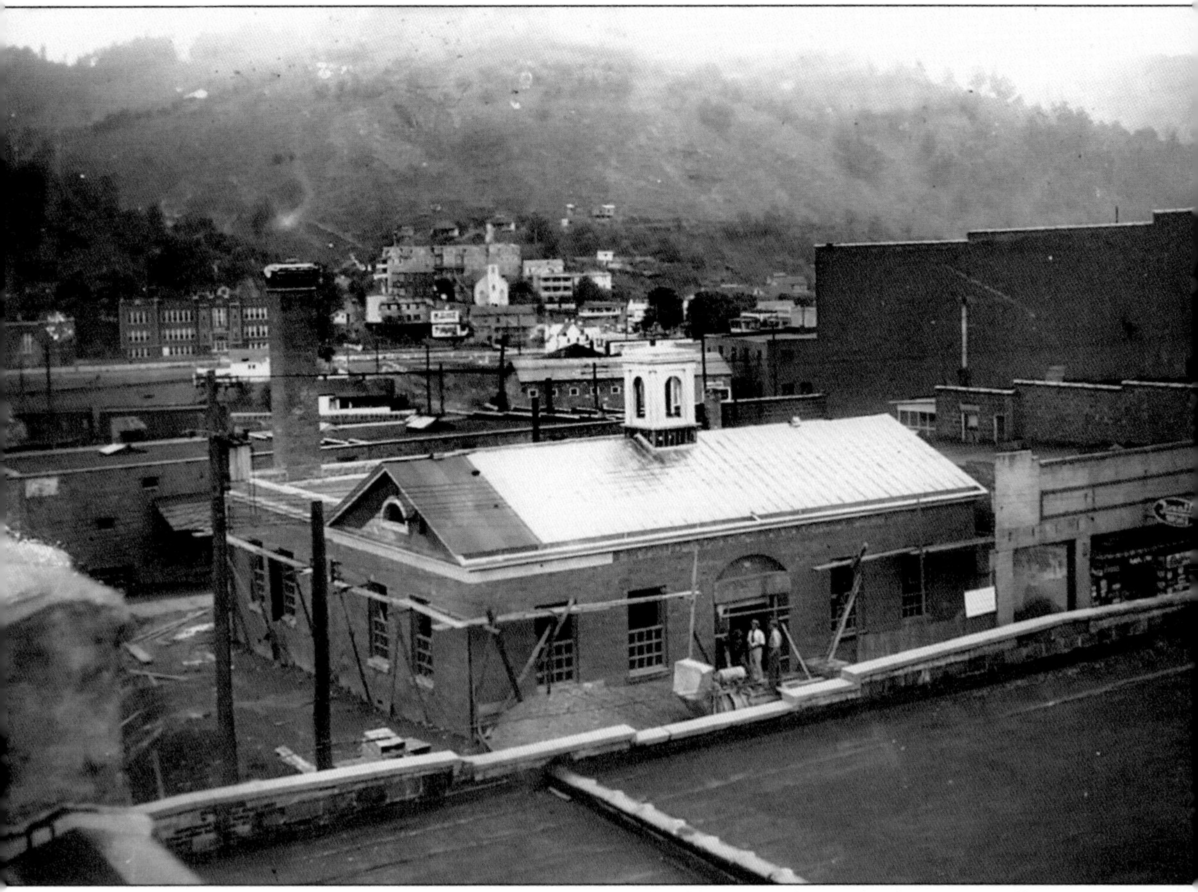

This is a photograph of the completed post office building. Richwood's first post office was located five miles away on Hinkle Mountain. The earliest approach to the town from the west was by way of Hinkle Mountain. Before 1900, there were more families living on the mountain ridge than in the valley.

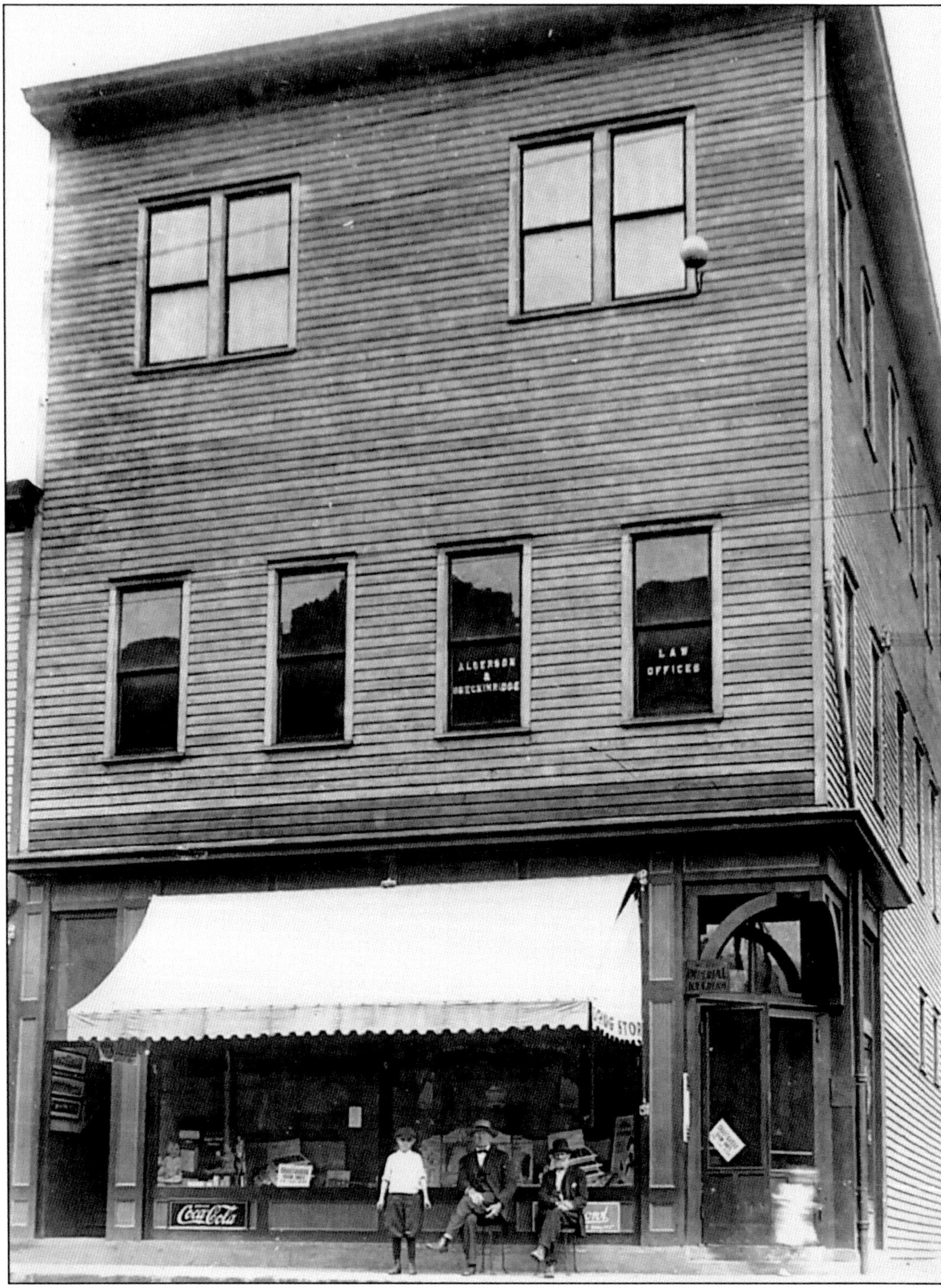


This was Richwood's first Masonic Hall (on the third floor). The second floor contained attorney's offices. The first floor housed the Richwood News Company, one of the main hang-outs for the youngsters of the town. Before the building was destroyed by a fire of unknown origin in November 1945. The American Legion Hall beside this building was also destroyed. The vacant space was soon filled by the Corner Pure Oil Station.

# *Four*

# Early Town Gatherings

*The following is from the Richwood News Leader, February 25, 1976: "Finley Taylor, for many years one of Richwood's colorful businessmen, died this week . . . He died Monday, February 23, 1976, at the age of 89. Finley Taylor was a photographer in Richwood for nearly half a century and took just about everybody's picture in the county during those years. Although Mr. Taylor was not a writer, he could still be considered Richwood's official historian. Through the medium of photography, film, he recorded—so colorfully—the growth of a city and the hopes, aspirations, emotions, good times and bad...wherever people were: wherever there was action: where history was being made or where there was fun and laughter, Finley Taylor was there with his big box–type camera."*

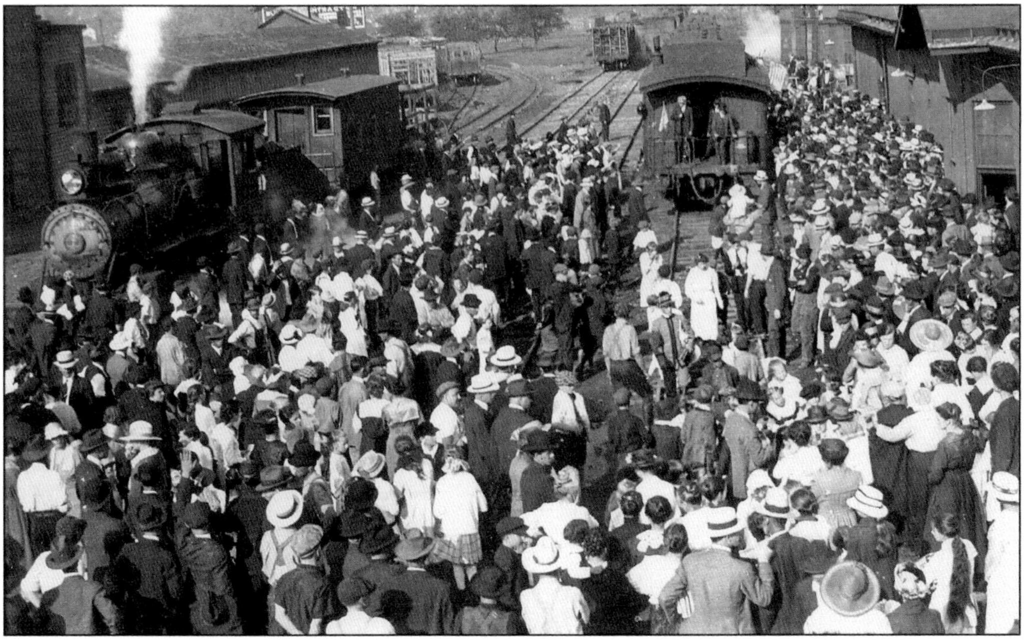

This is the second in a sequence of four photographs taken of the large crowd gathered to send off a group of Richwood's young men to serve in World War I. The first photograph in the sequence is this book's cover photograph. Finley toned his photographs in a sepia tone, like the photograph on the cover of this book.

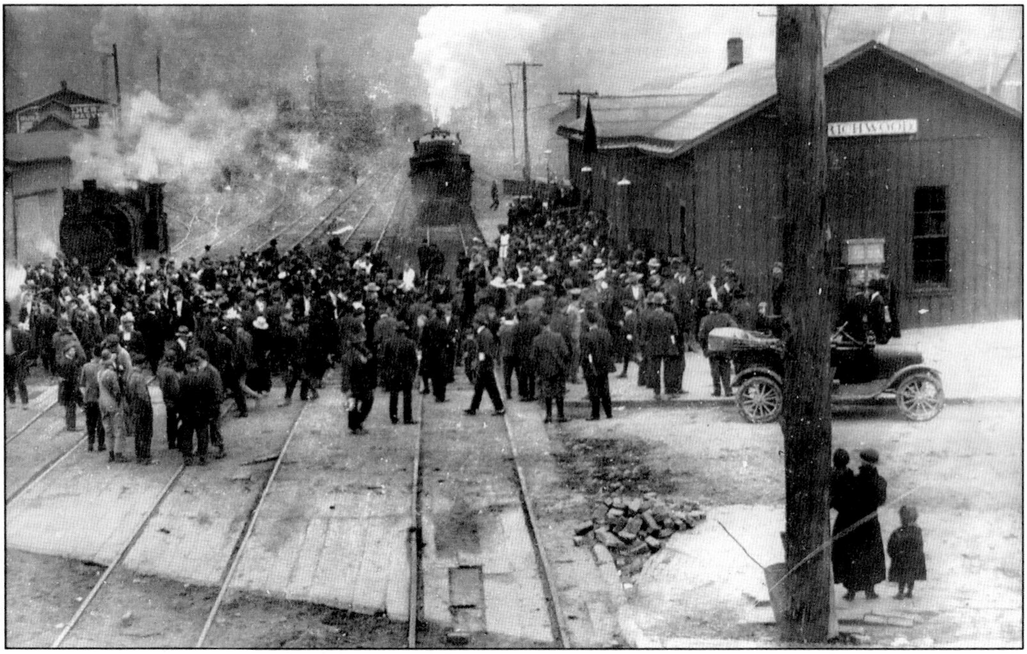

This photograph is the third image in the aforementioned sequence showing the town's send-off of recruits to fight in World War I. In this photograph, the train has moved well past the train depot and the crowd has begun to break up and mill around the area. Silhouetted in the lower right corner of the photograph is a woman holding a small child in her arms with another child standing beside her. This poignant image makes one wonder if she has just said goodbye to her son, or perhaps her husband.

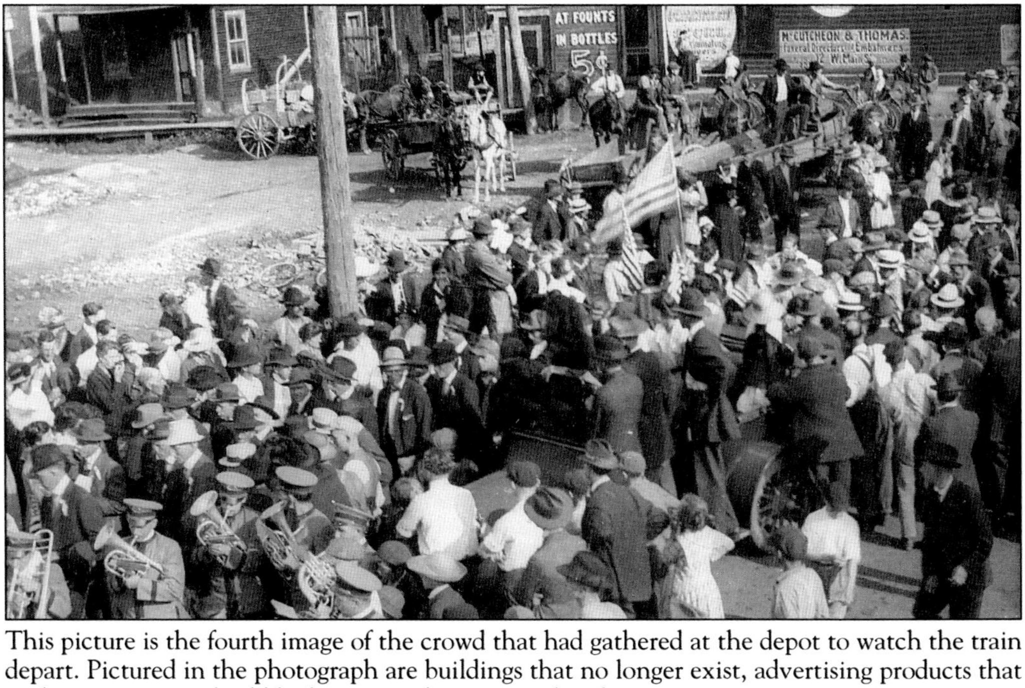


This picture is the fourth image of the crowd that had gathered at the depot to watch the train depart. Pictured in the photograph are buildings that no longer exist, advertising products that no longer exist, and sold by businesses long since closed.

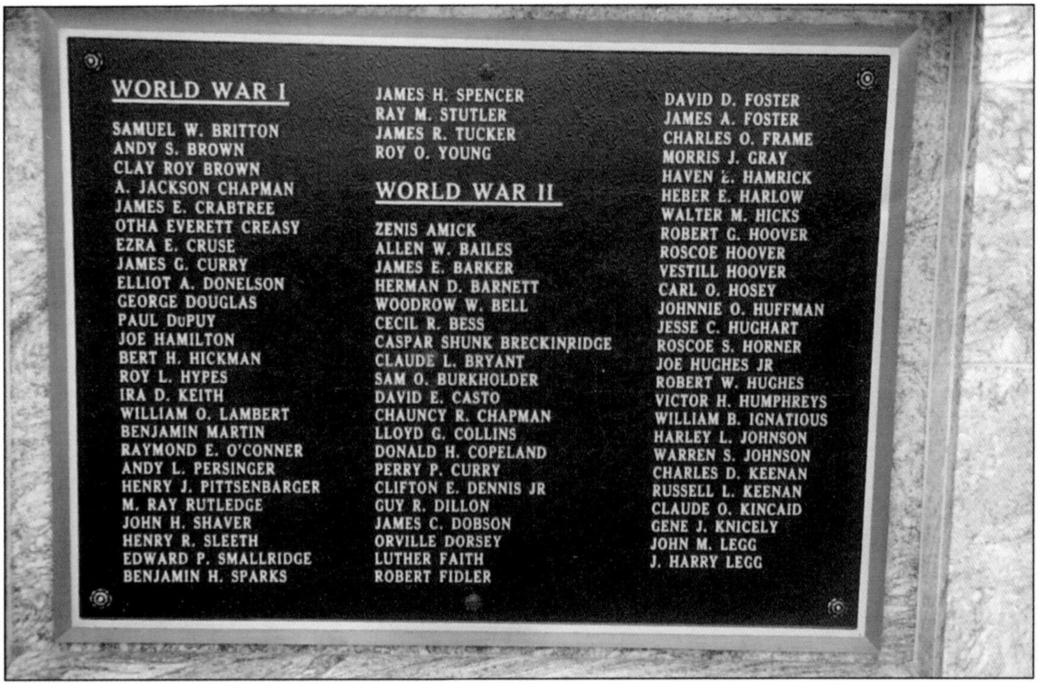


These are recent photographs of the plaques on the War Memorial Monument at Nicholas County Memorial Park in Summersville. They were erected by veterans to honor the soldiers from all of America's wars who gave their lives for their county. Missing from the plaques are Edward Kenneth Simms (World War II) and Berman J. Ganoe (Vietnam).

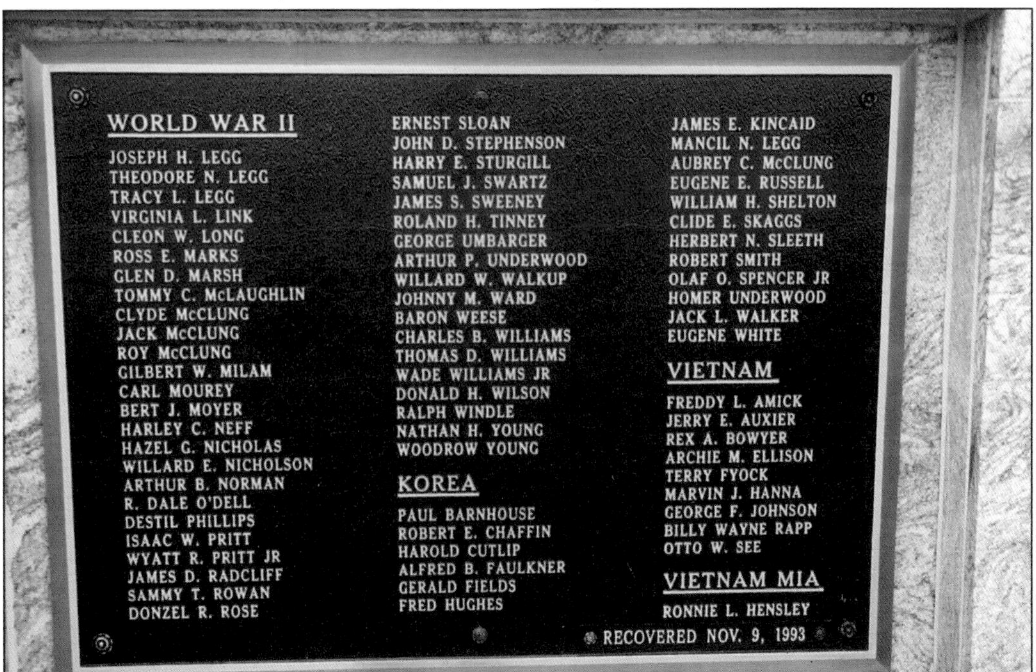

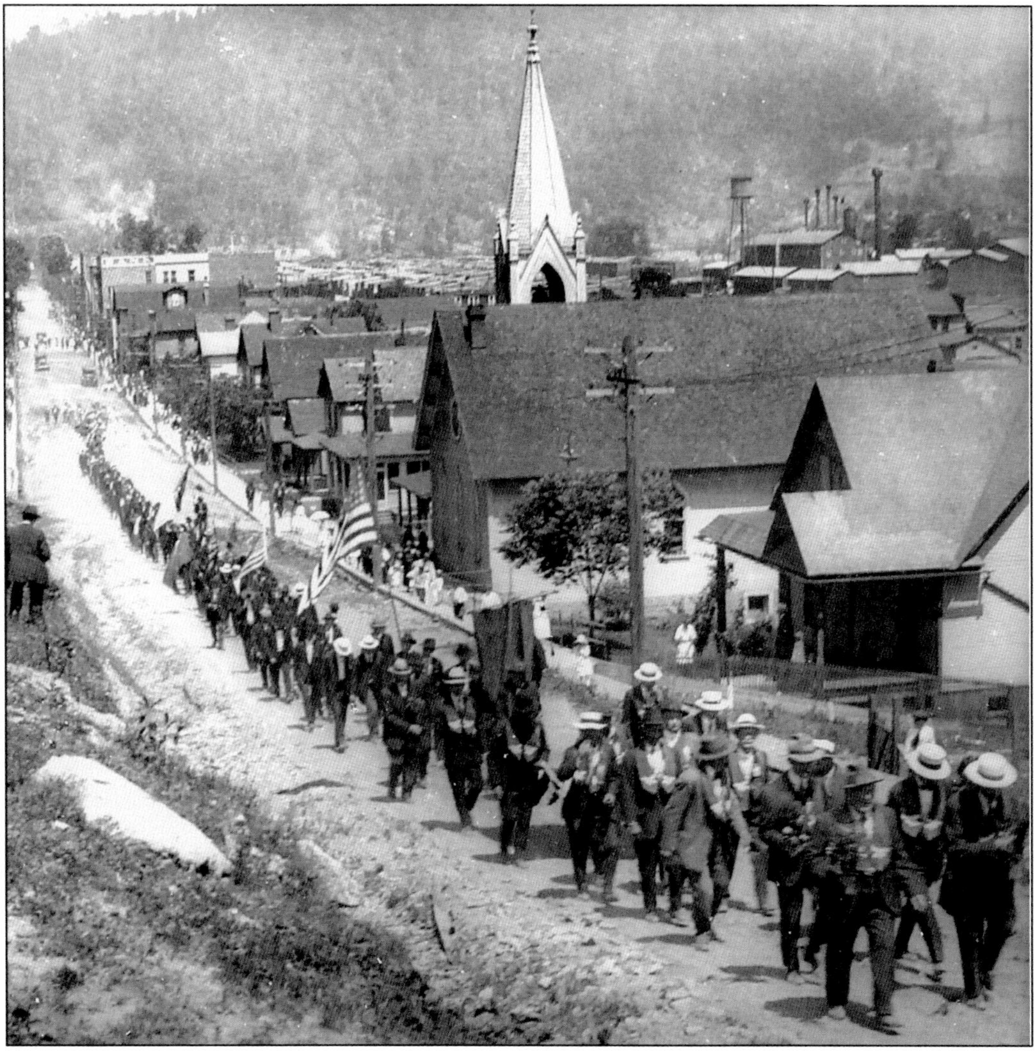

This marvelous image shows a funeral procession marching up Town Hill to Richwood Cemetery for the burial services of two men killed in the train wreck on Barrenshe. It was thought that this was one of Richwood's annual Memorial Day Service parades until Finley Taylor himself took a print of the photograph along with a print of the wreck (shown on page 40) to the *Richwood News Leader* office and clarified the purpose of the parade.

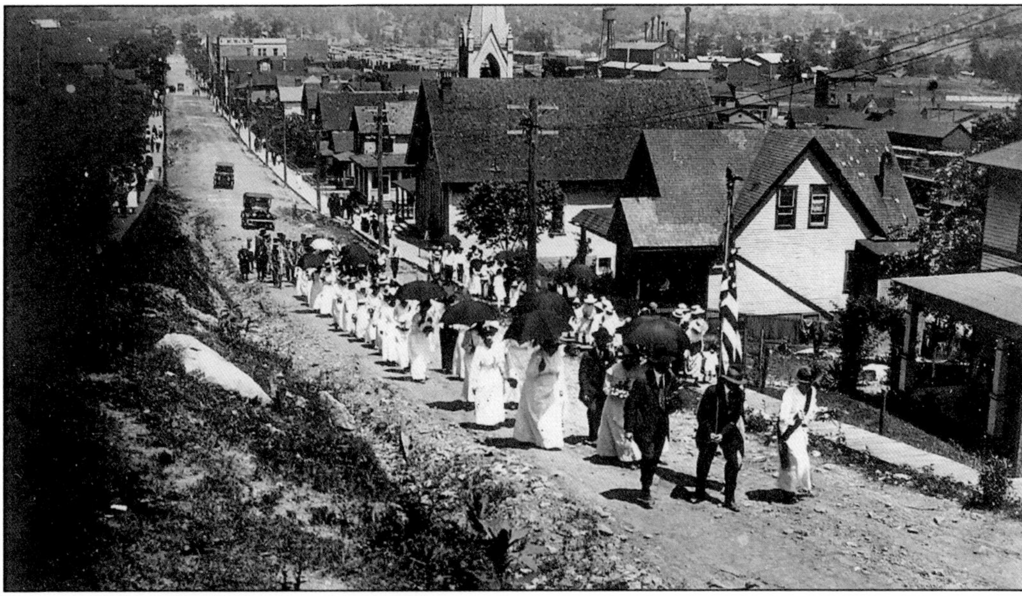

Above is an image of the wives of the Masons marching in a Memorial Day procession to Richwood Cemetery. The photograph below shows a parade celebrating the Fourth of July. The town of Richwood proved very early in its existence that it knew how to do parades, and that tradition has continued.

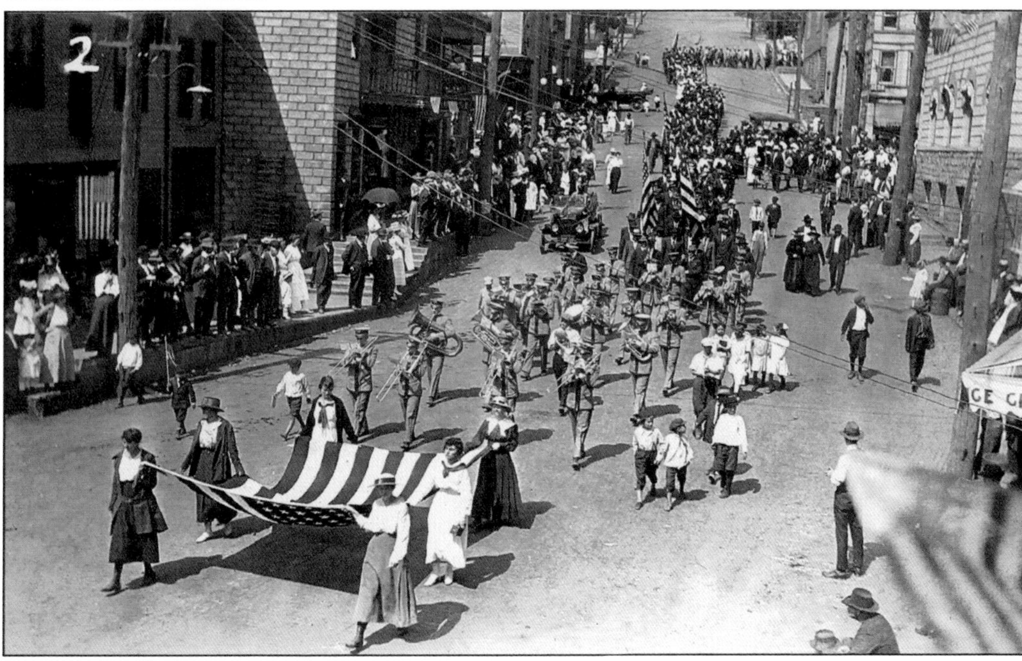

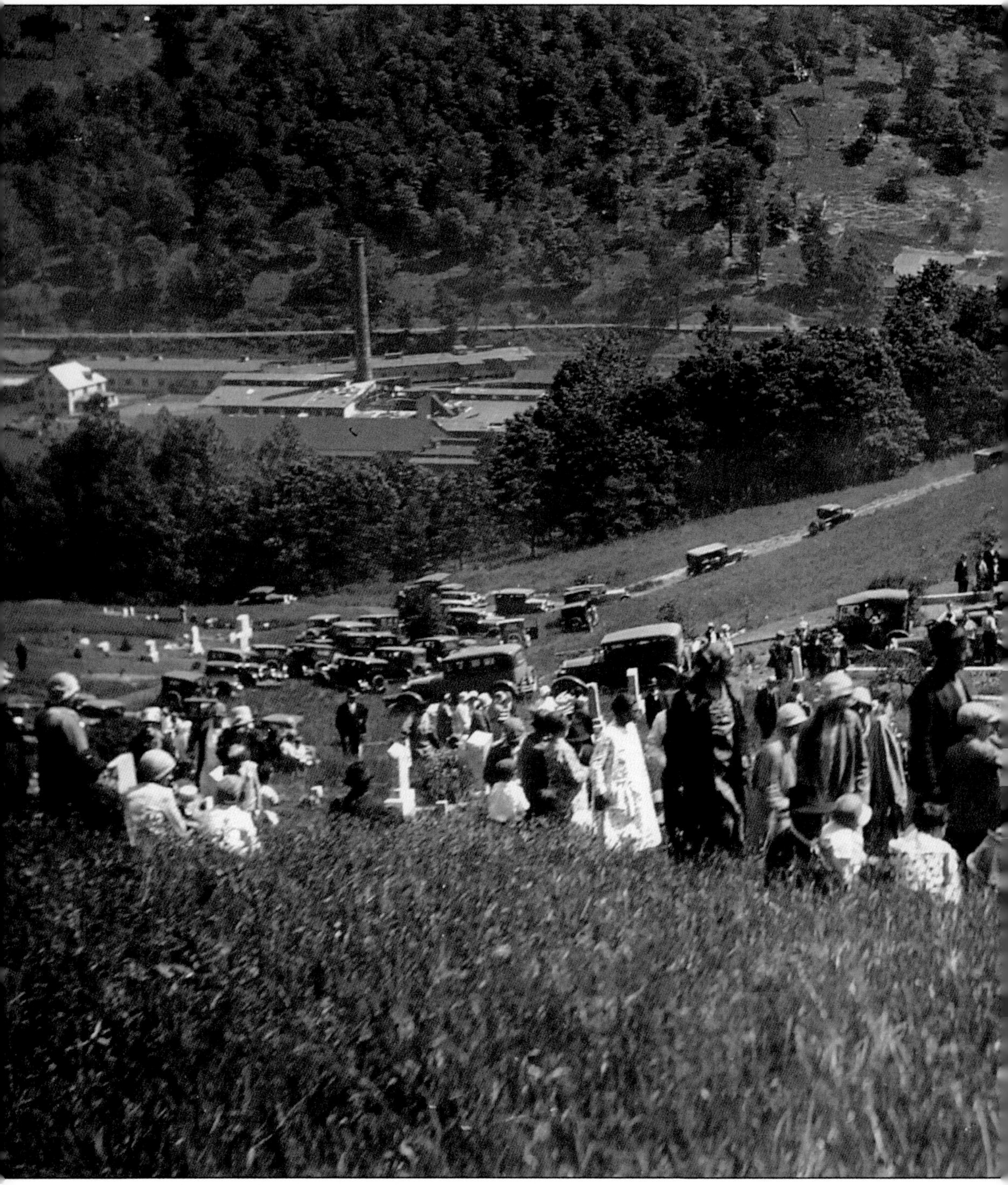

This is a photograph of Richwood Cemetery. Judging by the large crowd, the town's people have turned out to honor prominent citizens. As was the case for most of the town's residences, the cemetery was located on the hillside instead of the level land reserved for mills and small

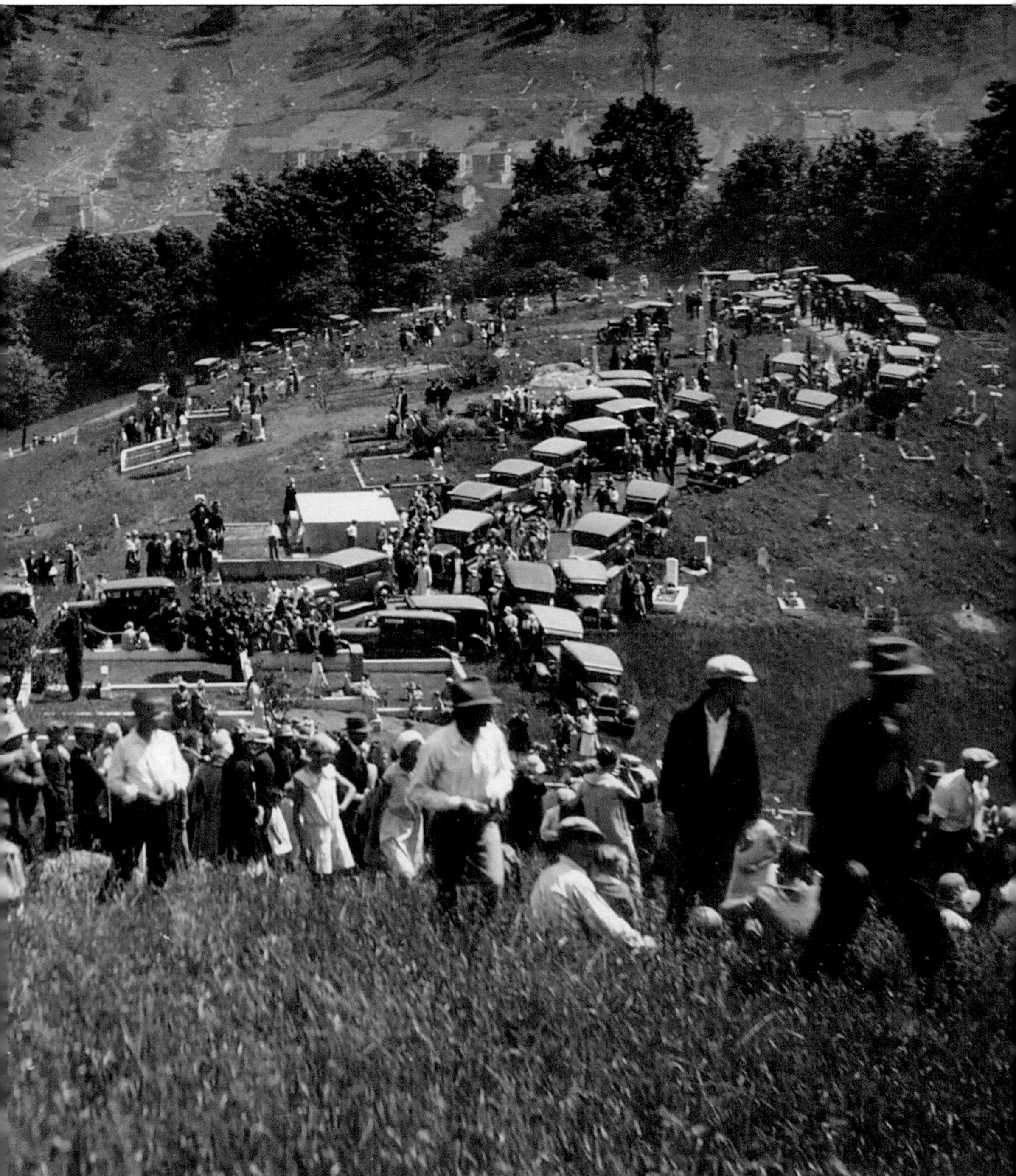

business (and a park). In the background on the left side, a portion of the tannery can be seen.

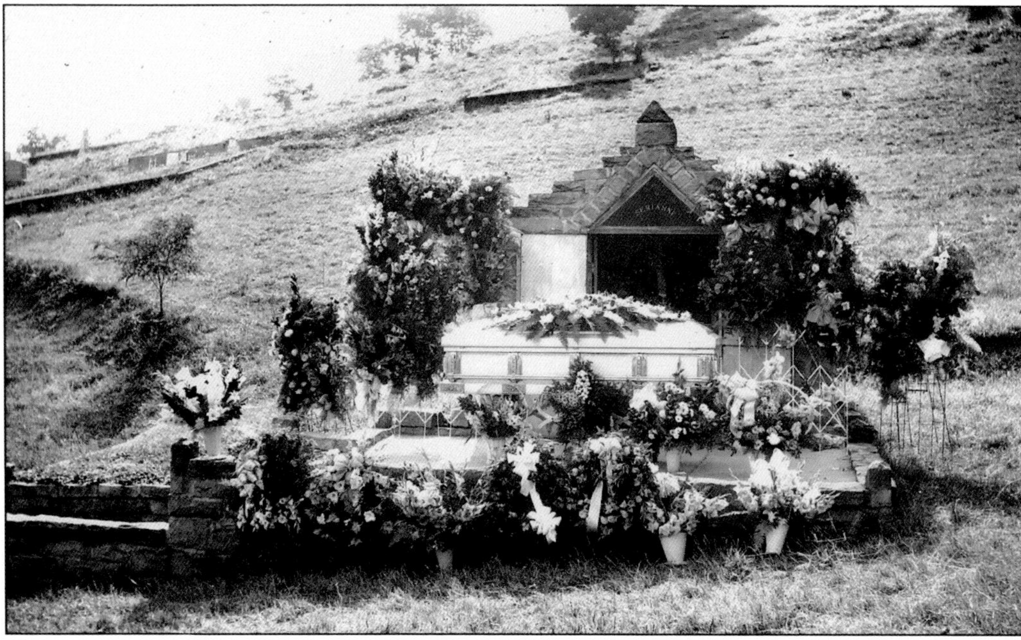

Shown above is the coffin for the funeral attended by the many townspeople shown on pages 52 and 53. The identity of the deceased is unknown, though the coffin is resting in front of the Serianni family tomb. The early date of this photograph and the later dates of the burials in the tomb indicate that the deceased was not interred in the Serianni family tomb, however. Apparently, the level platform in front of the tomb provided a convenient place for the casket and flowers brought to the cemetery. The touching photograph shown below is one of many that Finley Taylor took at the wake of townspeople who had passed away. It was a common practice for families to have photographs made of their departed loved ones in the first half of the 20th century and earlier.

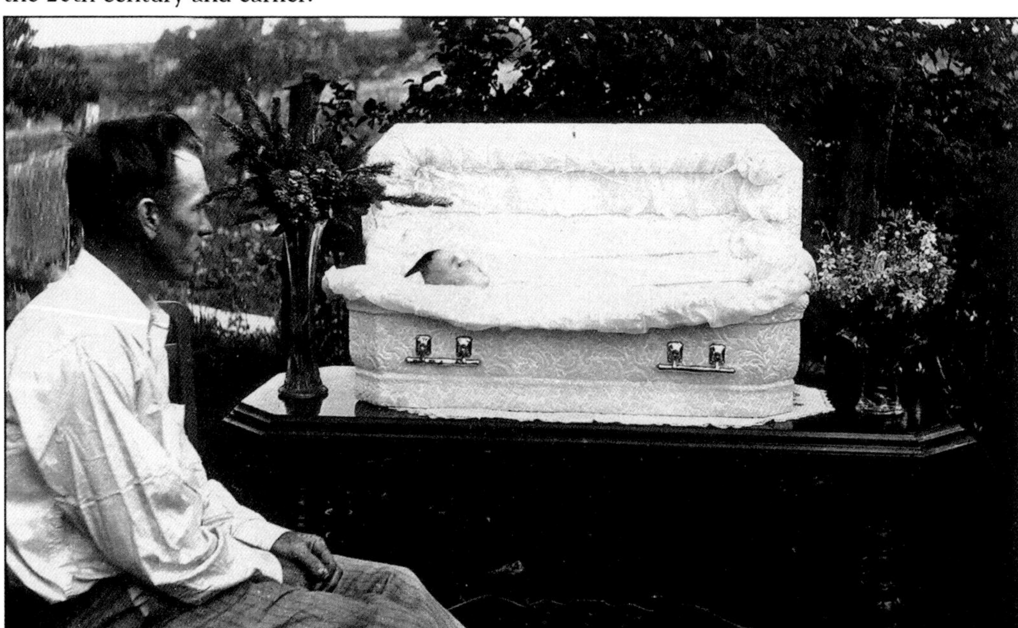

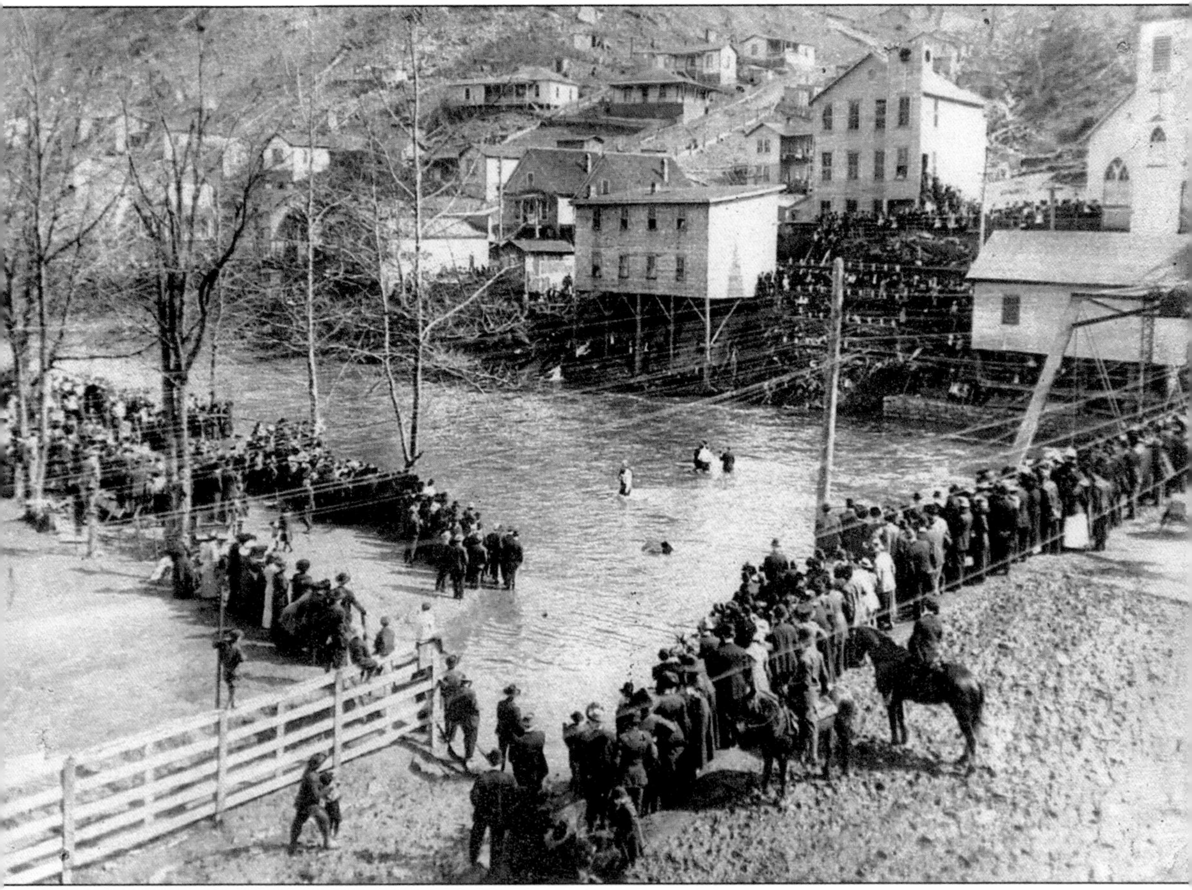

This is one of the many baptisms performed in Cherry River on either side of the steel bridge at the south end of Oakford Avenue. This bridge and identical bridge down river leading to the tannery were constructed about 1906. The lower bridge was privately owned and provided rail access to the tannery and the paper mill. The bridge pictured here was for automobiles and wagons, but it was mostly used by people crossing the river on foot. This bridge was replaced in 1921. The lower bridge stood until its foundation was undermined by flood waters in 1954, causing it to collapse. It was then torn down but not replaced because the tannery and paper mill were long gone.

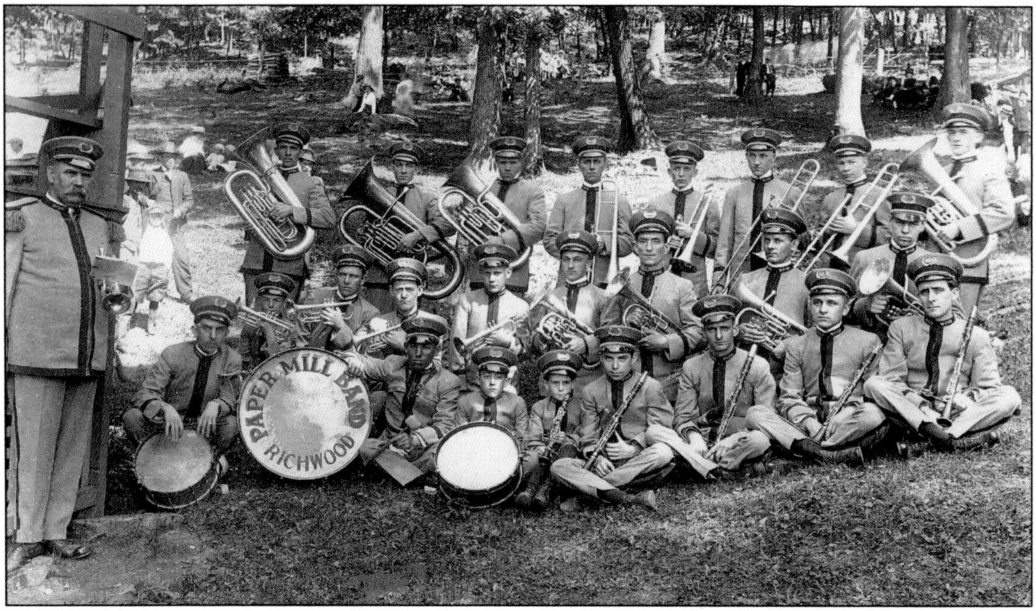


Two images of community bands are seen on this page. Richwood always had a rich sense of community. This was true of the town as a whole and also with respect to the employees of the various mills. The mills had their own bands and ball teams. In the picture above, John Shinn, band master, is beside the bandstand on the extreme left. In the front row, starting at the left, Wheeler Green is holding the snare drum; the next three members are unidentified; Wendel Holt is next holding a clarinet; and the last three are unidentified. In the second row, the first man is unknown; Gun Shinn is holding the trumpet over the drums; the next two are unidentified; George Finlinson is holding alto; the next person is ? Gainer; and the last two are unidentified. In the third row, "Tubby" Shinn is center trombone; the next two are unidentified; and finally ? Roberts, Frank Collins, Bill Davis, Harold Wolfe (with trombone), and Jim Finlinson (with baritone) are shown. Below is a photograph of the American Legion Band performing in front of the old Masonic Hall.

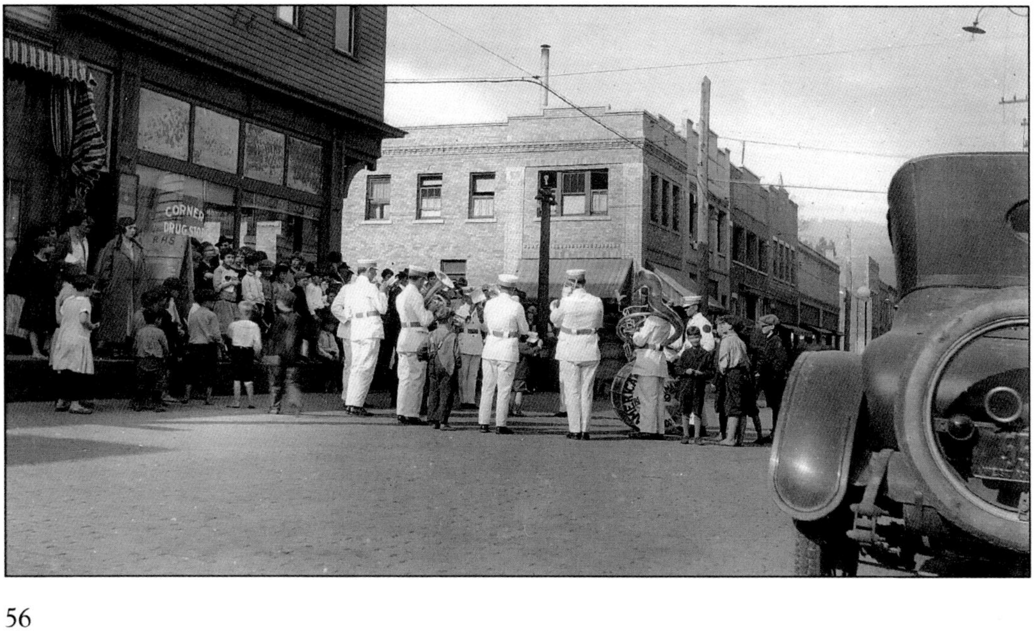

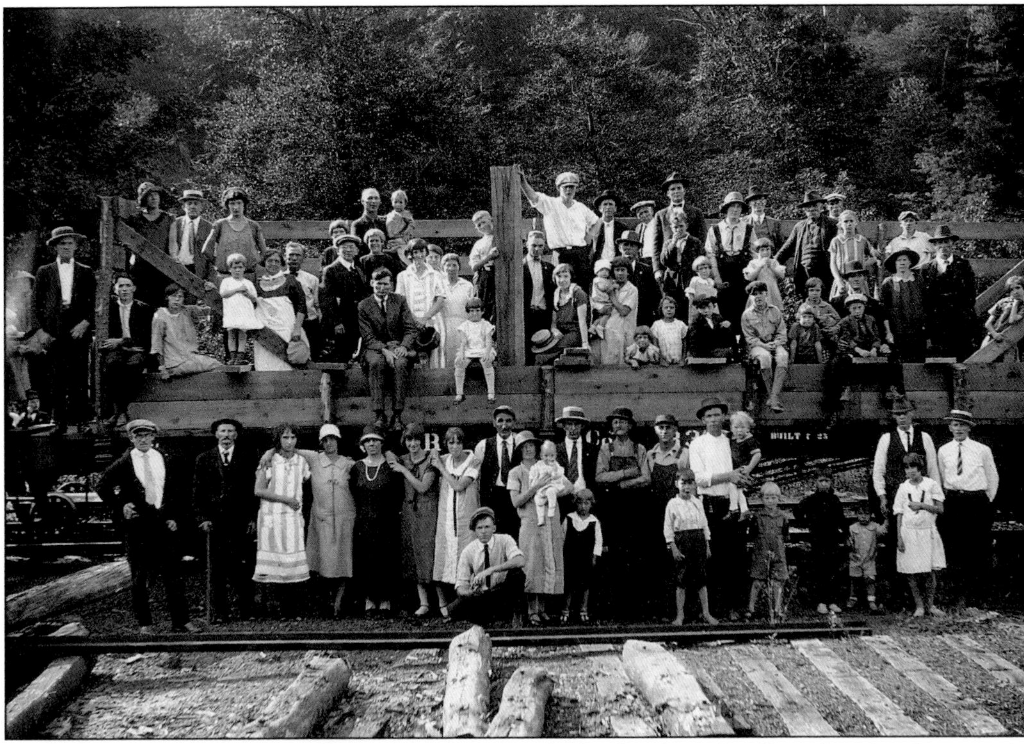

Shown above is the paper mill "dinky" packed with the families of mill workers heading out for a company picnic. Pictured below is a group of Big Mill families heading for a Sunday picnic on another day.

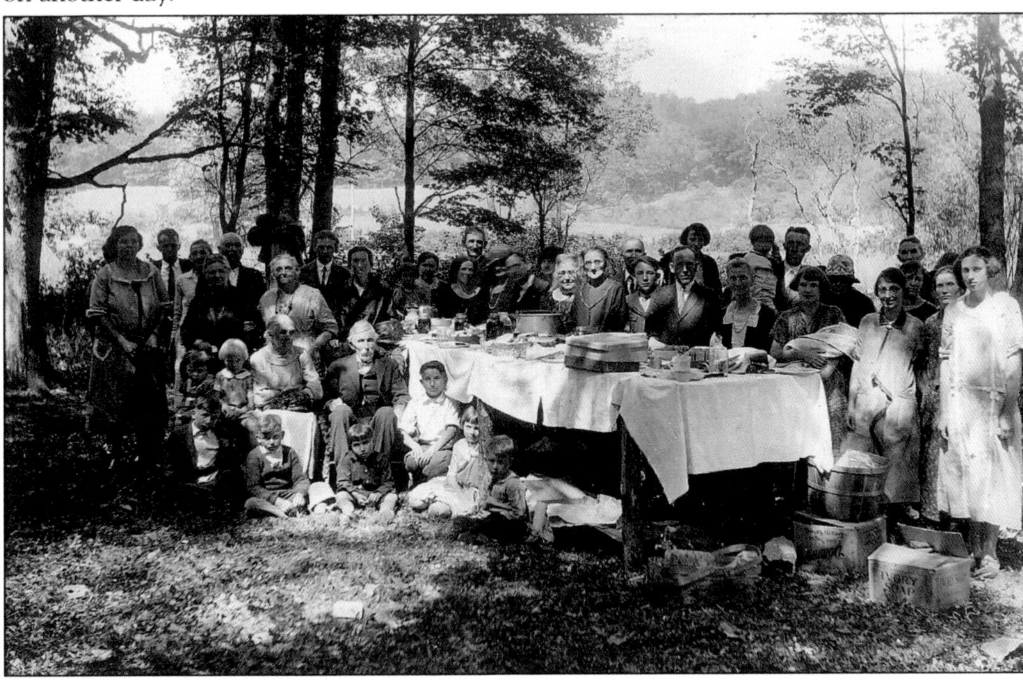

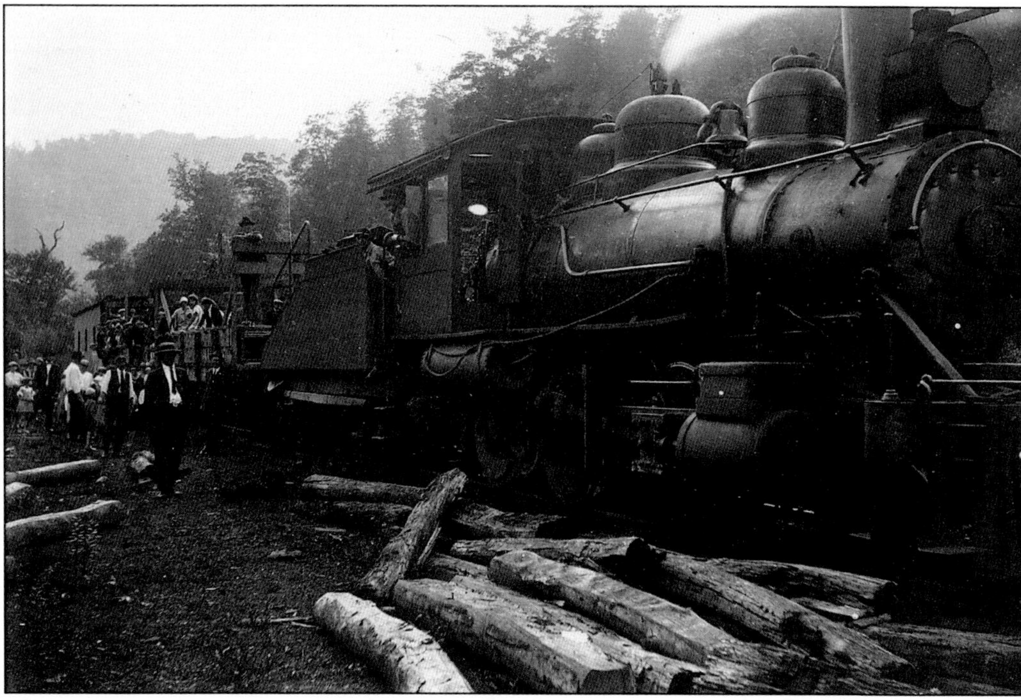

These images show what picnicking families did when they arrived at their destination. Cranberry Bottoms, the site of a small logging community before it became a Civil Conservation Corp camp, was one destination for early picnickers. Other sites included Camp Splinter on Cranberry River and North Bend on Cherry River.

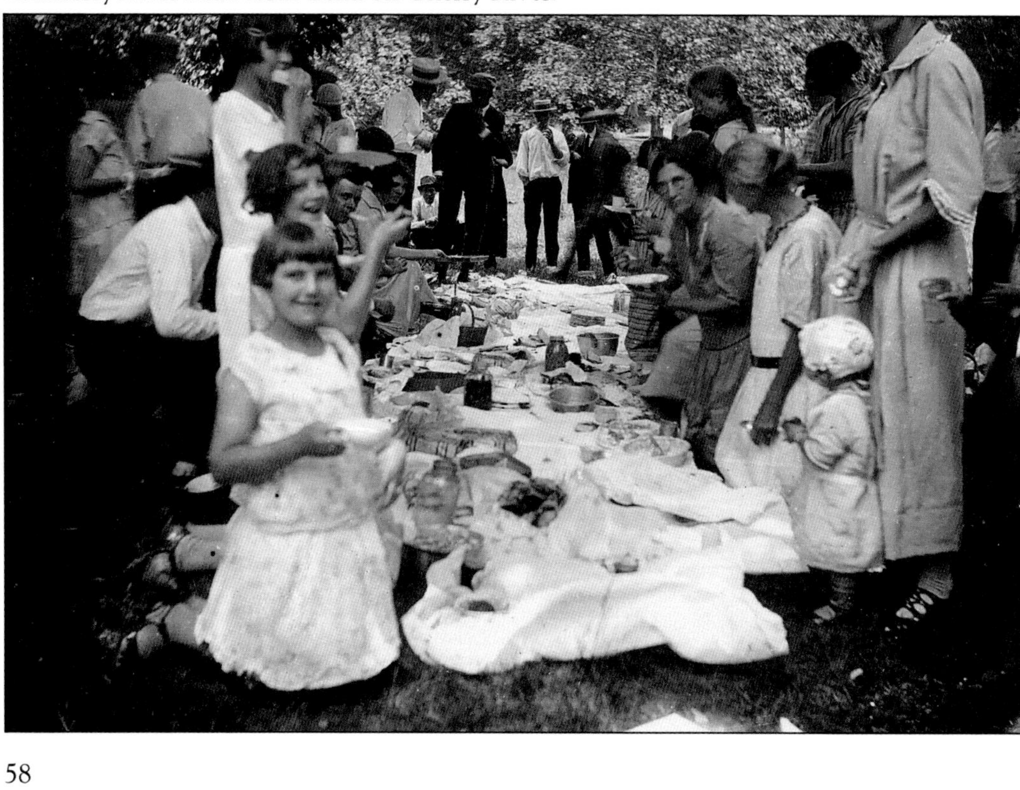

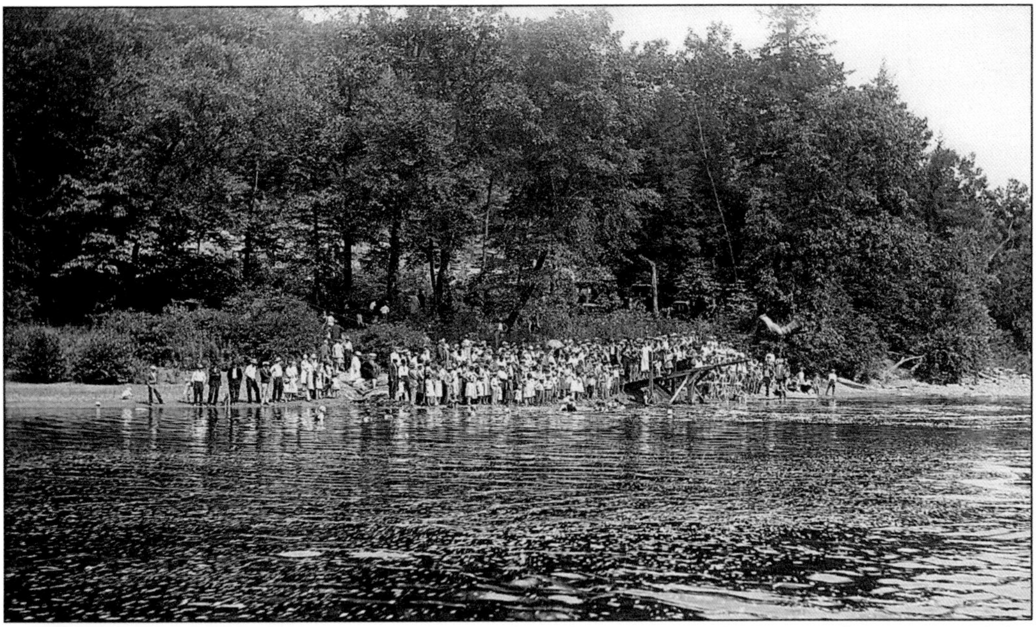

Above we see a large group of picnickers gathered at Camp Splinter watching some of the youngsters in the group enjoy one of the town's favorite swimming holes. Note that Finley caught the diver in mid-air, at the "peak of action point." Below is a close-up of swimmers taken several years later showing a rope rigged for additional excitement at the old swimming hole. What fun!

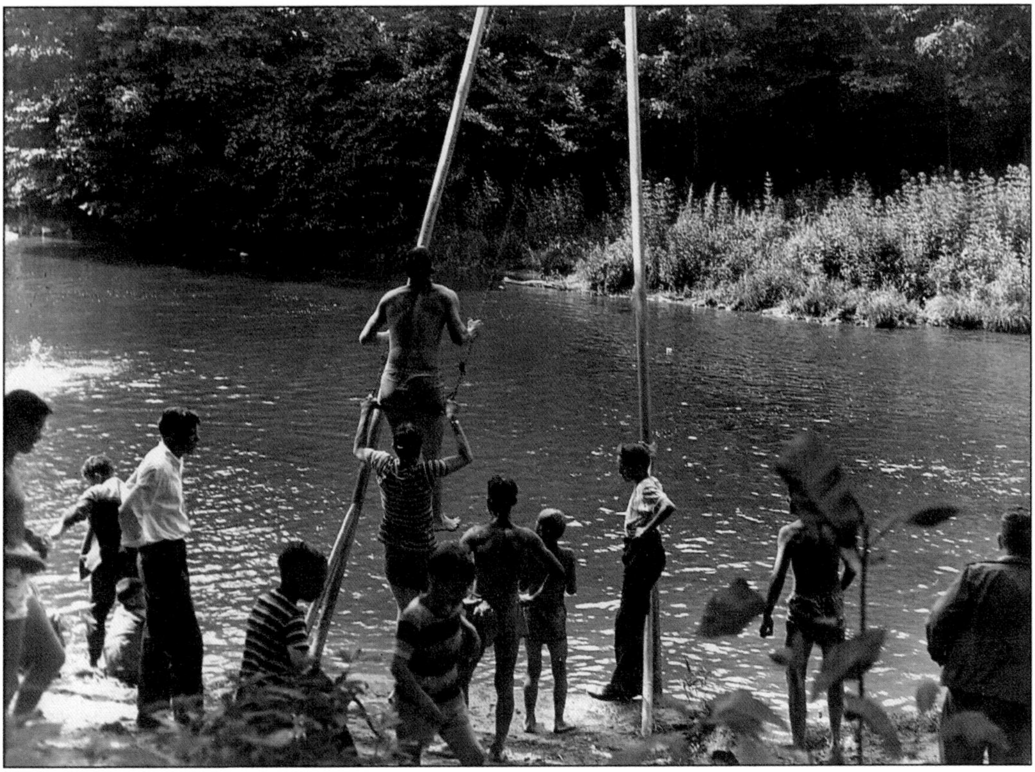

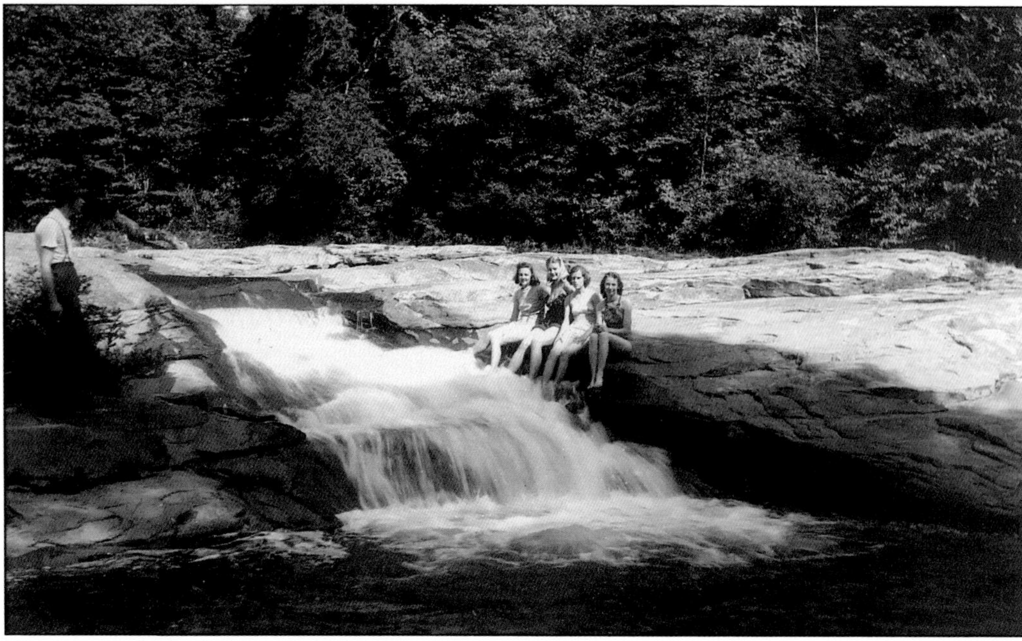

This is another of the town's favorite swimming holes. This spot, called "The Falls" on the North Fork of Cherry River, lies within walking distance east of town. On this day the usual beauty of the spot is enhanced by (from left to right) Ann Taylor, Ellen Hamilton, Irene McElwee, and Jeanette Richards.

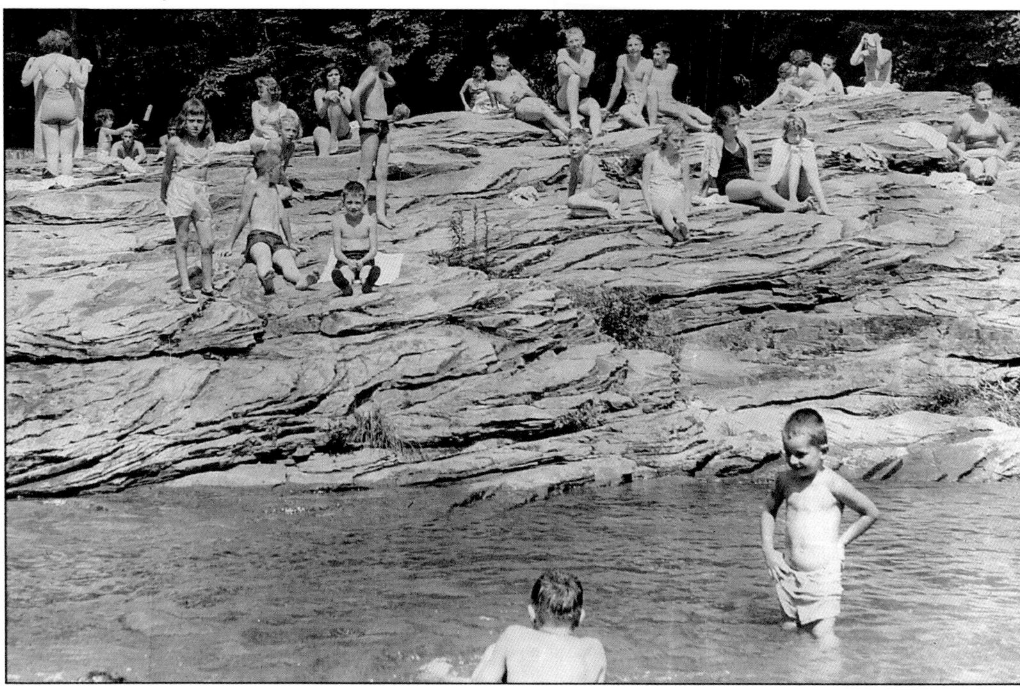

This is a close-up of The Falls that shows youngsters and adults enjoying a day at the river. Before the city built a large pool in City Park, there were so many swimmers at The Falls that it was difficult to find a spot on the rocks above the pool to lie down and soak up the rays. (*Richwood News Leader* photograph.)

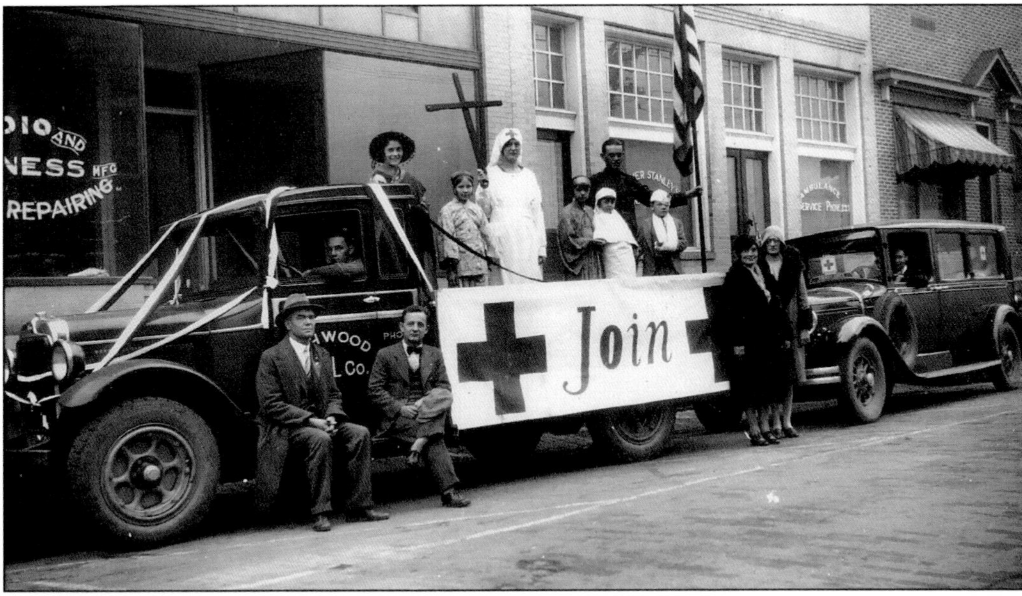


In the early years, Richwood always planned parades and other fun activities for Memorial Day and the Fourth of July. Another aspect of the town's sense of community was the various drives they carried on to support worthy causes, including the American Red Cross. The town conducted annual membership drives to recruit individuals to assist with helping the needy. The local Red Cross organization was very active and provided significant support to needy families in the community, not just in war zones. In 1932–1933, 240 volunteers worked 1,554 hours sewing 8,000 yards of government-donated material into 3,714 garments given to 428 families and 2,145 individuals. They also distributed 10,500 sacks of government-supplied flour and organized other support activities. Pictured above are individuals representing the local Red Cross in one of the town's annual membership drives. Newspaper articles indicate that the local Red Cross organization nearly always met their quotas in the membership drives. Pictured below is a large group of ladies at sewing machines in the town's Recreation Hall, where they gathered to sew the garments from cloth donated by the government.

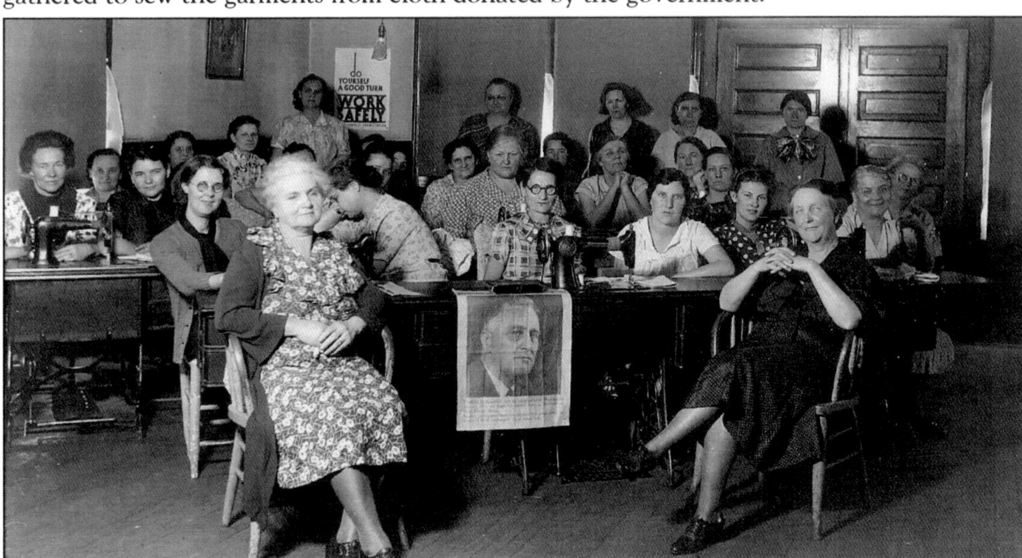

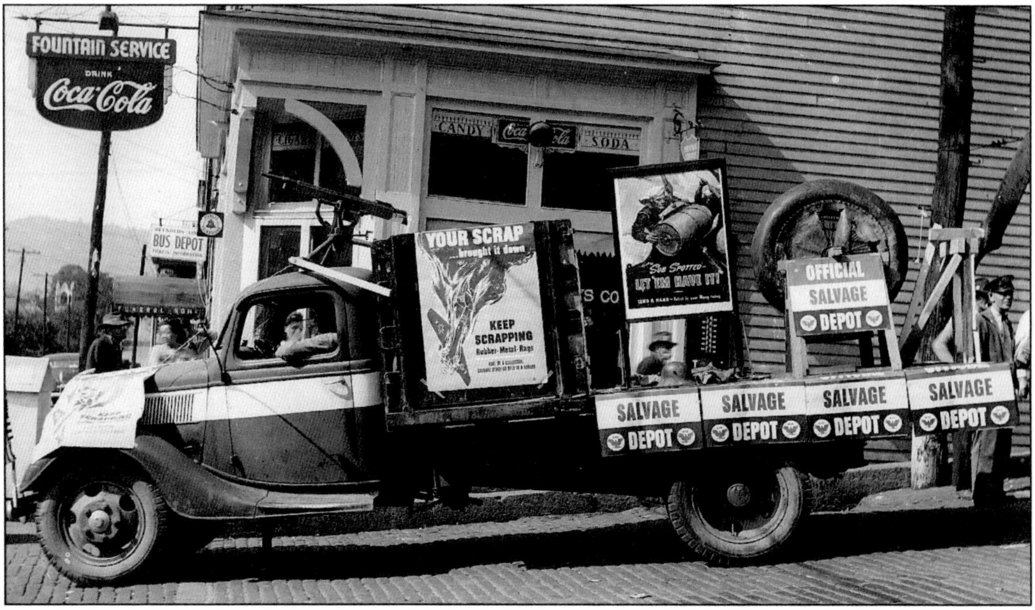


This great picture is of a truck decorated to draw attention to the town's patriotic efforts, which included a scrap metal drive, during World War II. The truck is parked at the corner of Main Street and Oakford Avenue by the Richwood News Company building. This building and the American Legion Building beside it were destroyed by fire just weeks after this photograph was made.

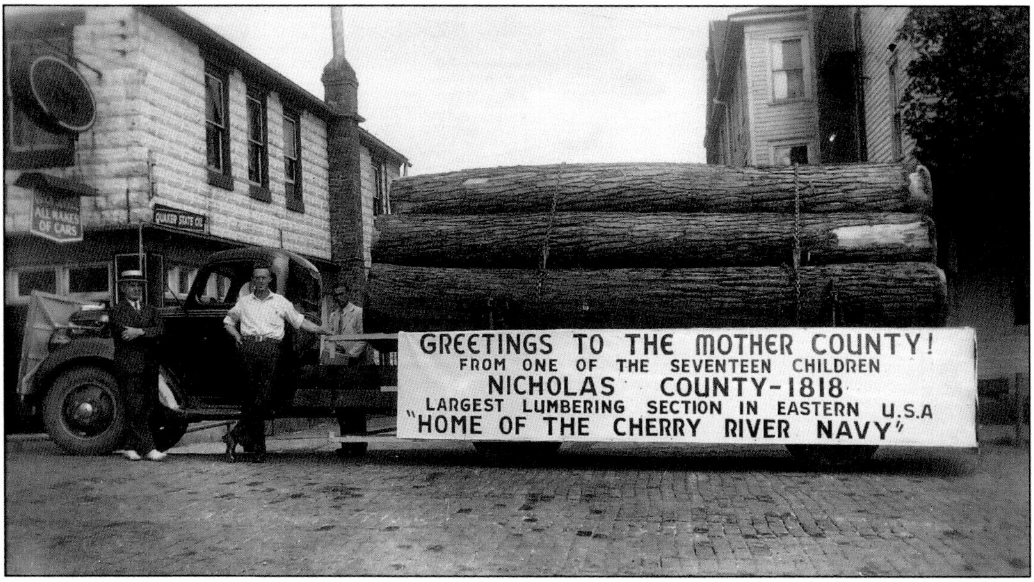


As if the town didn't already have enough reasons to plan a parade, it invented one of its own special events, the annual Spud and Splinter Festival. The Spud and Splinter Festival started in 1932 with activities scheduled for the first full week of August each year. Pictured above is one of the units from an early parade highlighting the town's lumber industry. Nicholas and adjacent counties have supplied timber for several famous projects including the construction of the *Titanic* in Great Britain, the remodeling of the USS *Constitution* in Boston Harbor, and most recently, the reconstruction of the famous covered bridge in Philippi, West Virginia.

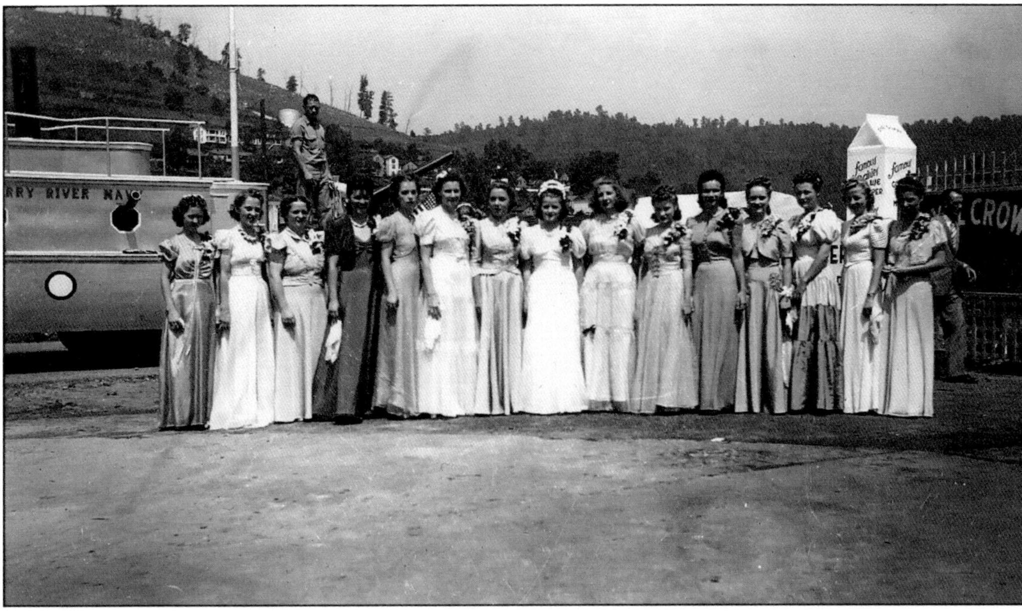

Every festival has its queen and her attendants, and the Spud and Splinter Festival was no exception. Pictured here is the 1940 Sweetheart of the Cherry River Navy, Helen McElwee (eighth from the left), and runner-up Marian Johnson (eleventh from the left). The attendants (not in any particular order) are Alma Ruth Tomlin, Marian Johnson, Mary Louise Morrison, Jennie Trimble, Frances Groves, Lucille Reynolds, Eleanor Carter, Camilla Coleman, Katy Hinkle, Pauline Jones, Eleanor Cutlip, Leona Hutchinson, and Zeta Lee Hanrahan.

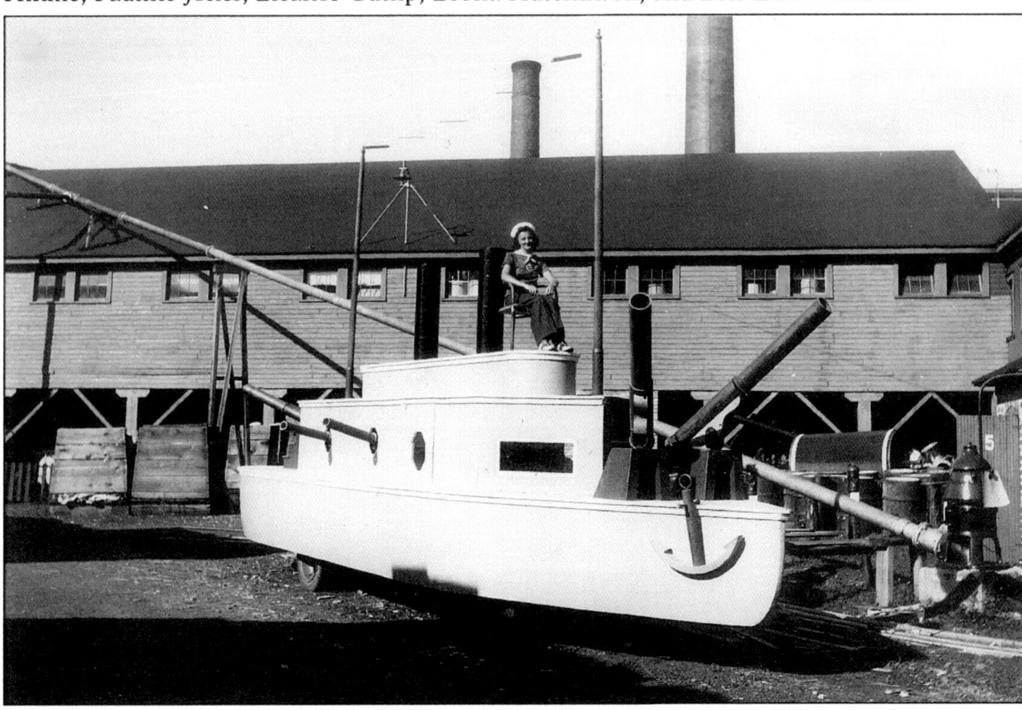

One of the unique features of the Spud and Splinter Festival parade was the Good Ship *Clothes Pin*. Pictured on the *Clothes Pin* is Jeanette Richards, 1938 Cherry River Navy Sweetheart.

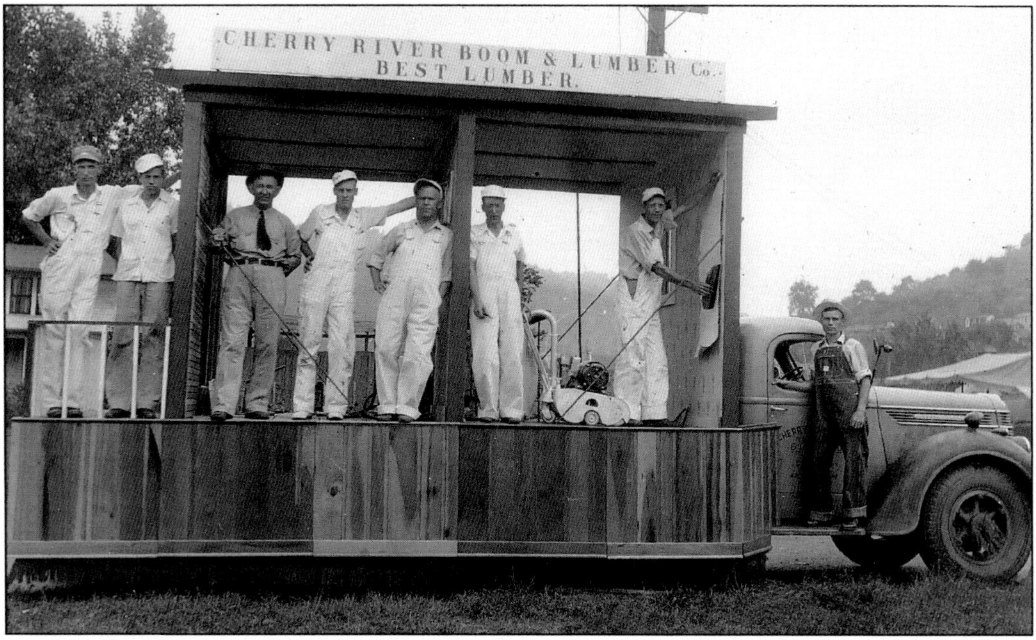


This is the 1941 float sponsored by the Cherry River Boom & Lumber Company. Pictured from left to right are Claude Tharpe, Howard Bennett, Gar Sturgill, "Red" Facemire, "Boss" Barnett, Dave Green, Howard Bennett, and Charlie Davis.

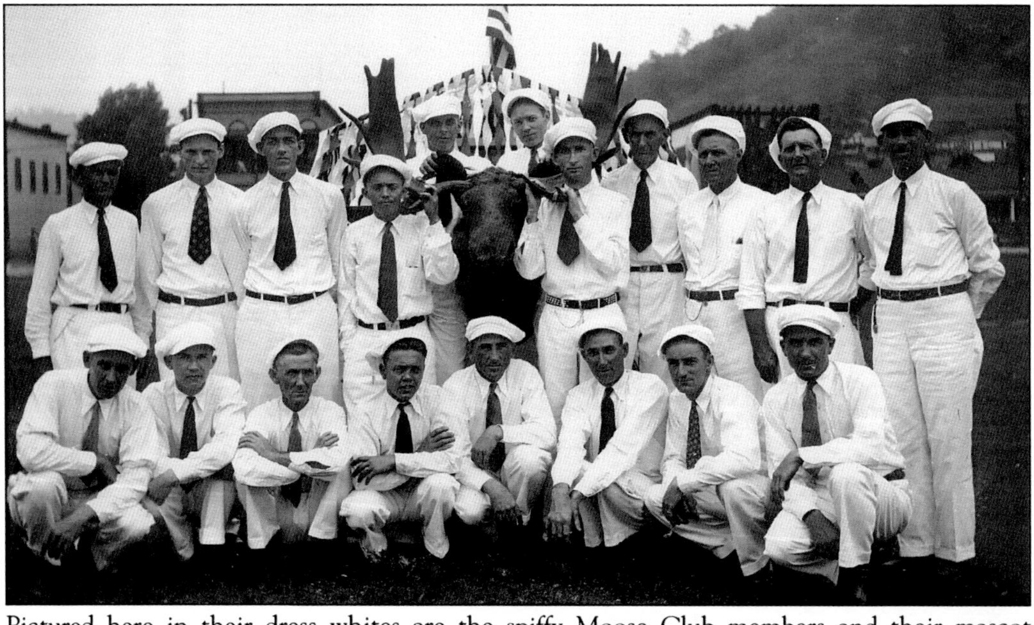

Pictured here in their dress whites are the spiffy Moose Club members and their mascot preparing to board their float for a Spud and Splinter parade. In the first row, from left to right, are Raymond Keeper, Delbert Miller, Morgan Brown, Lewis Wheeler, Lon Carter, Charley Giles, Russell Westfall, and Dice Snedeger. In the second row (from left to right) are Homer Doddrill, Bob Morton, Harley Bennett, George Wheeler, Jack Wills, Ivan Hunter, Dick Young, Bill Rigsby, and Tom Creasy. The men between the moose antlers in the rear are Arden Faulkner on the left and Earl Young on the right.

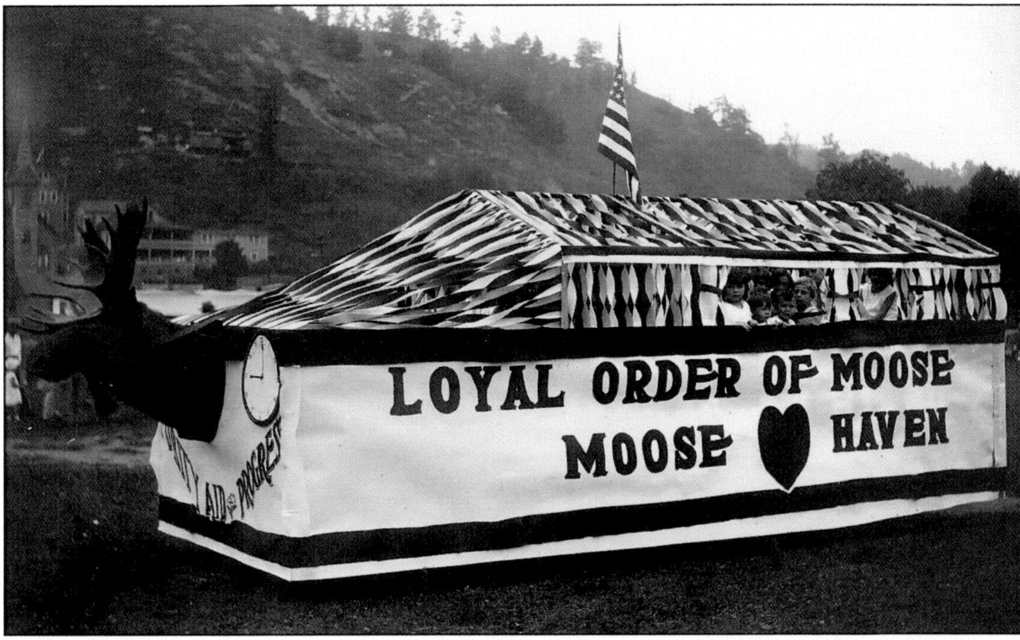


Pictured above is the Moose Club parade float. Pictured below is the 1938 Sweetheart of the Cherry River Navy and her attendants trying their hand at making splinters. From left to right are Irene McElwee, Jean Ellen Hamilton, Ann Taylor, and Sweetheart Jeanette Richards.

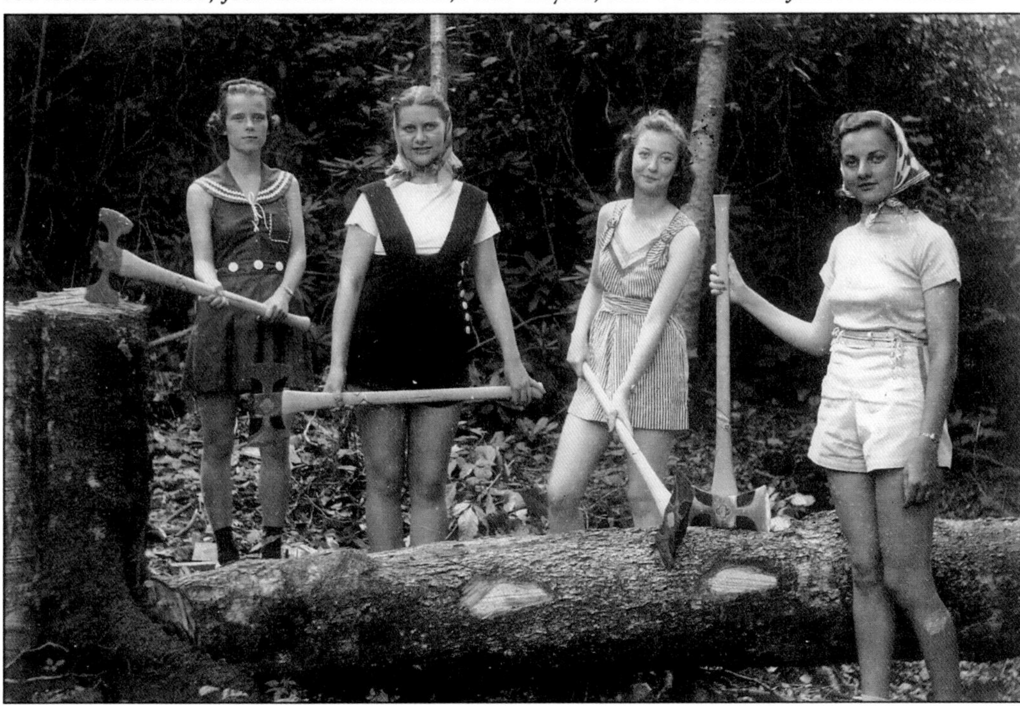

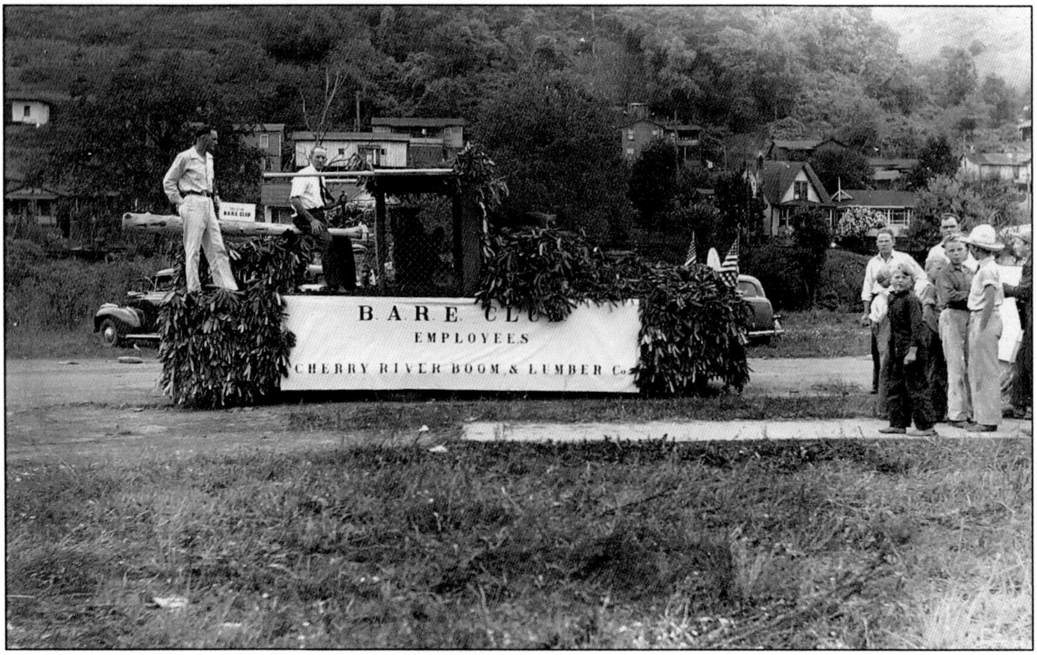


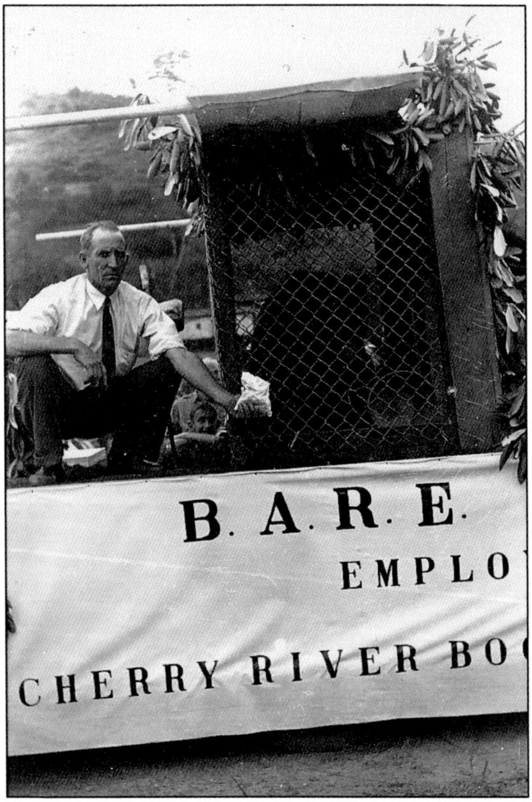


This page features two views of the Cherry River Boom & Lumber Company B.A.R.E. Employees Club float with their bear mascot. The B.A.R.E. Club was a club organized and managed by the employees to extend health benefits to participating members. In the 1930s the Richwood club chairman was Jennings Spencer and the Jerryville club chairman was Ed Hivick.

# *Five*

# STREET SCENES AND SMALL BUSINESSES

*"Richwood consists of a grass plot of several acres entirely surrounded by a well built city. Nobody ever thought it worth while to mention that right in the heart of town they have kept a fine park. It is the only town I know of in West Virginia that had the vision to do this..." (From the article, "Richwood in 1926, As Visited and Written about by Andrew Price," editor of* Pocahontas Times, *1929 West Virginia Blue Book.)*

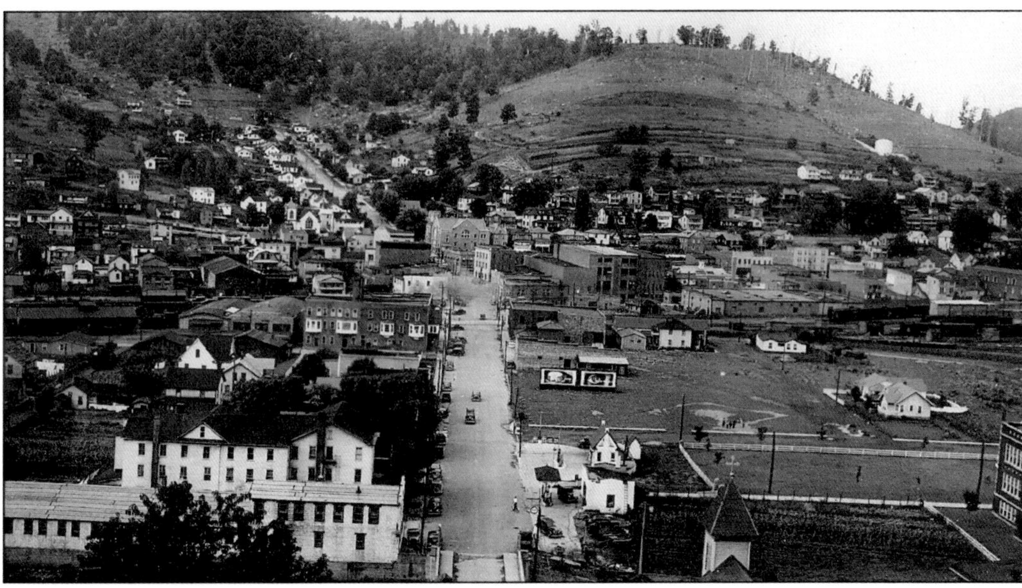

This is a view of the town showing Oakford Avenue running north and south and Main Street running east and west. The Big Mill can be see on the right of the picture and the pin factory just right of center in the foreground. The open area in the center is the fine park referred to in the chapter introduction on this page. After World War II when the paper mill was long abandoned, the paper mill became a new site for the city park and swimming pool. The open space in the middle of town was mostly taken over by residences and small businesses. The steep grade of upper Oakford Avenue was a favorite sled track for the town's youngsters in winter and remained so until a child was killed on the avenue when his sled collided with a car at the bottom of the hill.

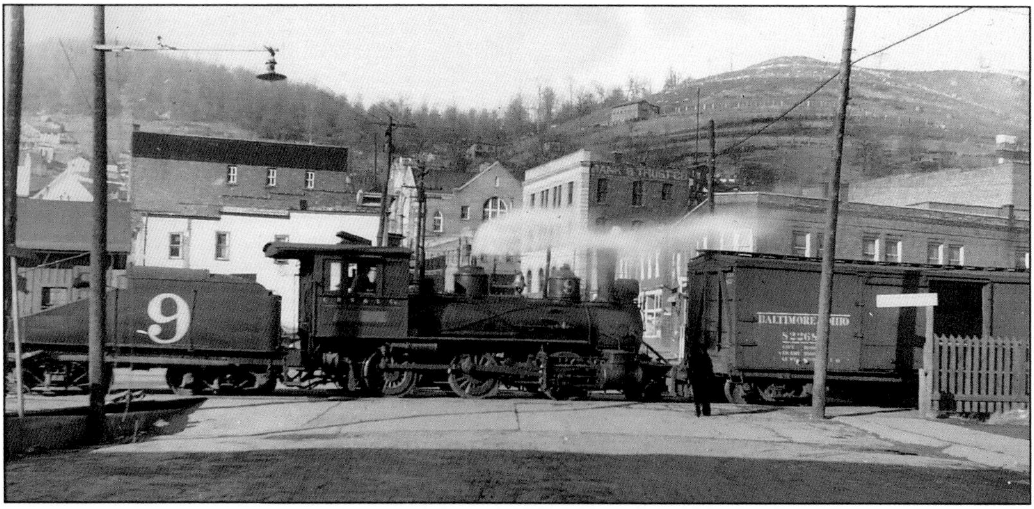


Above is the Cherry River Boom & Lumber Company rod engine No. 9. This was one of the oldest engines used by the company dating back to 1906. Railroad buffs report that this engine was fabricated from parts of three engines. It was used as a yard engine to switch cars in the lumber yard and around the mill. Rod engines (as opposed to shay engines) worked fine on level or nearly level grades. Another limitation for rod engines was that they could not operate on the company's railroads beyond the last trackside elevated water tank, regardless of the steepness of the grade. They had to take on water by gravity fed from above. Shay engines could siphon water from a stream or pond below the track and consequently could operate beyond the elevated water tanks.

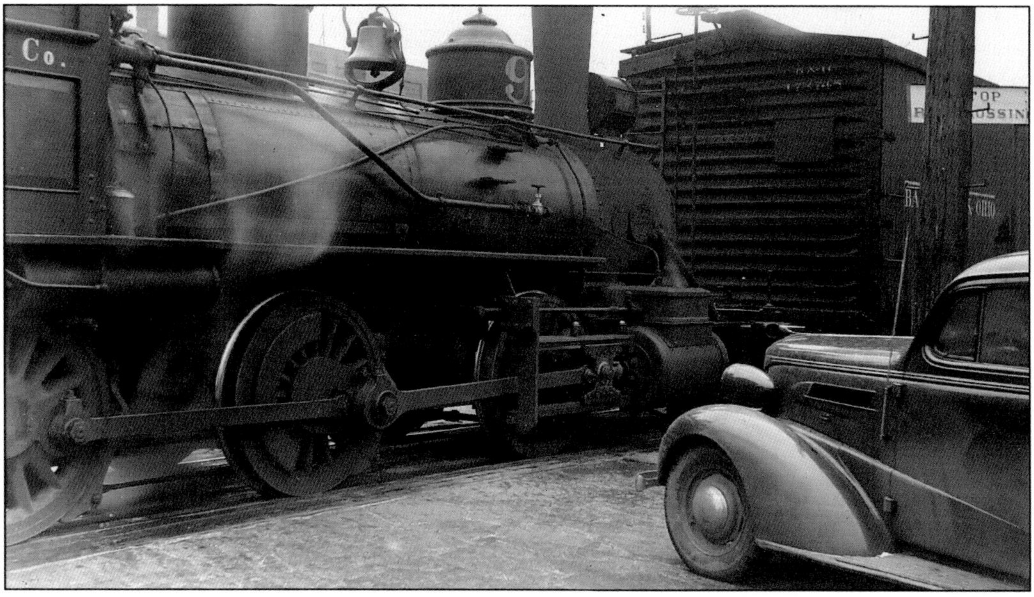


Here again is old No. 9 crossing Oakford Avenue pushing a boxcar. One of the interesting things about a mill town during the age of steam was that it was difficult to put a child to bed for a quiet nap. Mills blew their steam whistles several times a day to signal the beginning of the day, lunch time, end of lunch time, quitting time, and emergencies. In addition, locomotives blew their steam whistles every time they approached a railroad crossing. Under the right conditions, a steam whistle can be heard for several miles.

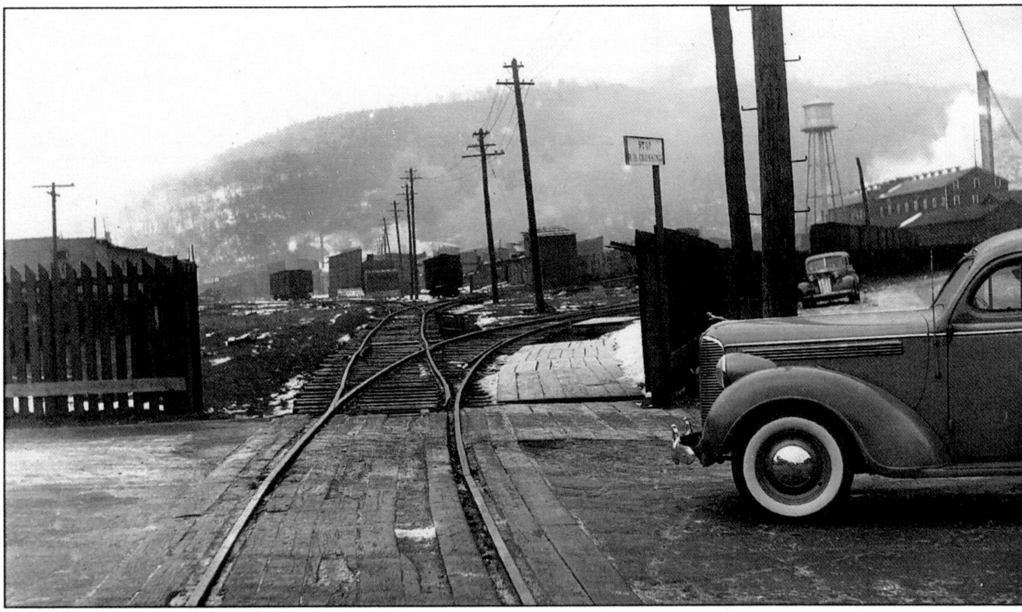

This is a view of the railroad tracks looking eastward. The track heading off to the right in the photograph is the track to the pin factory. The track going straight ahead is the access to the Big Mill. The Big Mill track had many branches providing access to the mill and to the many rows of lumber stacked in the lumber yard.

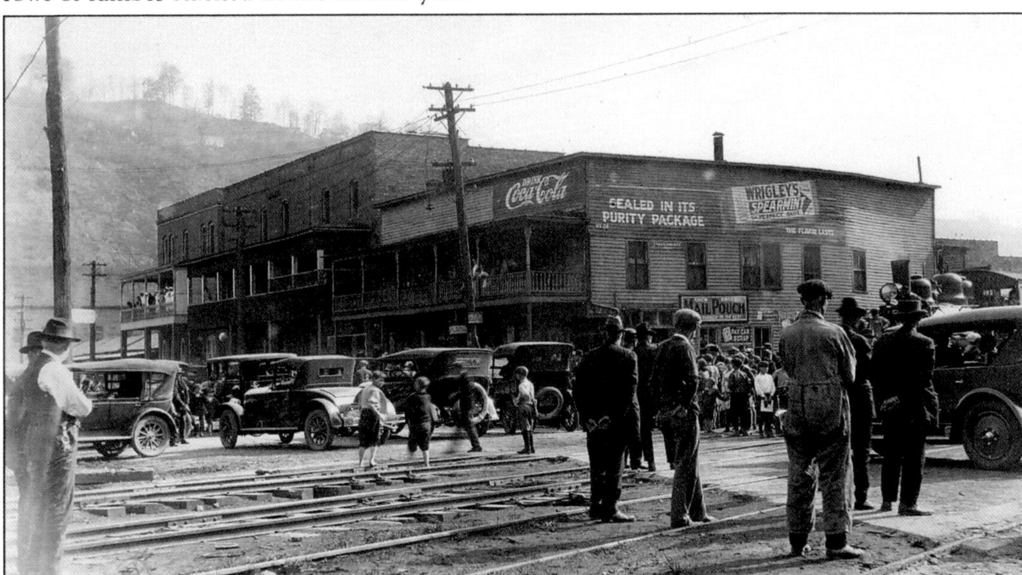


This is an earlier view of the same railroad crossing on Oakford Avenue when there were four tracks crossing the road instead of one. The railroad depot, just out of sight in the picture on the right, was quite a busy place in the town's heyday. In addition to the many carloads of lumber and wood products shipped out each day, there were many carloads of logs brought in and two Baltimore and Ohio passenger trains that arrived and departed each day. By the end of World War II, rail traffic had greatly diminished and the passenger service was cut to one train in and out per day.

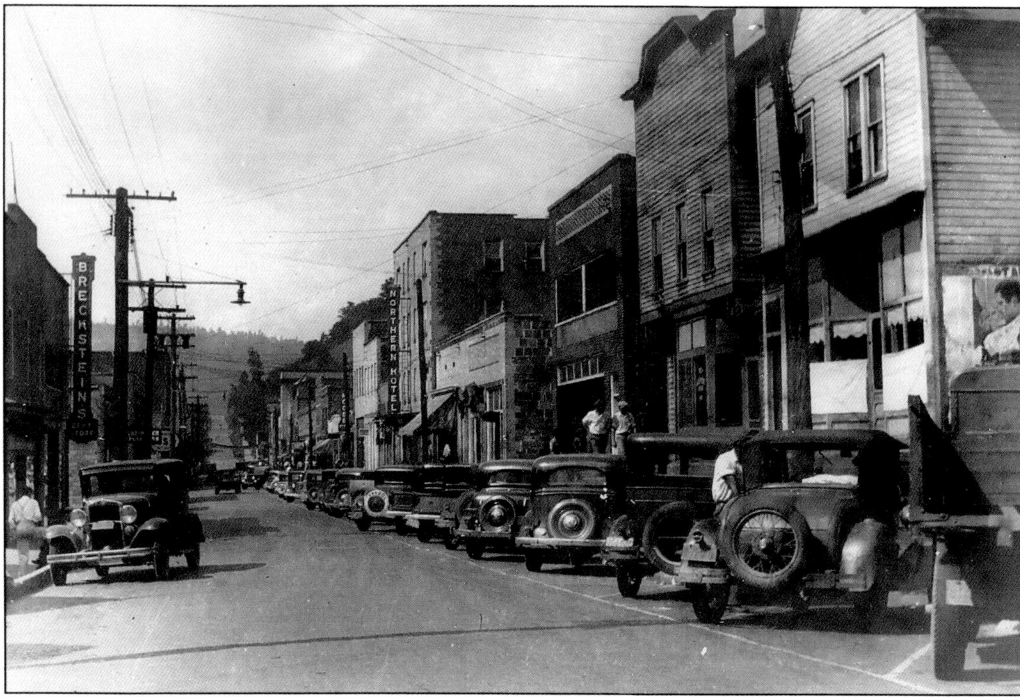


These are two scenes of Main Street when the wagons were mostly gone and automobiles had taken over. Automobiles were shorter then. Notice that parking on Main Street was diagonal until bigger cars made it necessary to change to horizontal parking. Even though vehicles became larger and larger, the width of the streets had to stay the same.

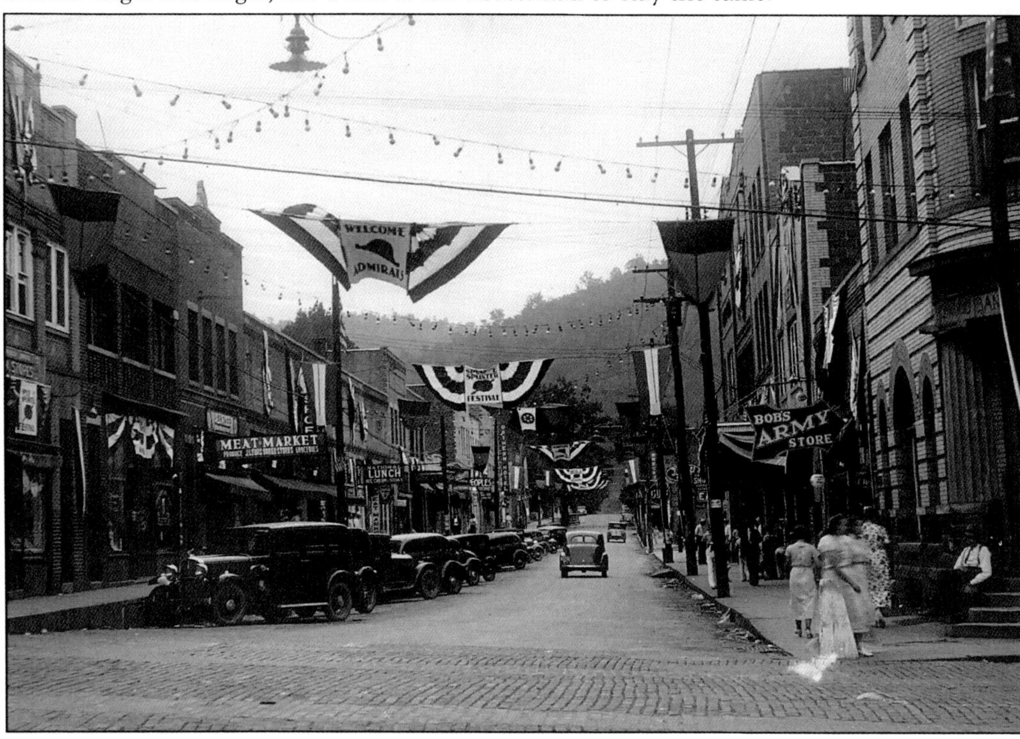

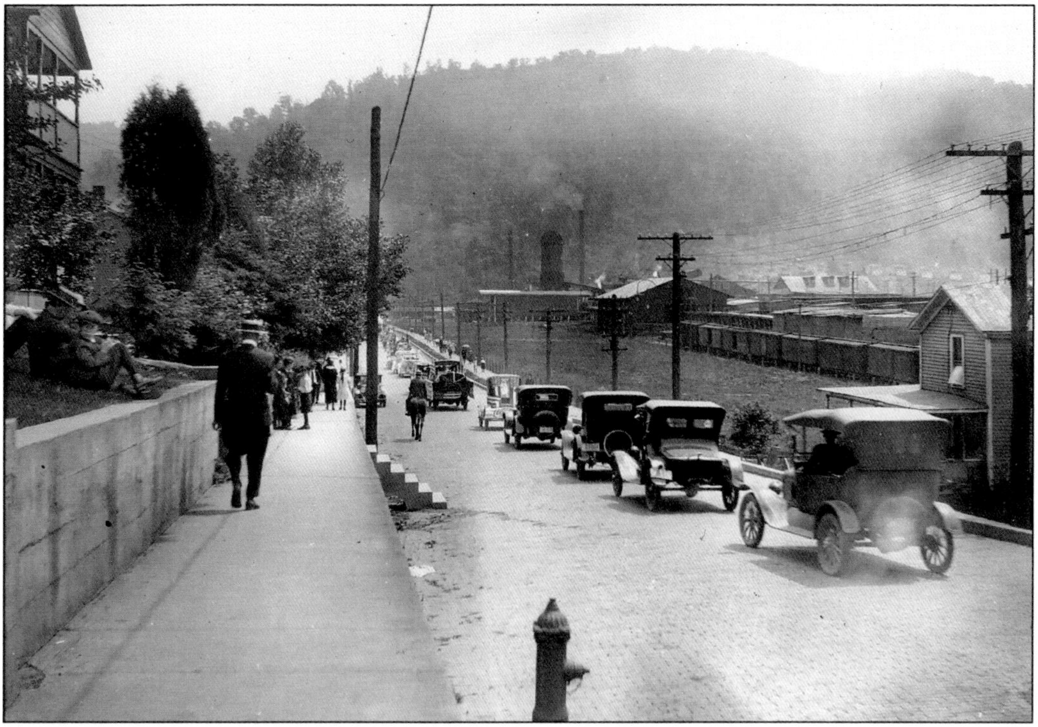

Pictured here are two opposite ends of Main Street. The picture above is a 1920s view toward the east end of Main Street. A few cars have fallen in behind the tail end of one of the town's many parades. On the right in the picture is the lower end of the Big Mill complex and a portion of the lumber yard. Pictured below is an image of the other end of Main Street at the top of town hill. A street crew is cleaning up after one of the many mud slides from the high bank on the left. These slides still occur today but there is a high brim that catches all but the worst of slides.

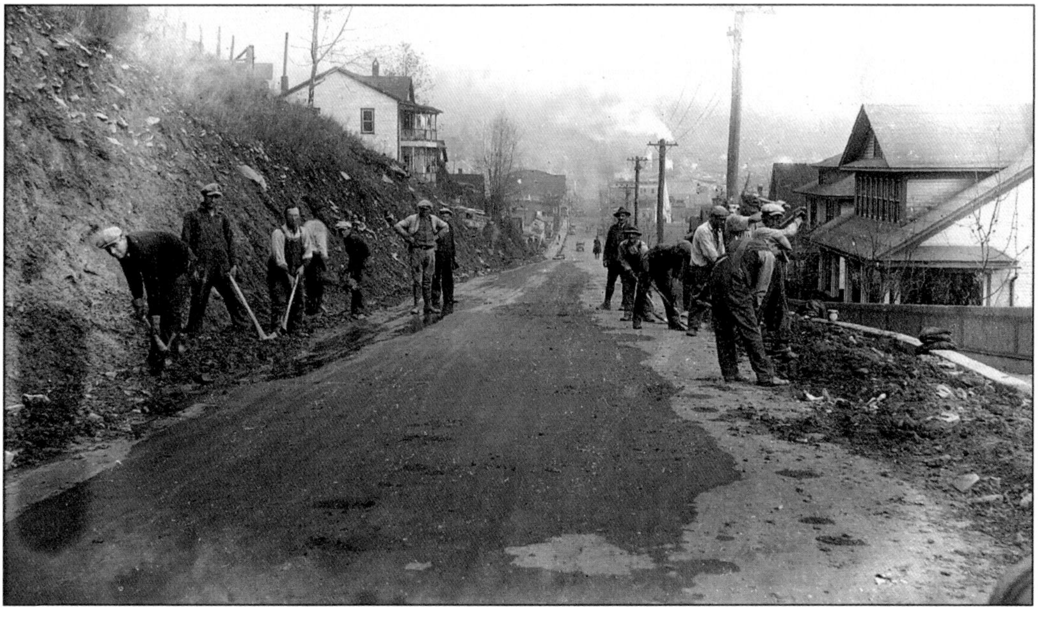

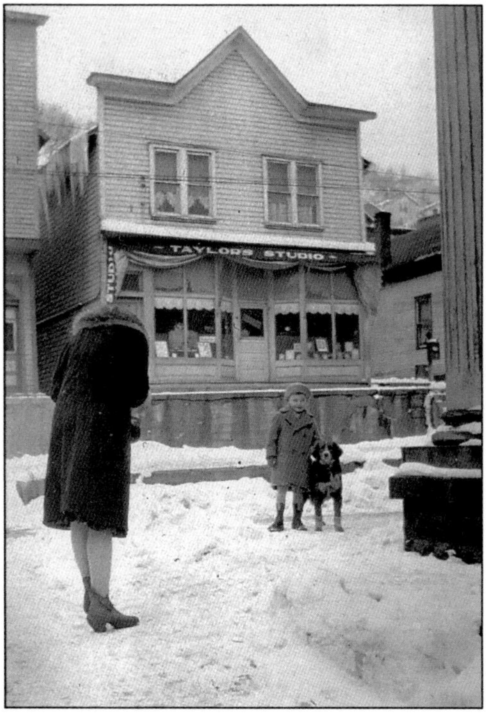


Here is an image of an unidentified woman photographing a child in front of the Taylor Studio. This could be Finley Taylor's wife and one of his daughters, Marie or Maureen. Although this cannot be confirmed, it seems highly unlikely that the composition of this photograph with the studio in the background is by accident. Additional support for this idea is the fact that this image was reprinted from an original photograph found among Finley's studio contents.

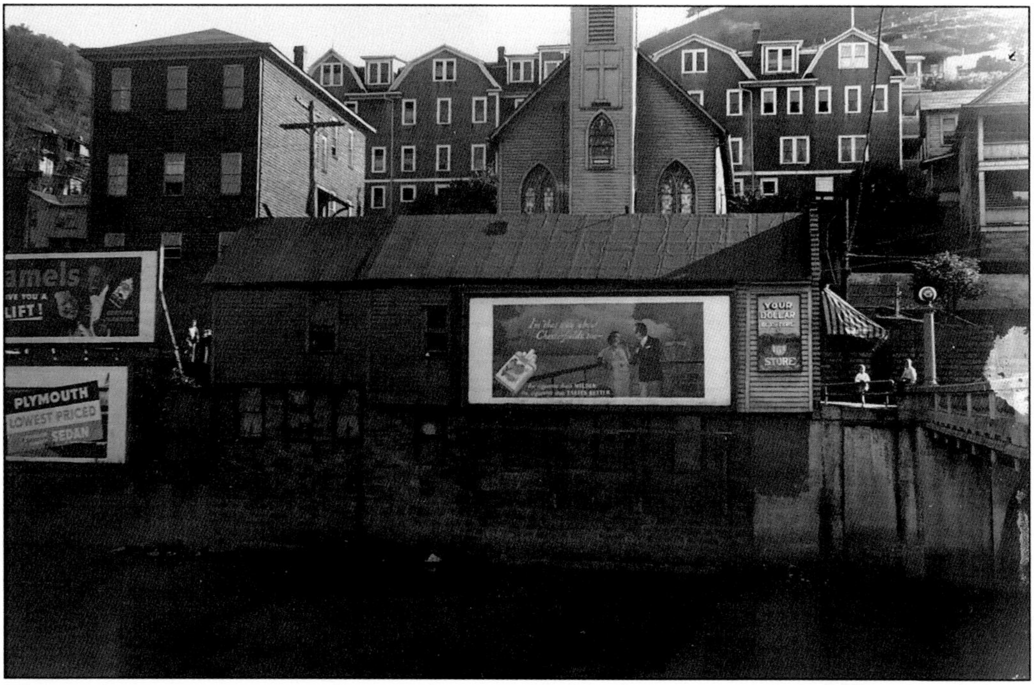


This is a fantastic street scene showing the end of Oakford Avenue. In the middle ground above the billboards is the Midget Super Market. In the background is the old Catholic Hospital, Holy Family Church, Holy Family School (to the left of the church), and the parsonage (to the right of the church). The hospital served Richwood until a new hospital was built on the site of the old tannery.

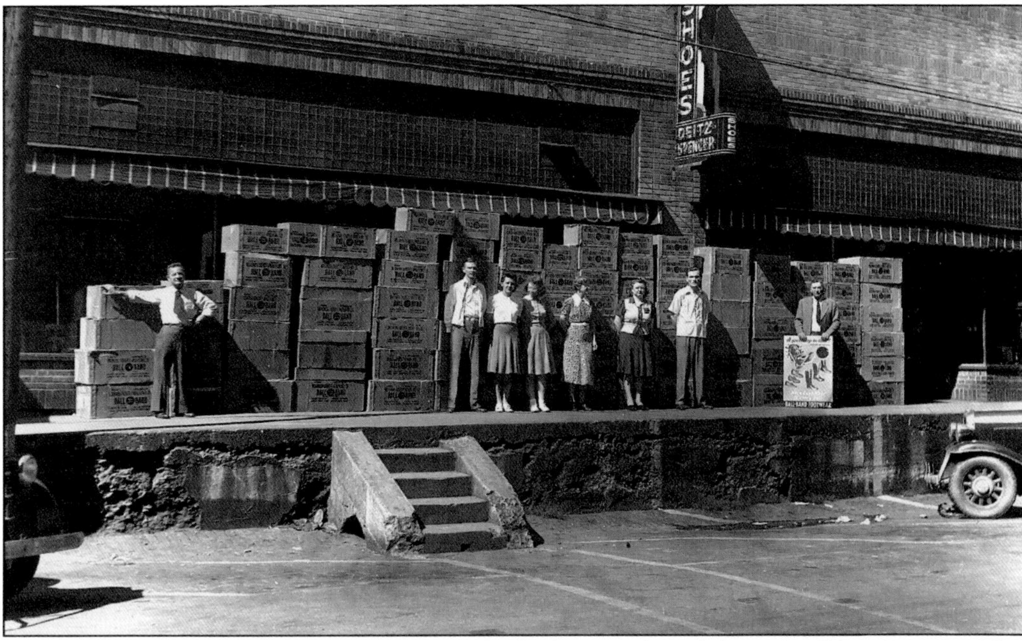


Here Finley Taylor has captured the arrival of a large order of shoes for Deitz-Spencer Shoe Store. Pictured from left to right are A.G. "Shorty" Spencer, Ray Friend, Freddy Perkins, Groetha Brice, Mrs. Emerson Deitz, Juanita Hall, Sam Hall, and a Ball Band footwear salesman.

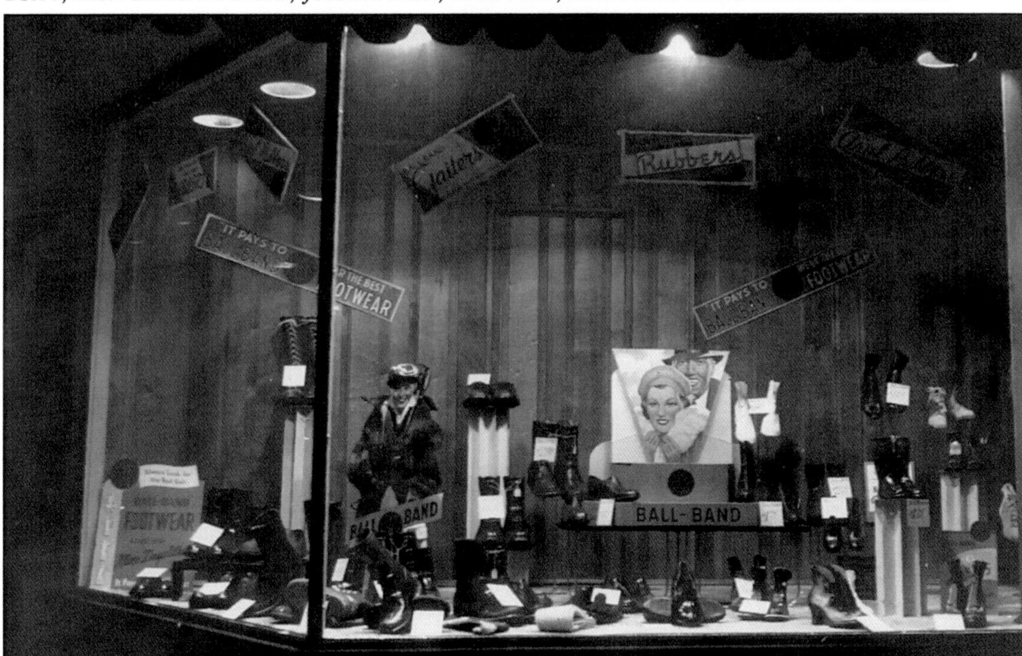


Pictured here is the Ball Band store window display that was set up after the arrival of the new shipment of shoes. Finley had to work within the limitations of the photographic equipment that was available to him. One type of photograph that worked well with slow lenses was a long exposure of artificially lighted scenes, such as store windows. Subsequently, he left behind numerous images of the store windows on main street.

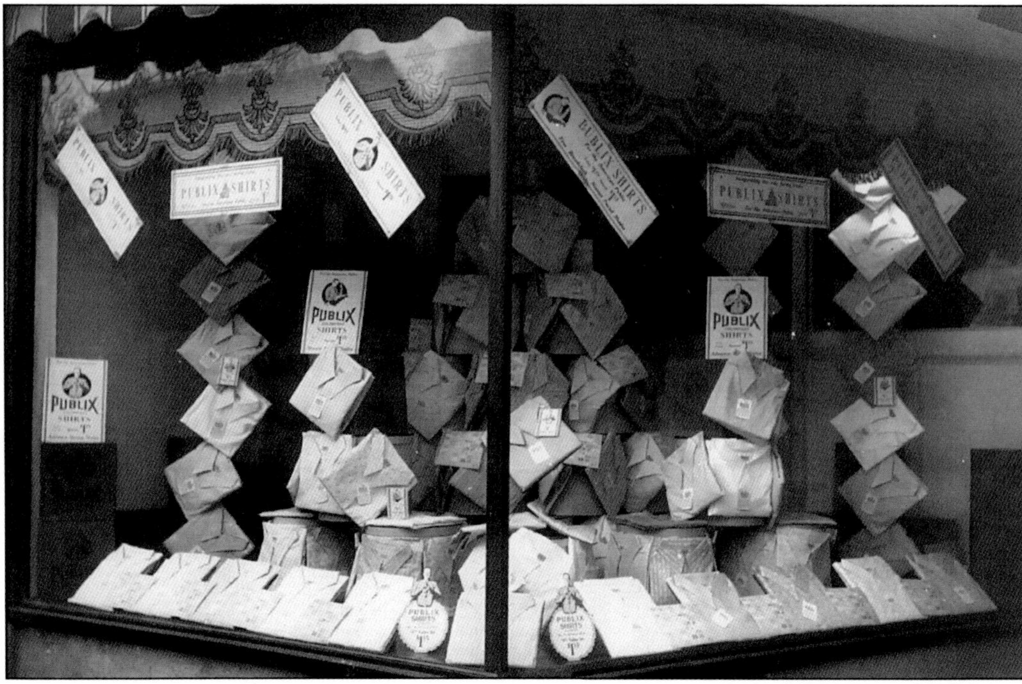


Pictured on this page are two additional store-front images. The top image is a display of men's shirts. The bottom photograph is a store window advertisement for Star Hams.

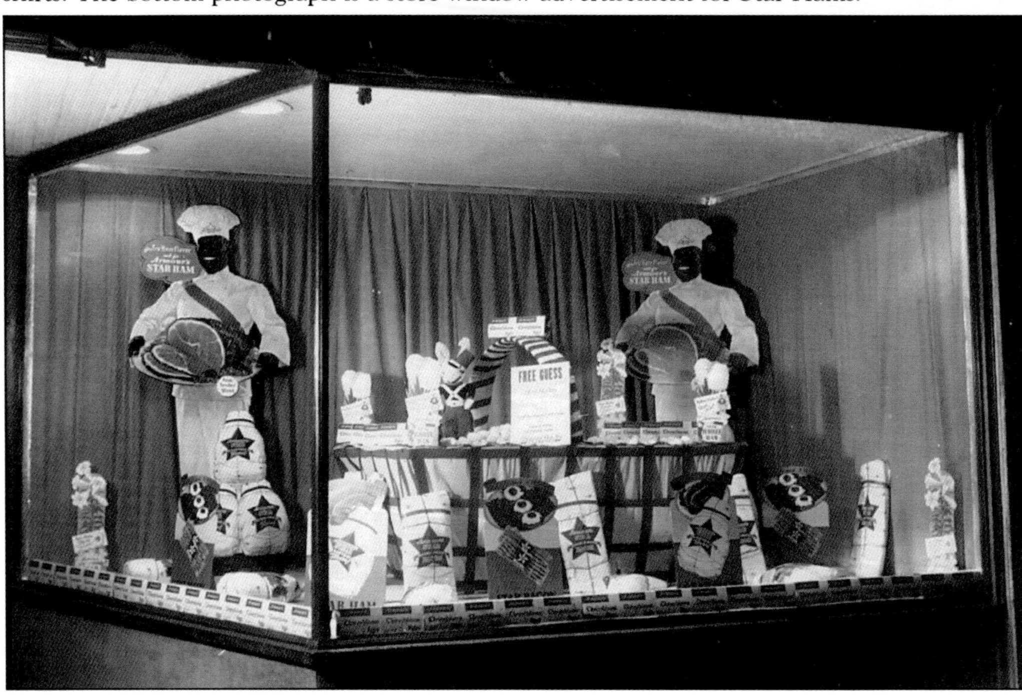

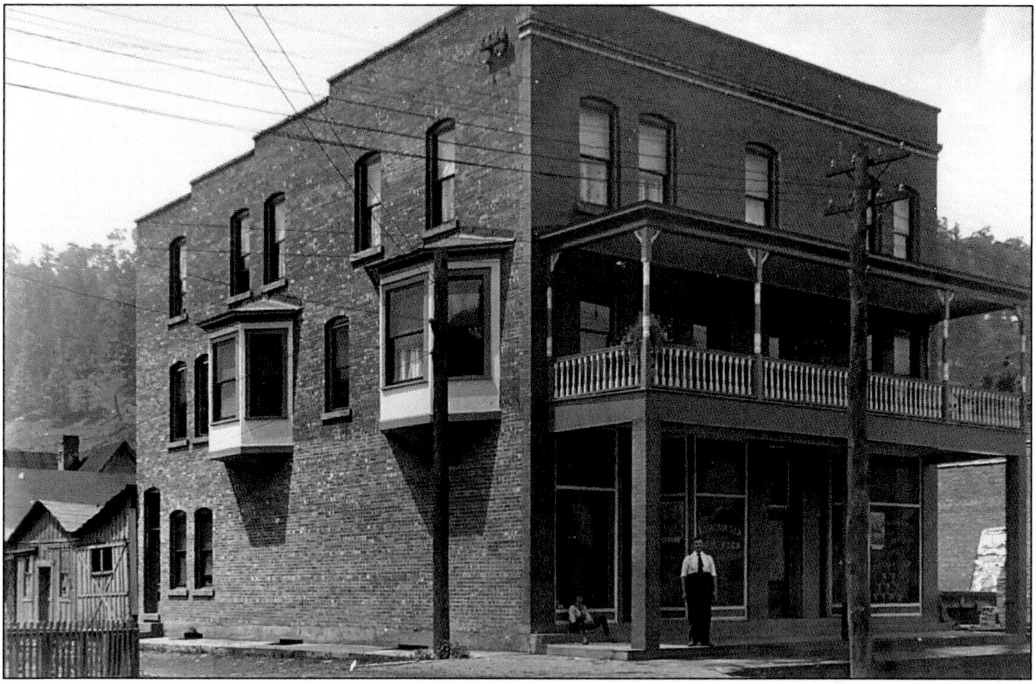

Here is the A.J. Krashowitz Building when it was a pool room. Later it would become the second McClung Hospital, as pictured below. Nurses are standing on the second floor balcony of the hospital. If you look closely on the left side of the building, you can see the outline of the original building above. The building was enlarged to about twice the original capacity and an elevator was installed.

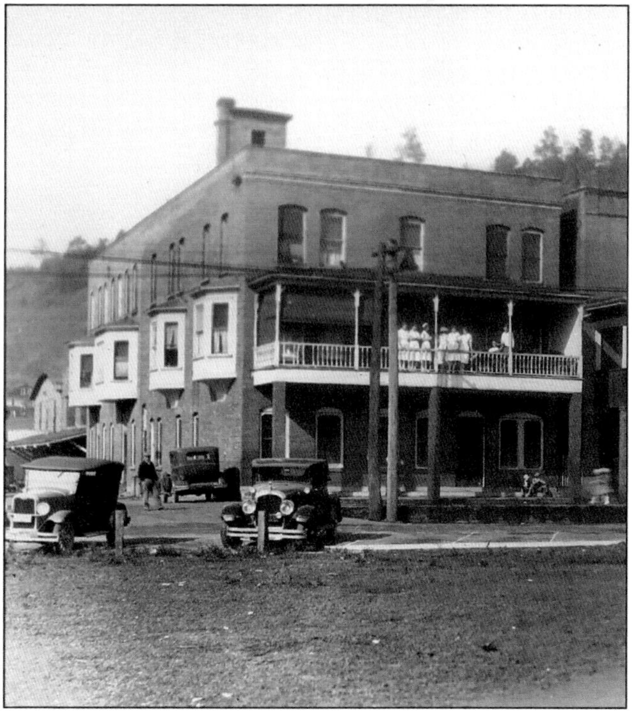

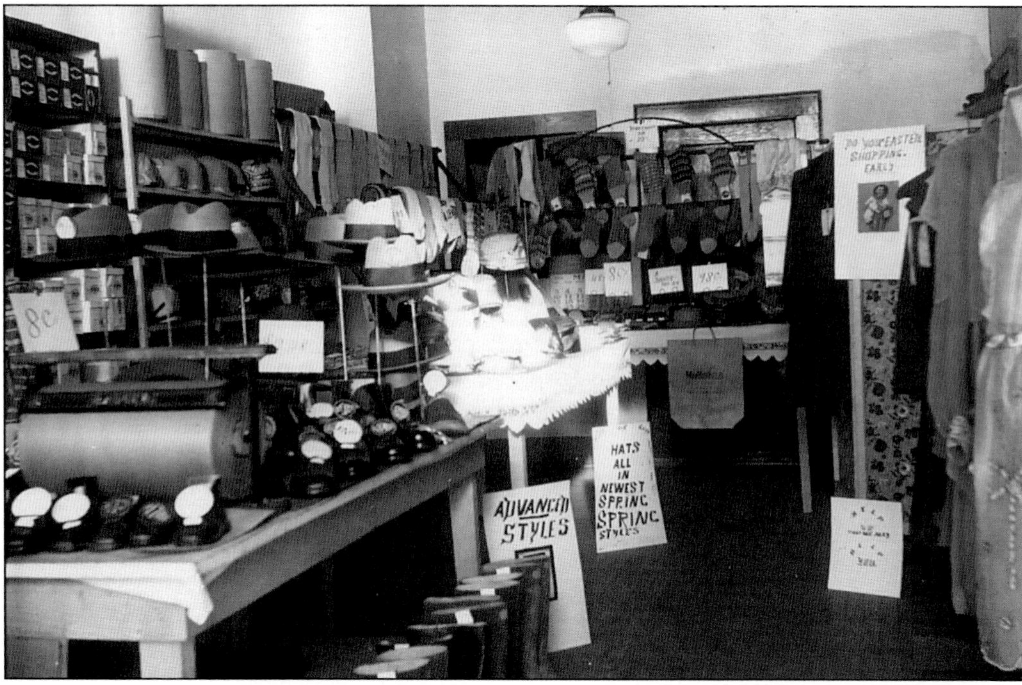


Here are two of many store interiors Finley photographed. The top photograph is a small clothing store prepared for that year's Easter fashion season. Below are some of the latest Westinghouse electric ranges then available at the Monongahela Power Company store outlet.

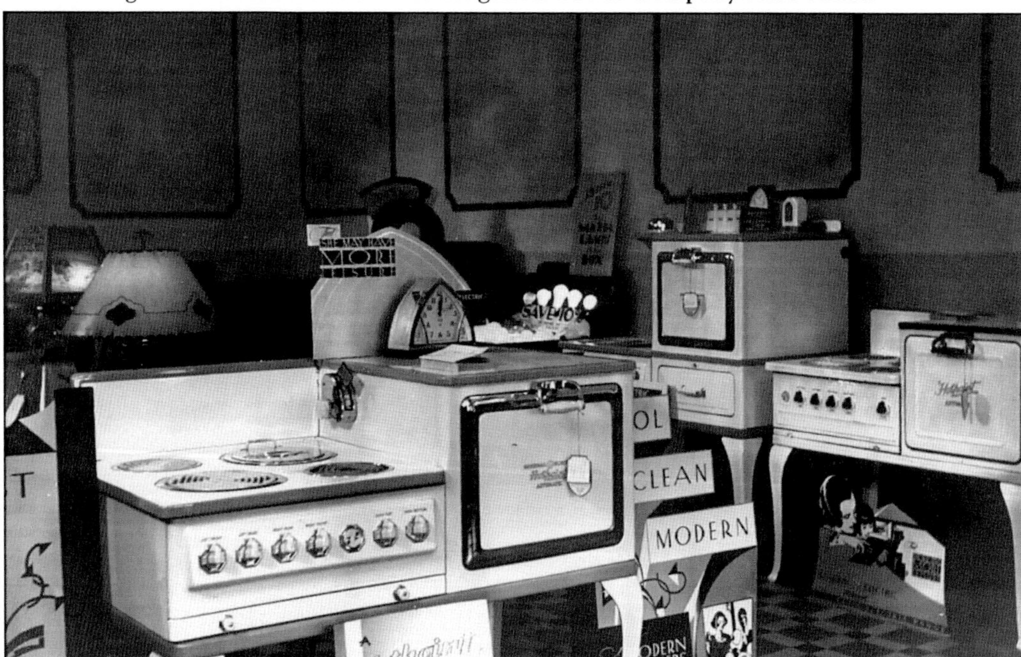

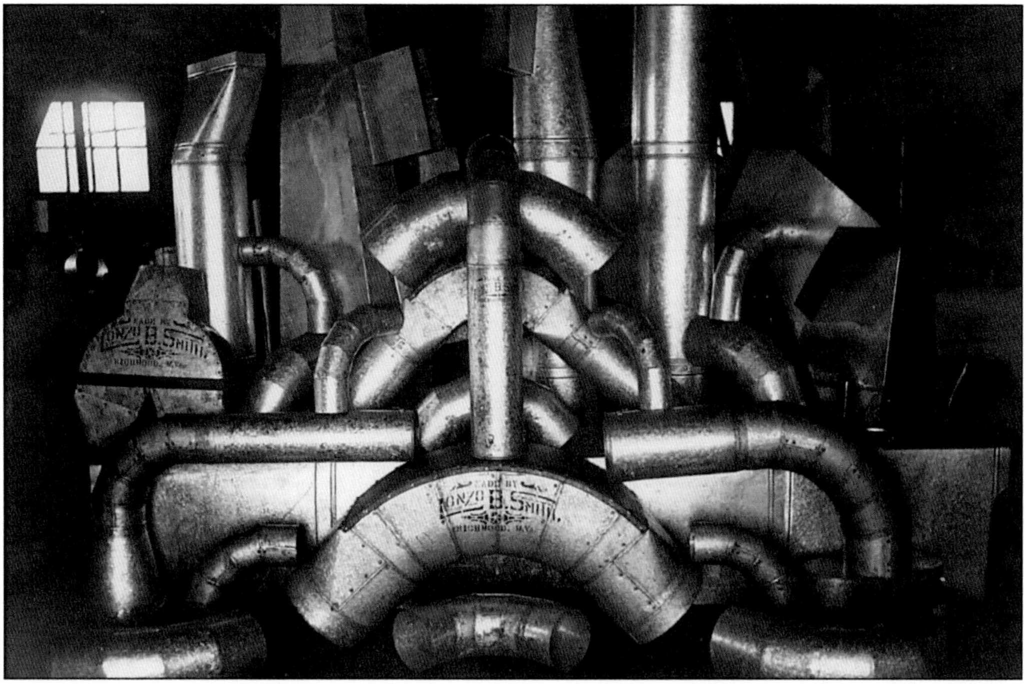

One of the most gifted businessmen in the town was Lonso B. Smith, a tinsmith extraordinaire. The photograph above shows some of the stove pipes and heating vents he made. The bottom photograph shows some other items he made including a sink, coffee urn, and a model locomotive. He was an engineer and craftsman who designed and erected a 150-foot chimney at the pin factory.

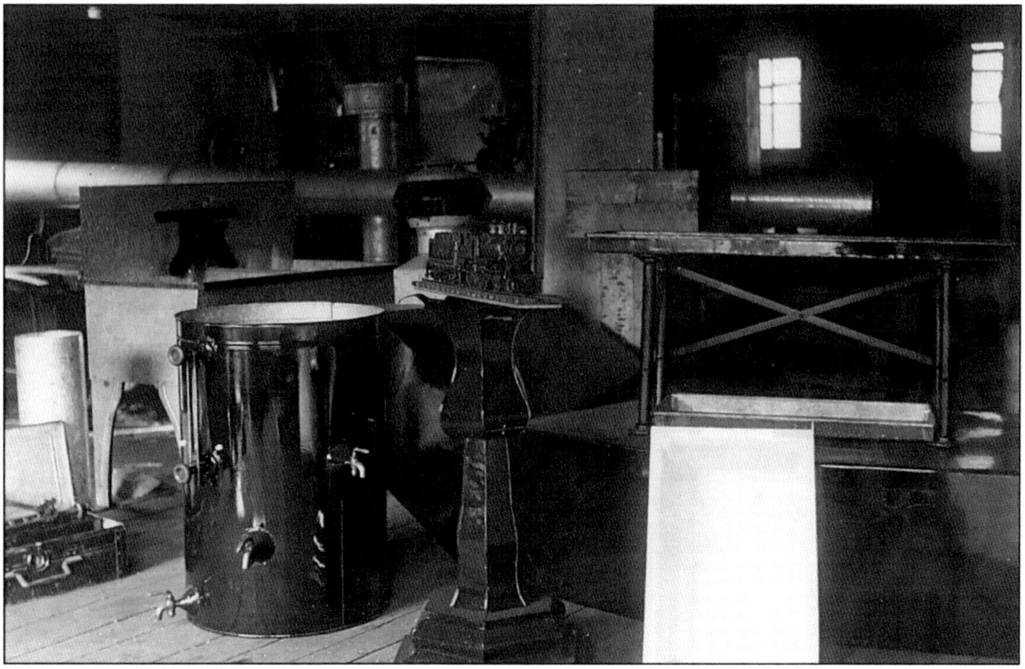

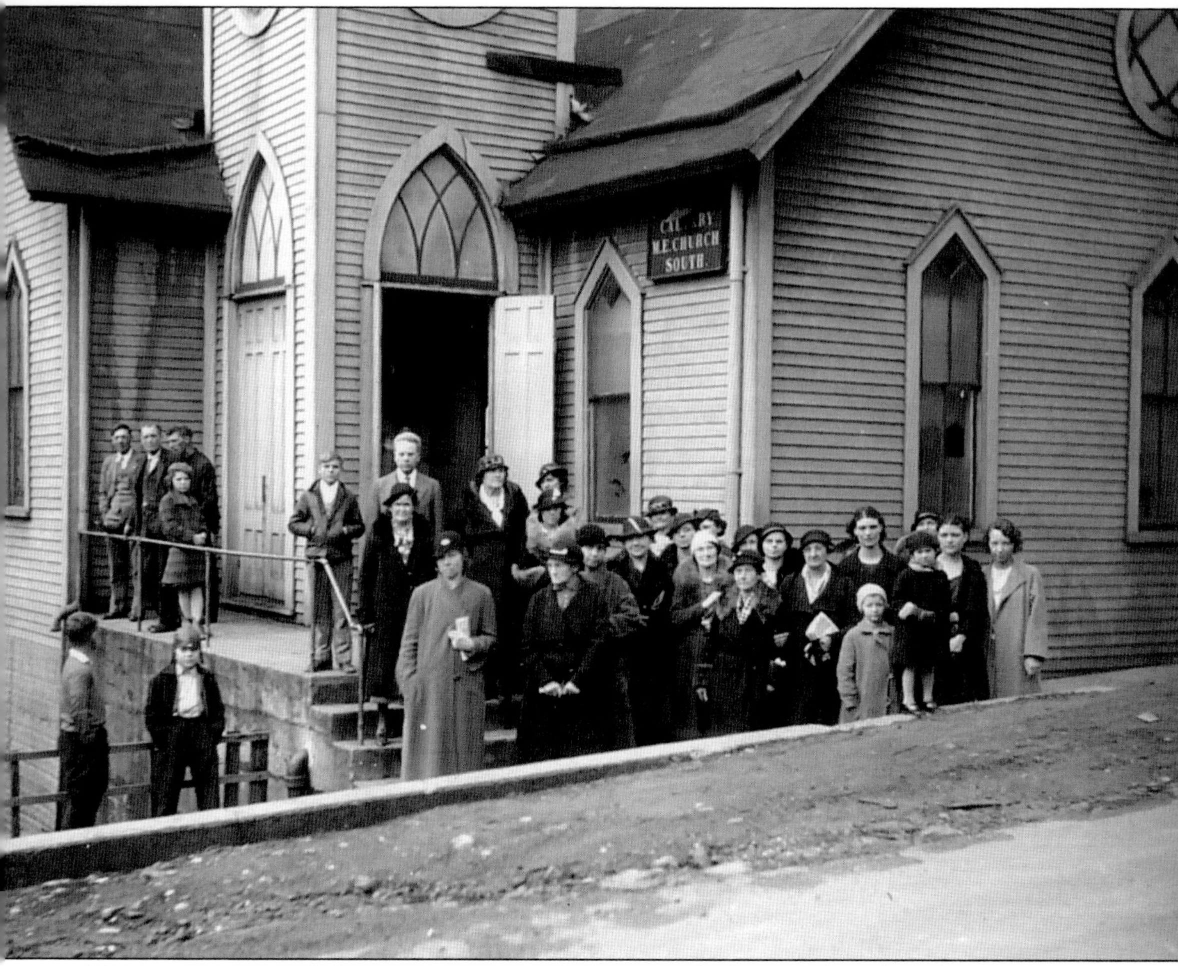


Here is an image of the congregation of Calvary Methodist South gathered after a church service. This photograph was taken after the congregation built a basement under the structure which included a kitchen and large dining room. It was taken long before the bell tower was replaced with a tall steeple.

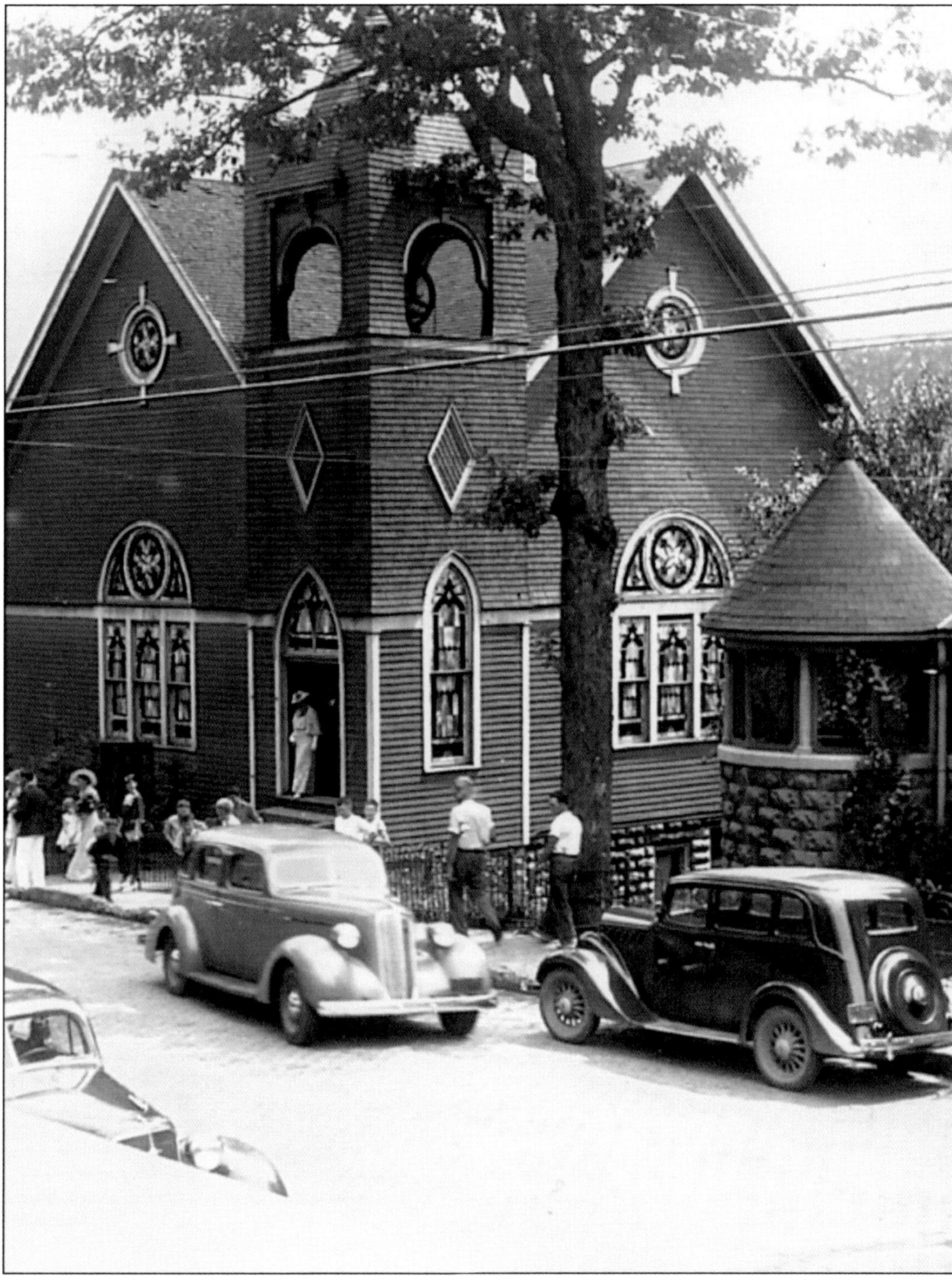

In this picture, Finley captured a wedding party gathered in front of the Presbyterian Church on Main Street. On the right of the church is the home of Dr. Jarrett, longtime town dentist. This is the second Presbyterian Church. It replaced the first church that was heavily damaged by fire in 1906. The Presbyterian Church was the first church established in Richwood in 1902.

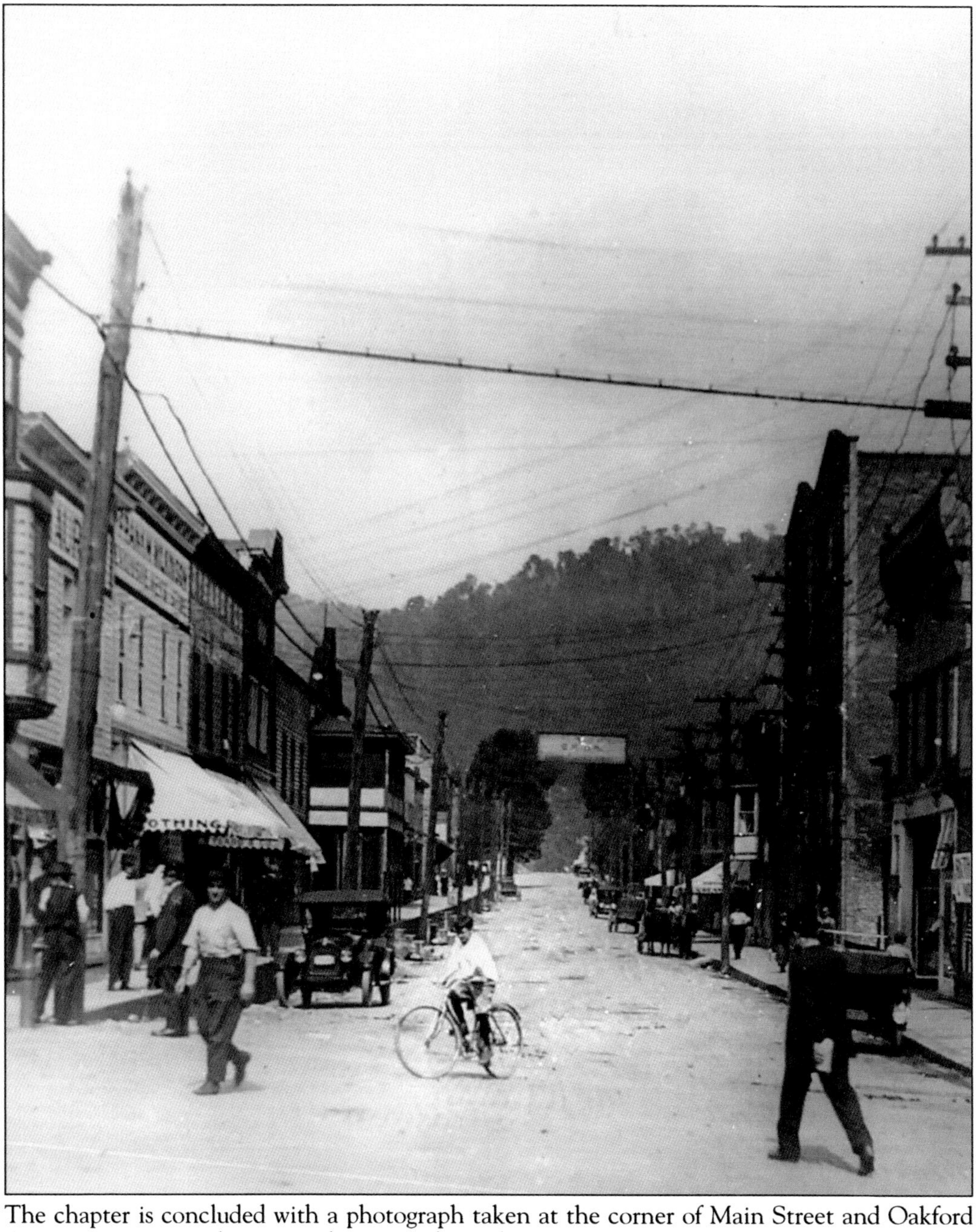

The chapter is concluded with a photograph taken at the corner of Main Street and Oakford Avenue. Townspeople are caught going about their everyday life as the town is decorated in preparation for the Spud and Splinter Festival coming in the first week of August.

# *Six*

# Formal and Informal Portraits

*"A home without beauty is not worth having. An enlarged snap-shot is often a piece of art." (Nicholas Republican advertisement for Taylor's Studio, 1926.)*

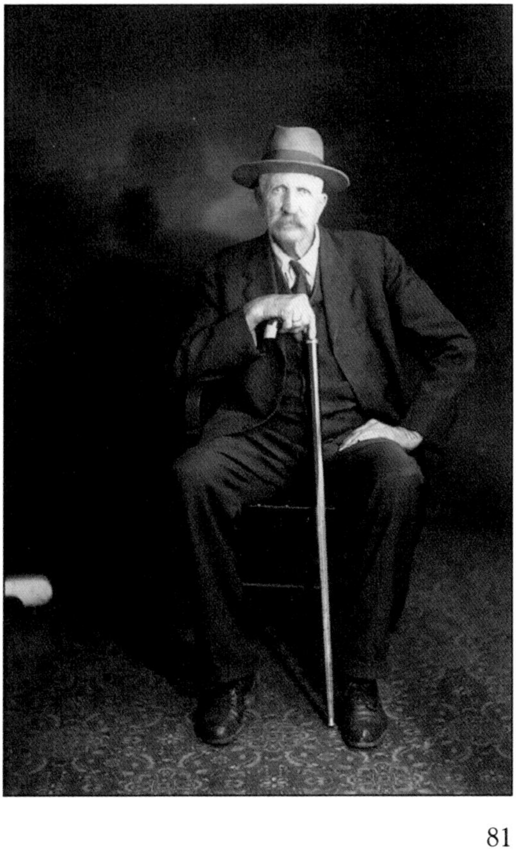

Intermixed in this chapter are portraits Finley Taylor took of individuals posed in his studio and of people caught in their own environment outside of the studio. Considering the collection of images he left behind as a whole, it must be said that Finley was a people person. For example, of almost 500 images he left of logging operations taken in Nicholas County, only about 40 of them are pictures of equipment—and even they have people in them. Those that knew him say he was very pleasant to pose for. Pictured here in the studio is Charles William Bell on or around his 80th birthday. Born near Summersville, he lived in a cabin on Hinkle Mountain until he died. He traveled west when he was 25 and experienced Denver and the Silver Dollar Saloon when famous outlaws were around and about. He claimed to have seen Frank James, brother to Jesse, in Summersville shortly after a Huntington bank was held up.

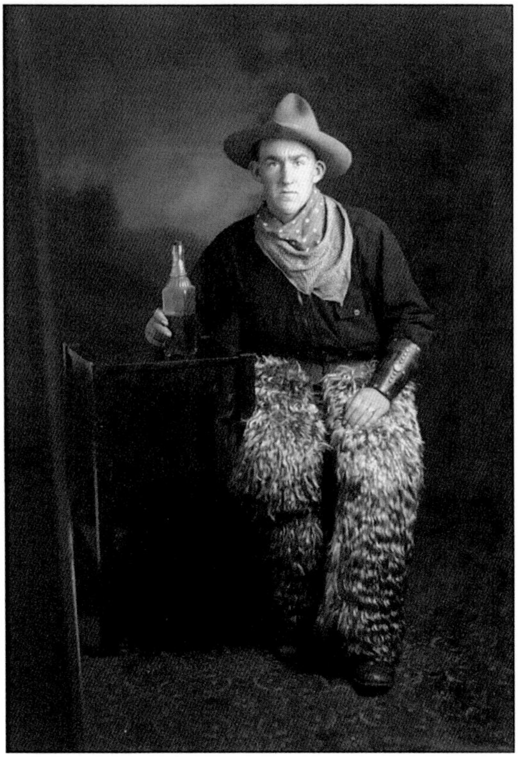

Pictured here is an unidentified individual who came to Finley's studio and was photographed with some of the props he had on hand. Lots of men had their pictures made with this same bottle, sheepskin chaps, and leather cuffs. I have the leather cuffs—minus the rhinestone decorations that once adorned them.

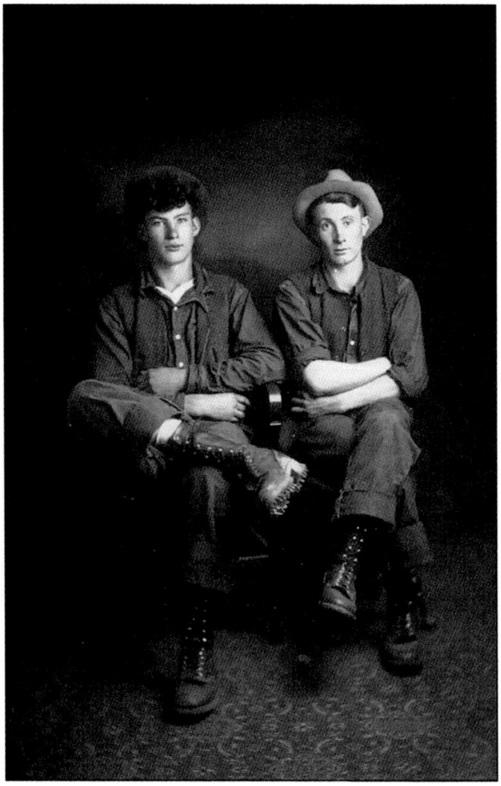

Here is Billy Hammonds and Raymond Fletcher. Billy reports that this photograph was made in June 1937. His entire working life was spent in the logging industry for several companies in the county. The cork shoes he so proudly displays helped the loggers keep their footing on logs when working around log landings. The price for cork shoes in 1937 was $8.

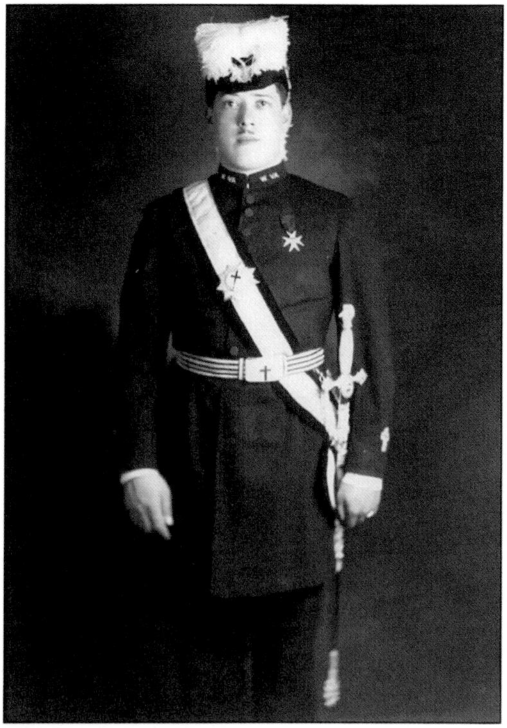

Pictured on this page are two members of the Masonic Order. The studio portrait taken above is of Farley Bowers, a resident of South Side in Richwood. The outdoor portrait taken below is of Victor Morrison. Victor and his brother Tom were retail merchants in Richwood for many years while operating the Morrison Brothers IGA store on Main Street. In later years after Victor's death, Tom moved his store to Commercial Avenue below Main Street.

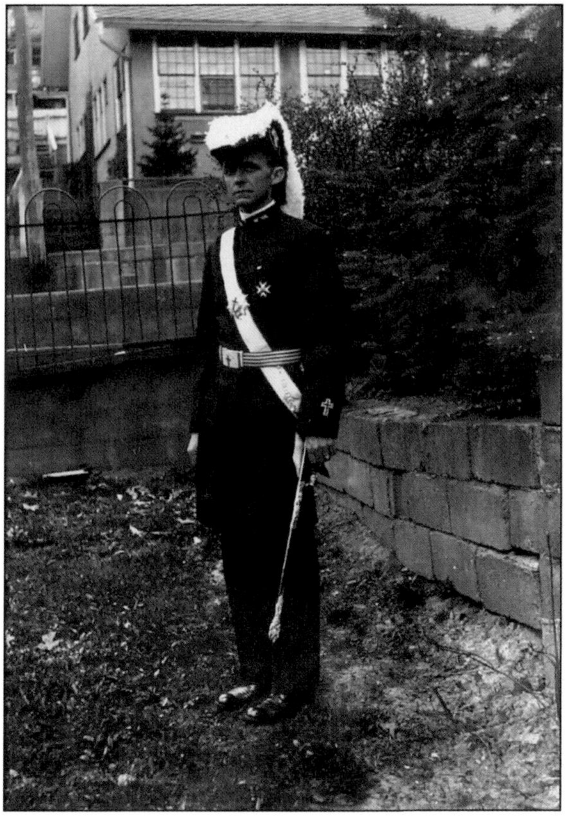

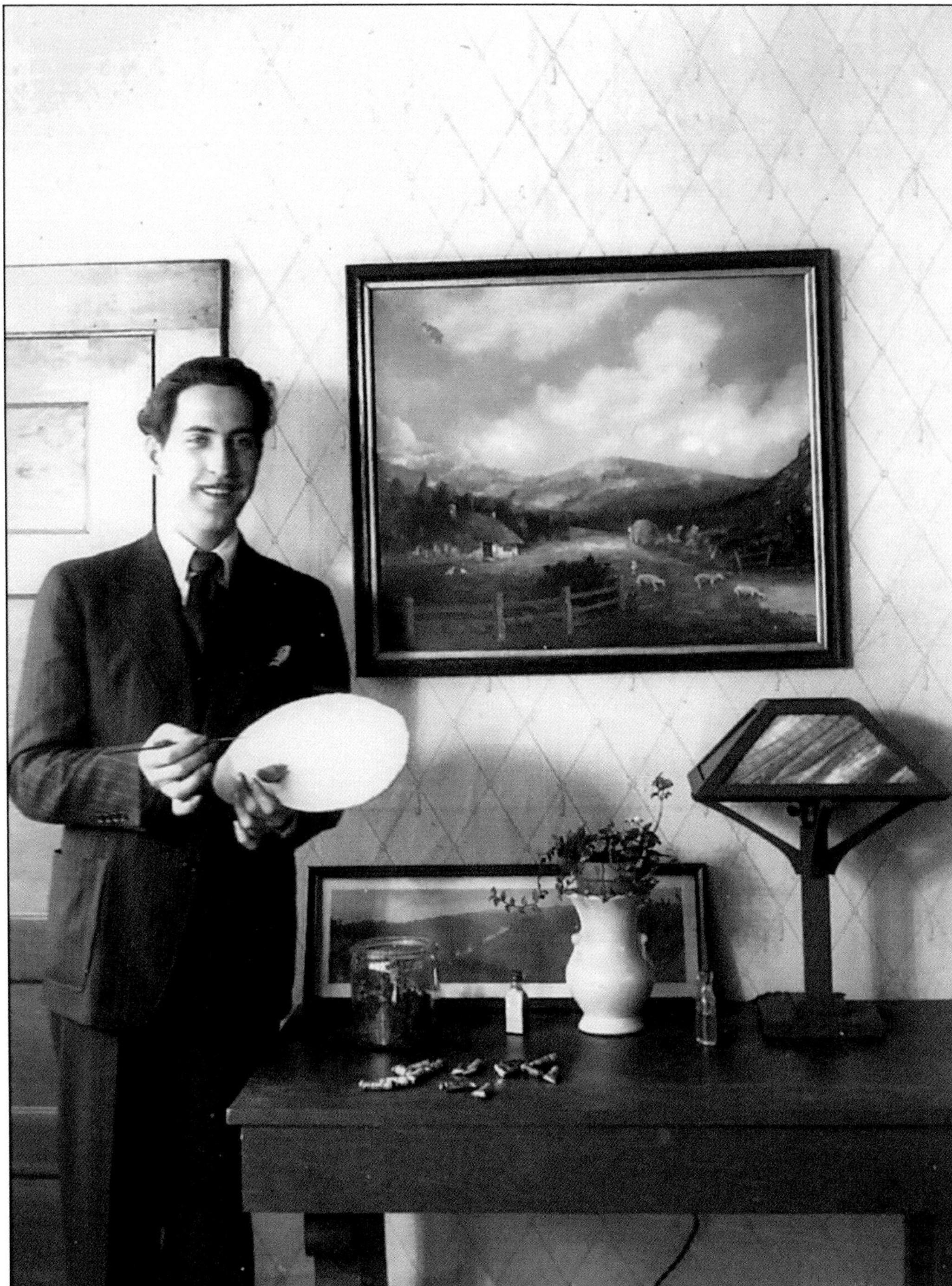

This is a portrait of Gayle Surface taken in his home with his palette and oils. Gayle was a well-known local artist who won many awards during his lifetime. He has left behind beautiful murals in local churches and public buildings as well as hundreds of treasured oils in private residences. The author's favorite is a mural entitled "The Ascension of Christ," which hangs behind the pulpit in Fenwick United Methodist Church.

Here is another of Richwood's talented craftsmen, Lonso B. Smith. On page 77 is some of his handiwork. Although a tinsmith by trade, he could make just about anything. Here he holds a model of a ship. He was also an inventor, engineer, and maker of banjos. He left Richwood after the Depression and went to work in a shovel factory in Parkersburg. He continued to craft banjos and in 1979, upon a prior request by Jim Comstock, he delivered a beautiful banjo to Jim to be donated to the Cultural Center in Charleston, where it still resides today.

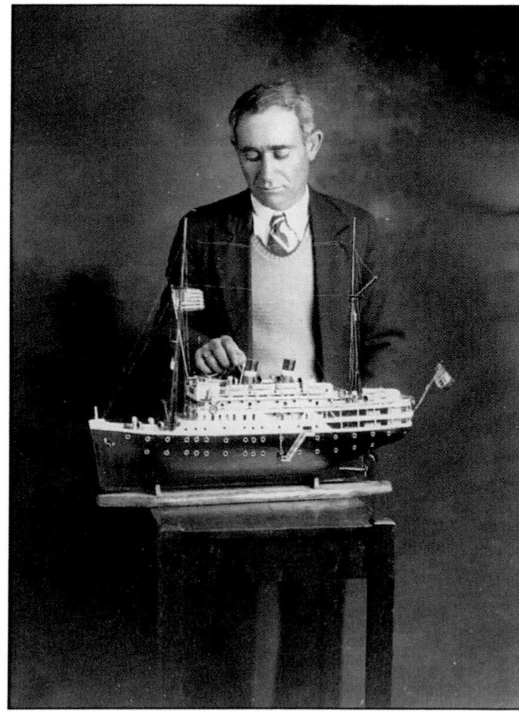

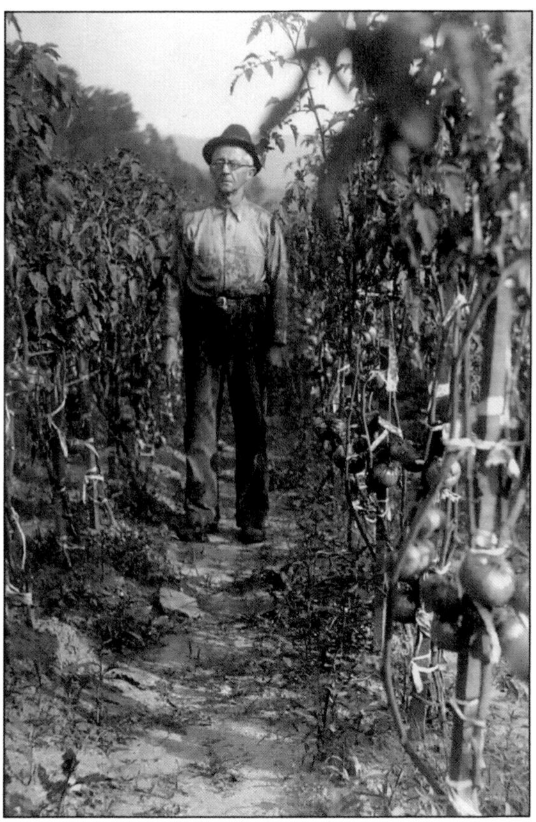

This is an unidentified and very serious looking vegetable gardener in his tomato patch. After the Depression, many of the townspeople looked about for land to raise vegetables to supplement their food supplies. Newspaper reports from the time indicate that several families were able to utilize land vacated by the handle factory in Weber City.

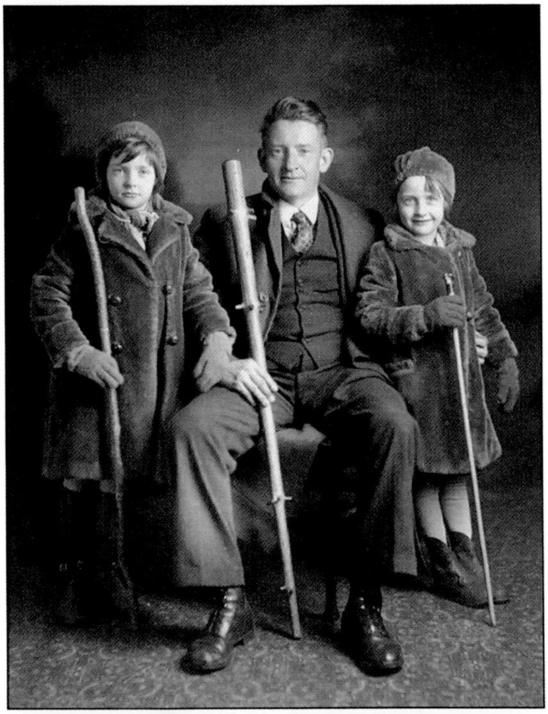

Here is one of Richwood's longtime weekly newspaper editors, C. Donee Cook, and two unidentified children. They all seem to be very proud of their canes. C. Donee Cook was the editor at different times of two weekly newspapers based in Richwood. He first edited *The Advance* and later edited the *Nicholas Republican*. He continued to do job printing and maintain an office and school supply business when he retired from editing.

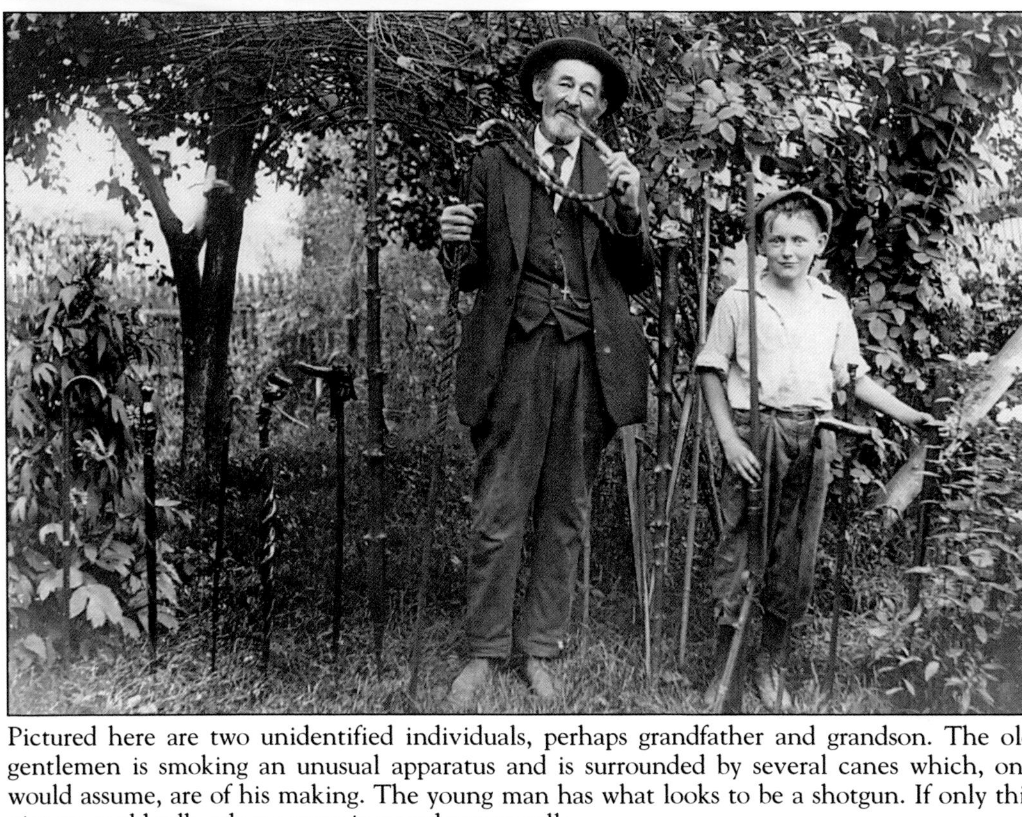

Pictured here are two unidentified individuals, perhaps grandfather and grandson. The old gentlemen is smoking an unusual apparatus and is surrounded by several canes which, one would assume, are of his making. The young man has what looks to be a shotgun. If only this picture could talk, what a story it must have to tell.

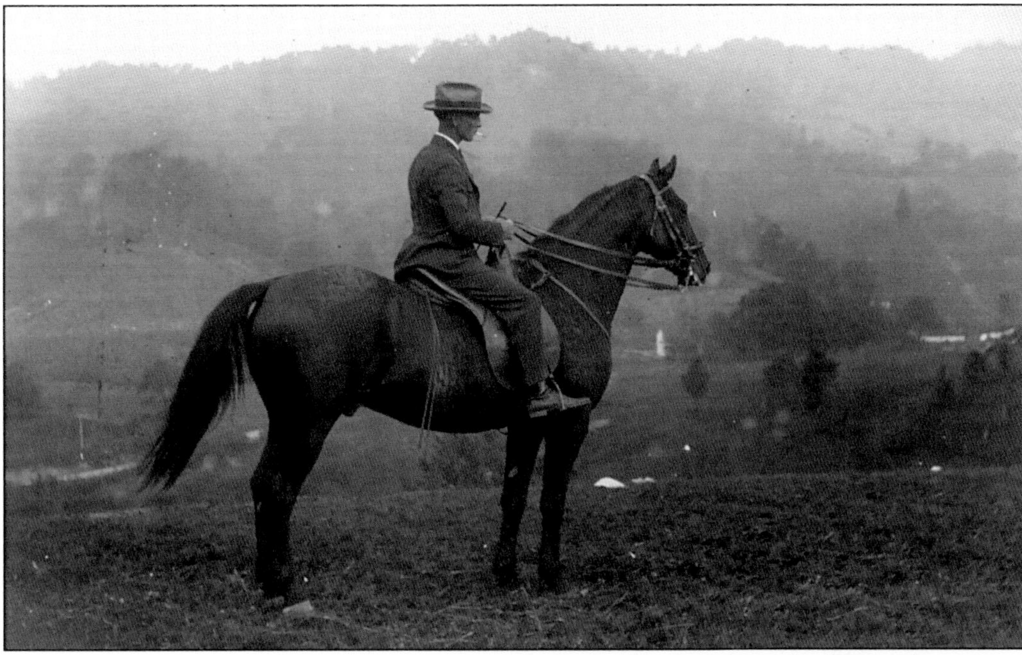

Pictured here is Dr. Hill, a Webster County native who had his office 20 miles west of Richwood in Camden on Gauley. He had hospital privileges at the McClung Hospital in town. All of Richwood's early doctors traveled on horseback to see patients during that era.

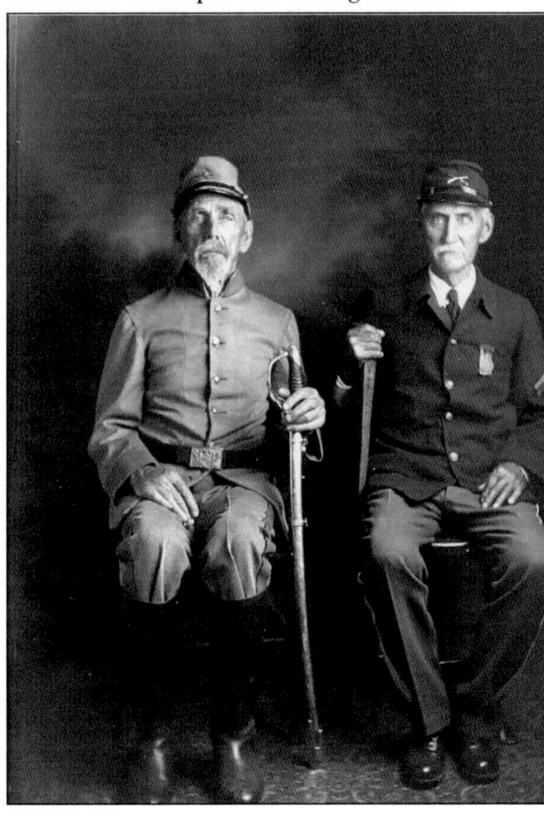

In addition to serving as the portrait photographer for the home-town folks, countless individuals from other towns and communities sought out Finley Taylor's services. Probably none are more interesting than these two distinguished Civil War veterans. It is believed that the Confederate veteran on the left is Capt. John J. Halstead of Keslers Cross Lanes. The *Nicholas Republican* reported on his visit to the town in December 1926, at the age of 89. He is reported to have gained much distinction for his valor in the war. The union army veteran is probably Adonijah Richards, who was reported by the same paper to have passed away at the home of his grandson, Fred Jones, in February 1933, at the age of 90.

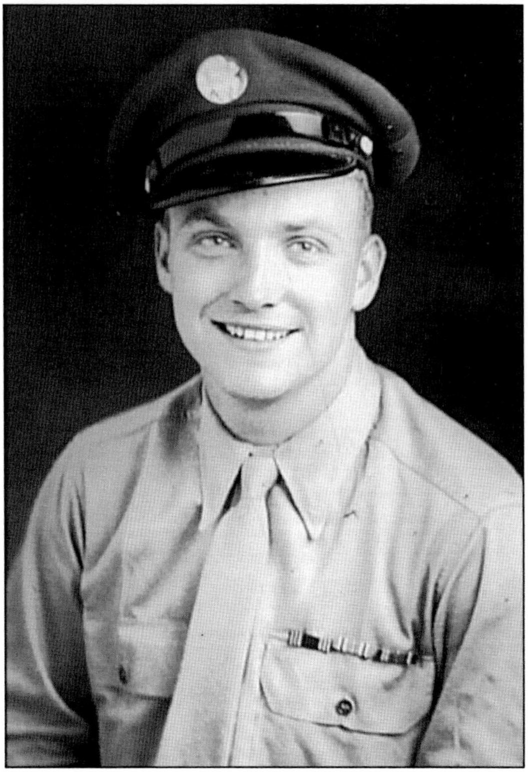

The earliest documented portrait by Finley Taylor the author has seen was dated 1912. Finley would then have been 25 years old at the time. He most certainly took portraits of World War I soldiers, but none are in the author's collection of Finley's negatives. There are, however, lots of World War II portraits, mostly unidentified. On this page, shown as representatives of the many wartime portraits Finley made, are two individuals known to the author. The young man in the army uniform above is Ferrell Johnson. After the war he was a prominent and successful businessman in the county. He was a state delegate, 32-degree Mason, and member of other organizations too numerous to list. The young man below in the Marines uniform is Holman "Scrubby" Denna. Scrubby was a member of the locally famous "Cuspie" Bragg platoon that was recruited in Richwood in honor of "Cuspie" Bragg, who was captured by the Japanese early in World War II. Scrubby worked for C&P Telephone Company for many years.

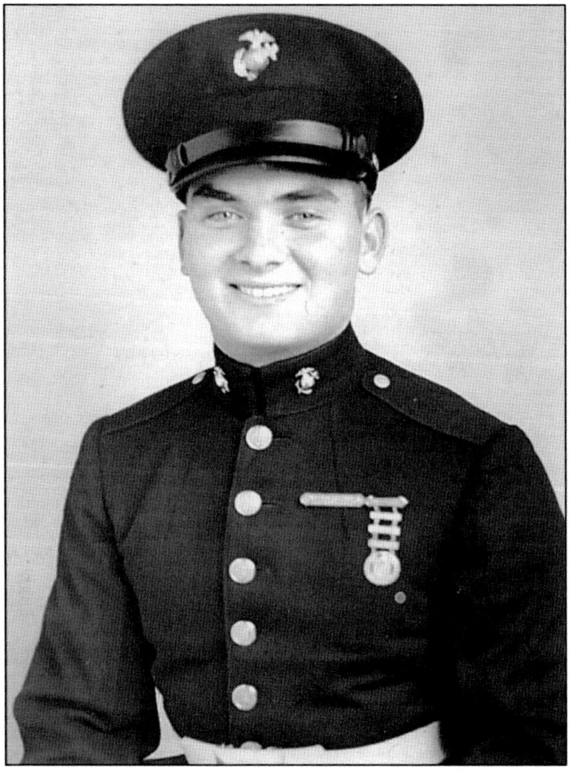

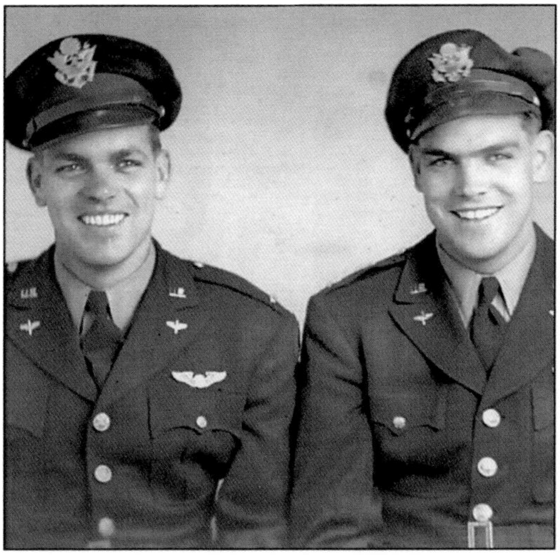

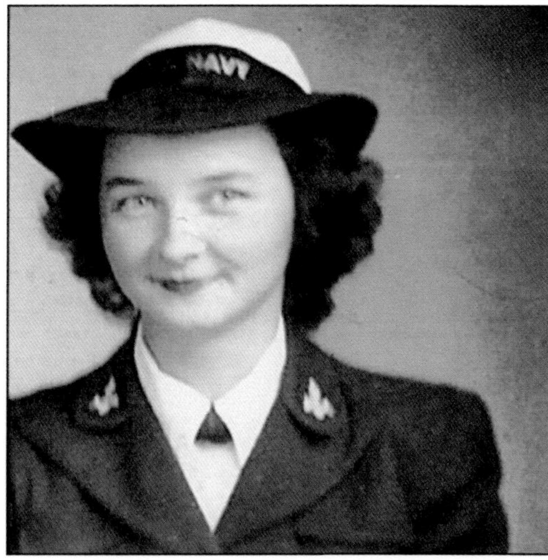


Pictured above are two local flyboys Finley captured in his studio. On the left is Glenn "Puffy" Spencer and on the right is Earl Spencer, both sons of Lon Spencer. In the photograph on the right is an unidentified representative of the Navy. Finley took many yearbook and senior pictures of Richwood High School students over the years. Included below are two young ladies, Wanda Taylor (left) and Hilda Taylor (right).

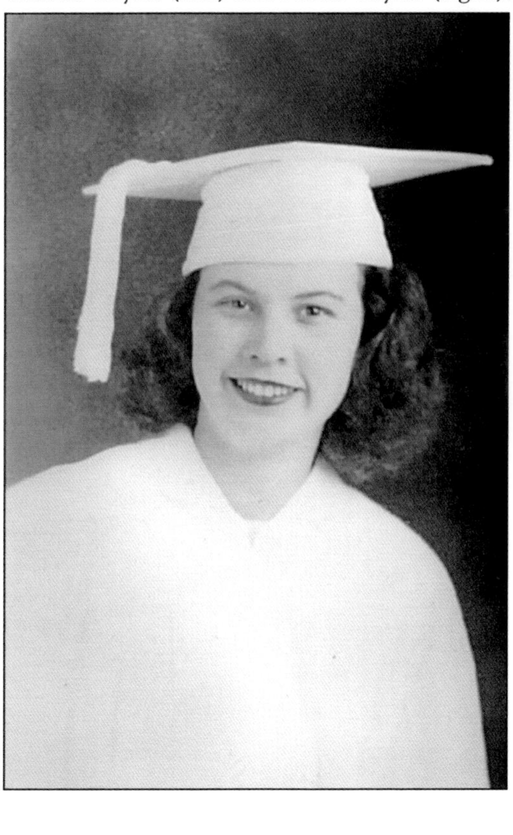

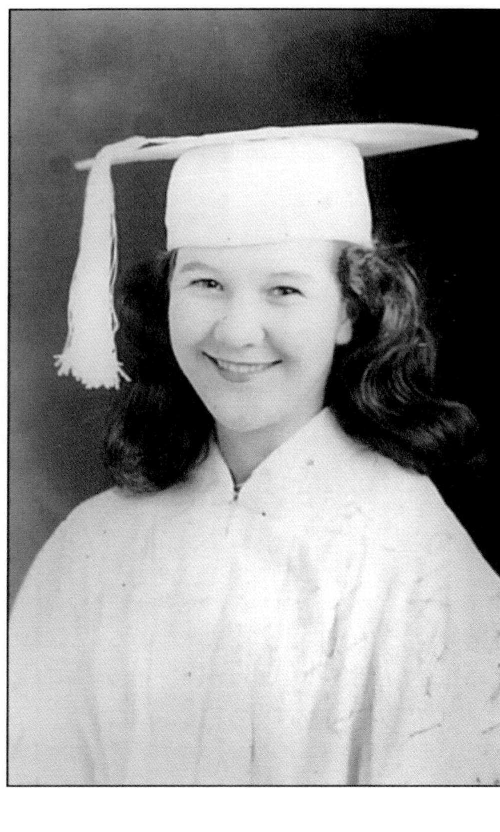

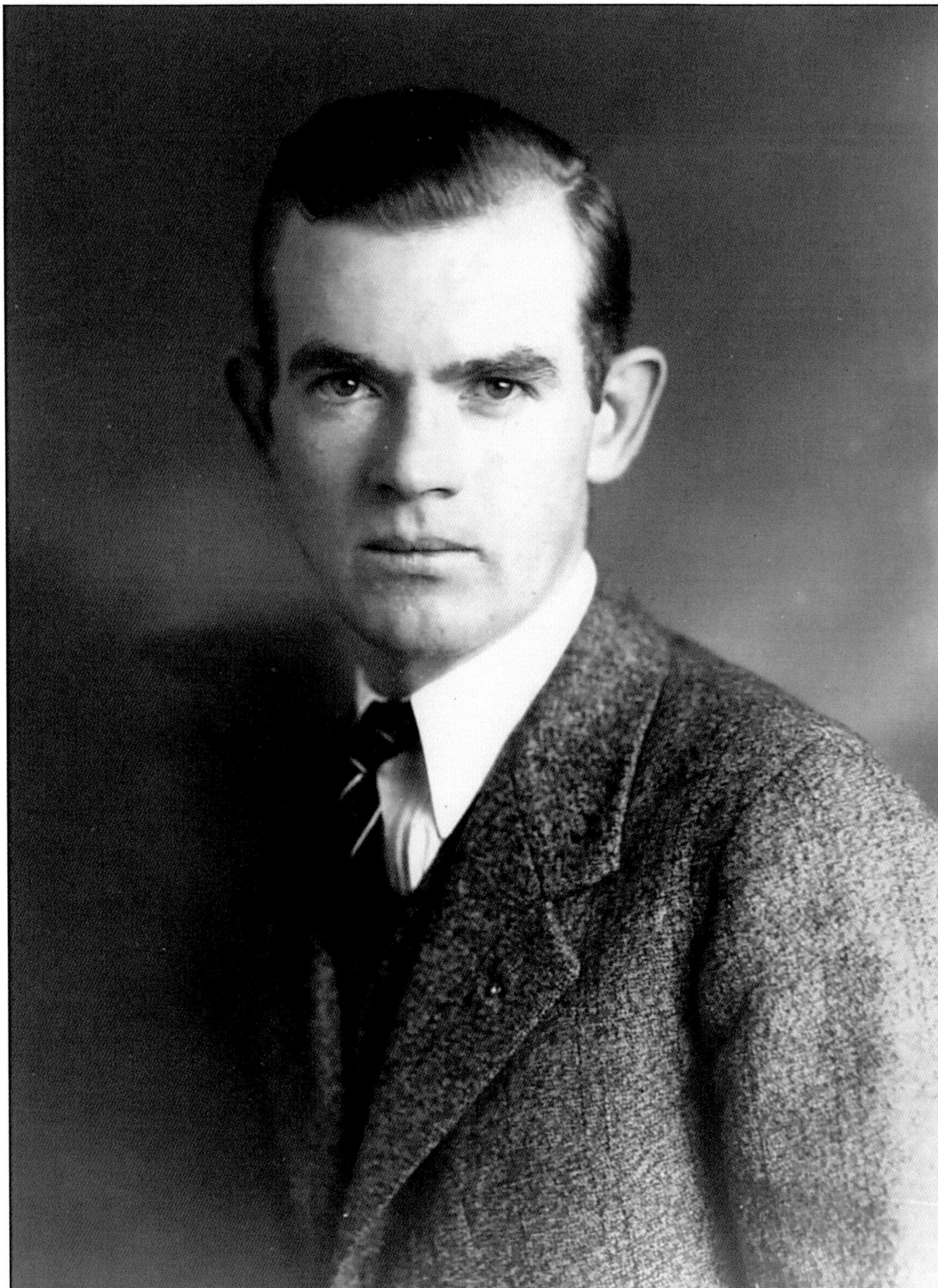

Shown here is longtime Richwood High School principal Edgel Dean. Mr. Dean was a very well respected educator in the state and in his community. In addition to his academic pursuits and academic accolades, he was a lover of the outdoors. He was active in the town's sportsman clubs and was past president of the Nicholas County Rod and Gun club.

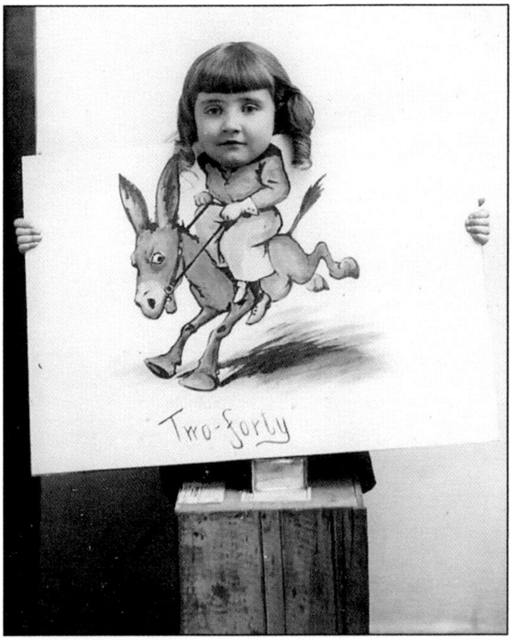


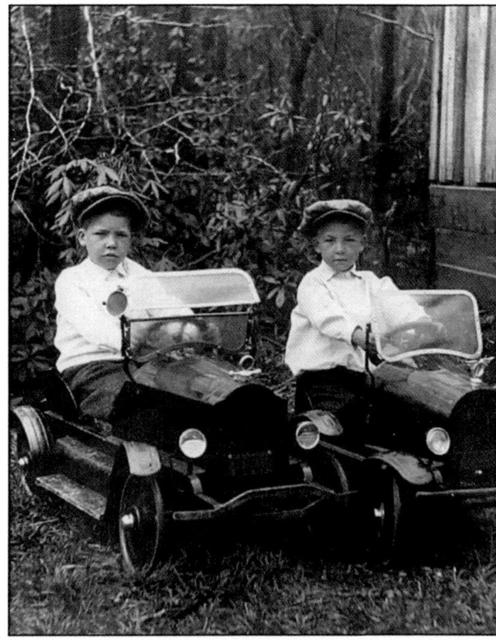

Pictured on this page are four Finley Taylor children's portraits. None of these children are identified, but I believe the Boy Scout is a very young Dr. Jim McClung.

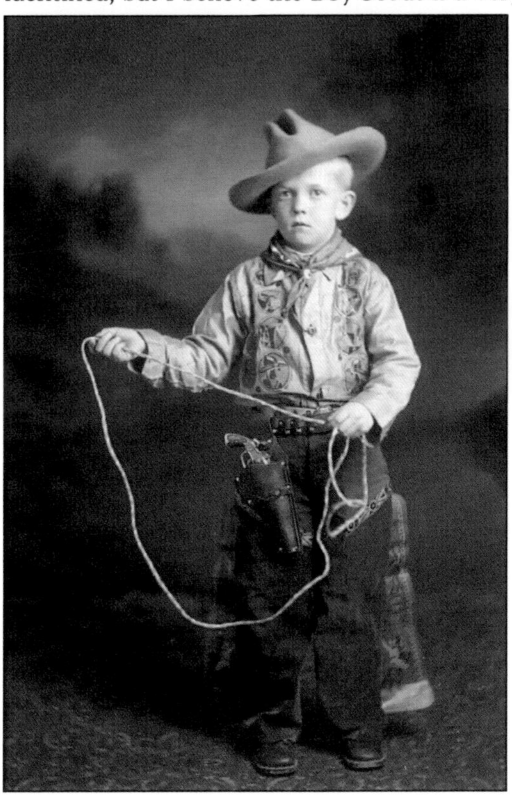

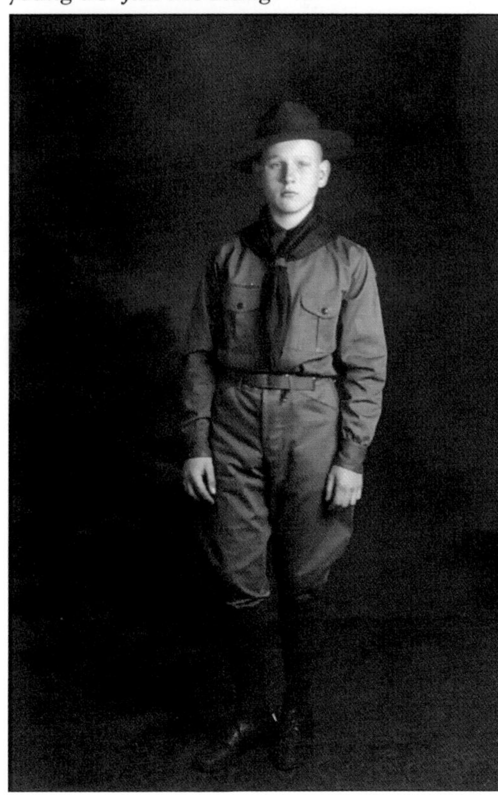

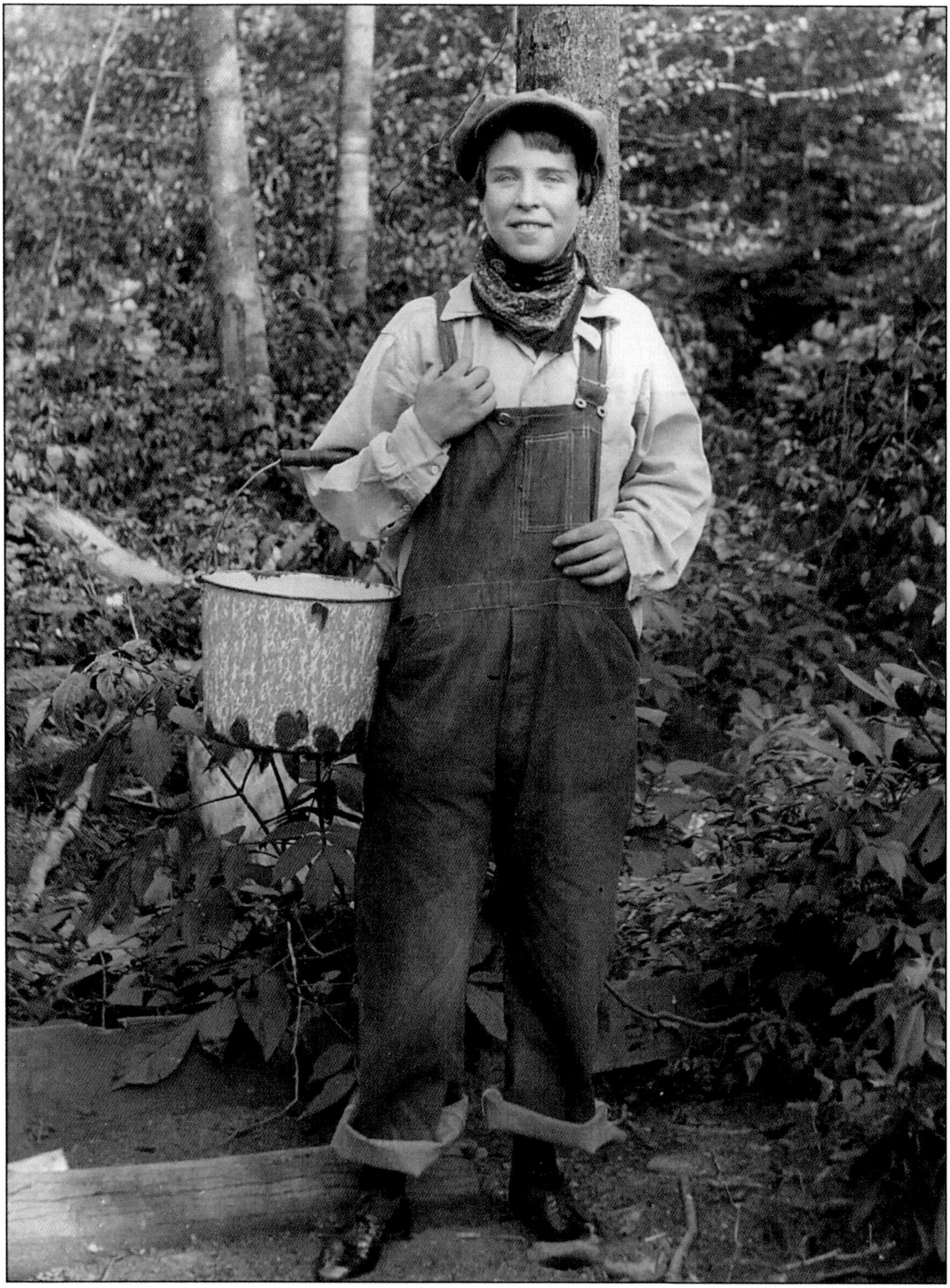

Apparently, one of Finley's Taylor's favorite subjects was the individuals who worked in the logging industry. Particularly in the first half of his career as a photographer, he traveled extensively to most of the logging operations in Nicholas and neighboring counties, seemingly photographing everyone that would pose for him. This unidentified girl is holding a graniteware water bucket.

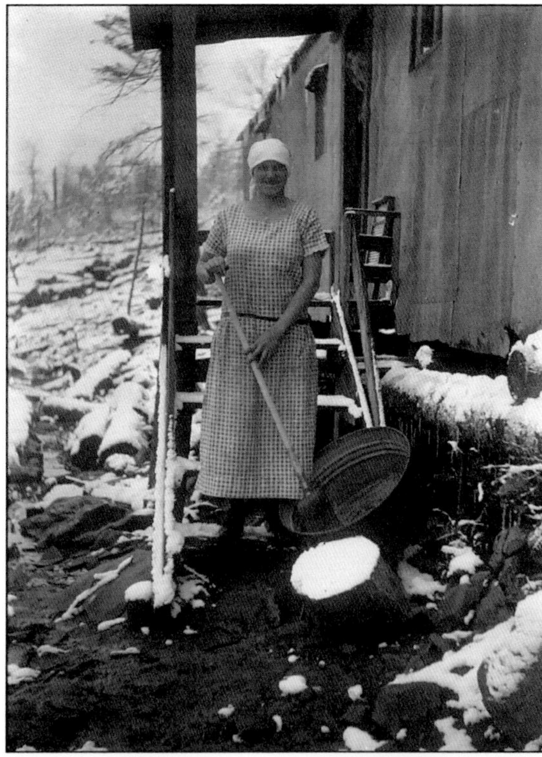

Pictured to the right is an unidentified young lady cleaning out a wash tub. Wash tubs were used for lots of purposes including dish washing and even as pots for cooking large amounts of potatoes or other vegetables. Pictured below is a young couple in front of their shanty supplied to them by the company at a cost of $2 per month. They are James Freeman and Josie Faulkner Freeman.

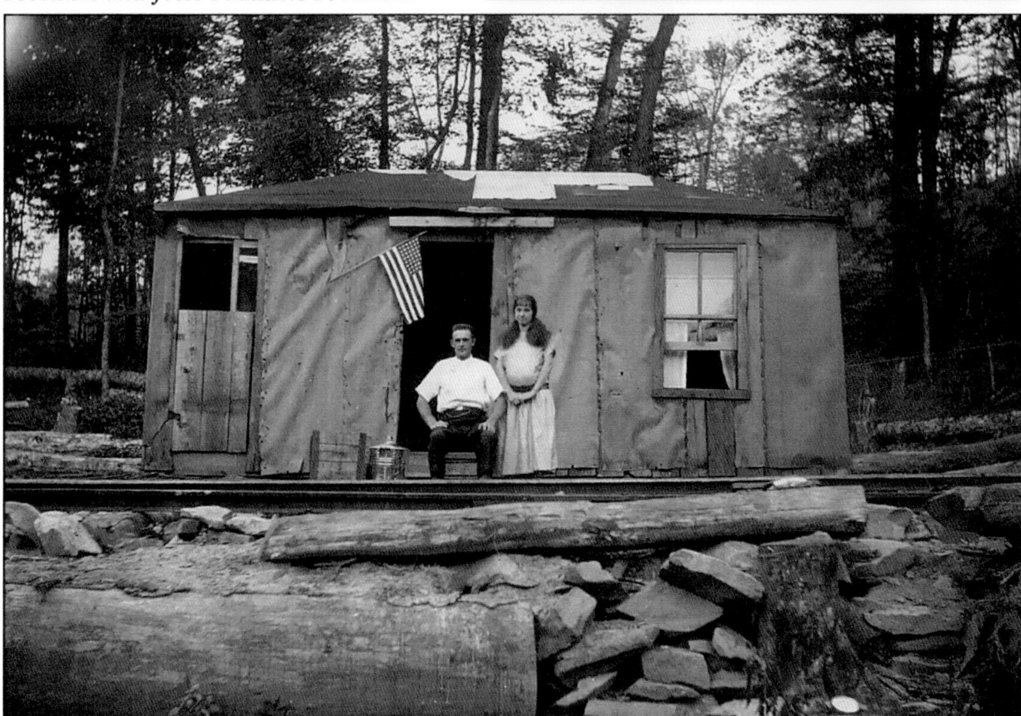

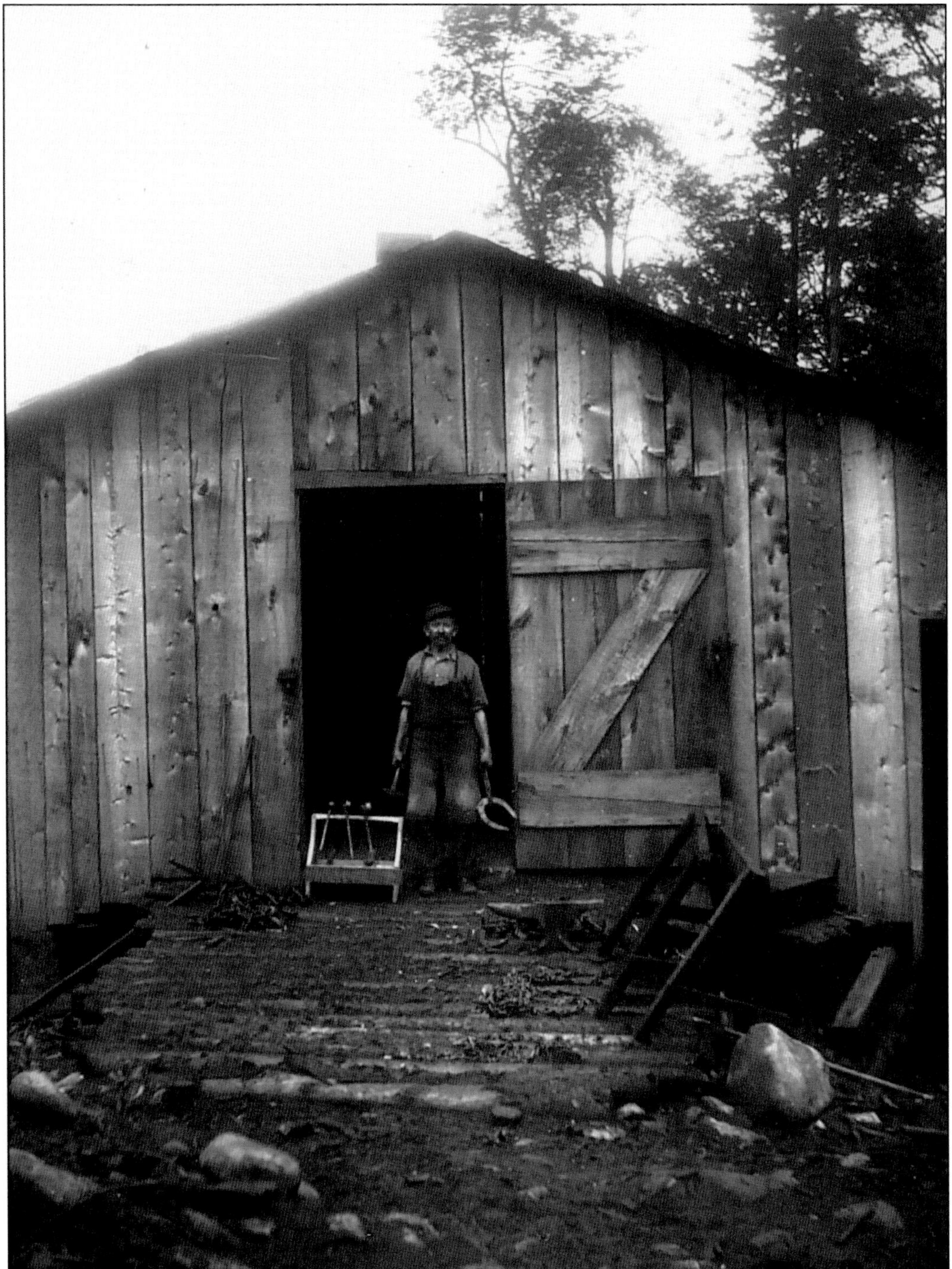

This blacksmith has a very important job in the logging operation. He has been identified as George Faulkner. The site is on the Middle Fork of Williams, three miles above the town of Three Forks, putting the site just below the mouth of Big Beechy Run. George is the father of Josie in the photograph on the previous page.

# *Seven*

# Hunting and Other Fun Things

*"During the heyday of these 'ignoramuses' I, along with several other idiots, killed and cut off the tails of more than one hundred waterdogs in one night. This happened along the Cranberry River middle section between the mouth of Jakeman Run and the mouth of Barrenshe Run. I am sure that this episode was being acted out by people doing the same thing along other streams." (Excerpt from newspaper article written by Beecher Hinkle in an attempt to answer the question, "What ever happened to our waterdogs?")*

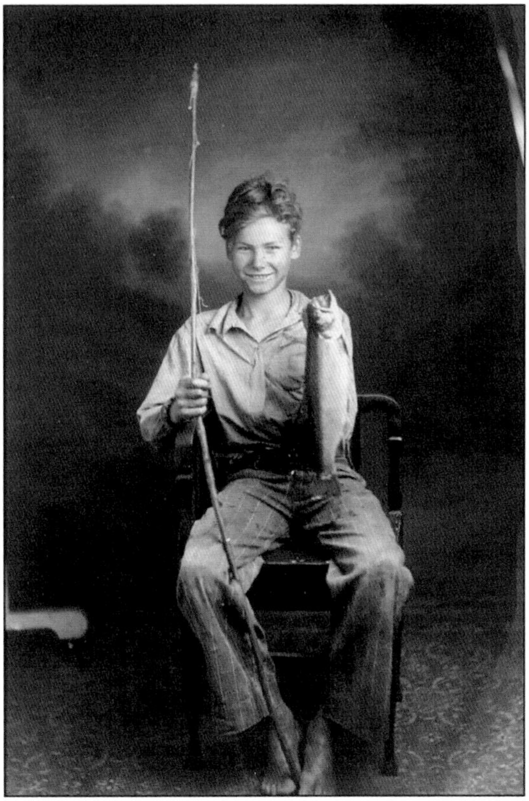

Pictured here is Clifford Cogar, who proudly displays a trophy brook trout he caught that won him first prize in a contest sponsored by Nicholas Hardware Store. The fish was 16 inches long. Clifford became the poster boy for later contests and this picture appeared in local papers a number of times.

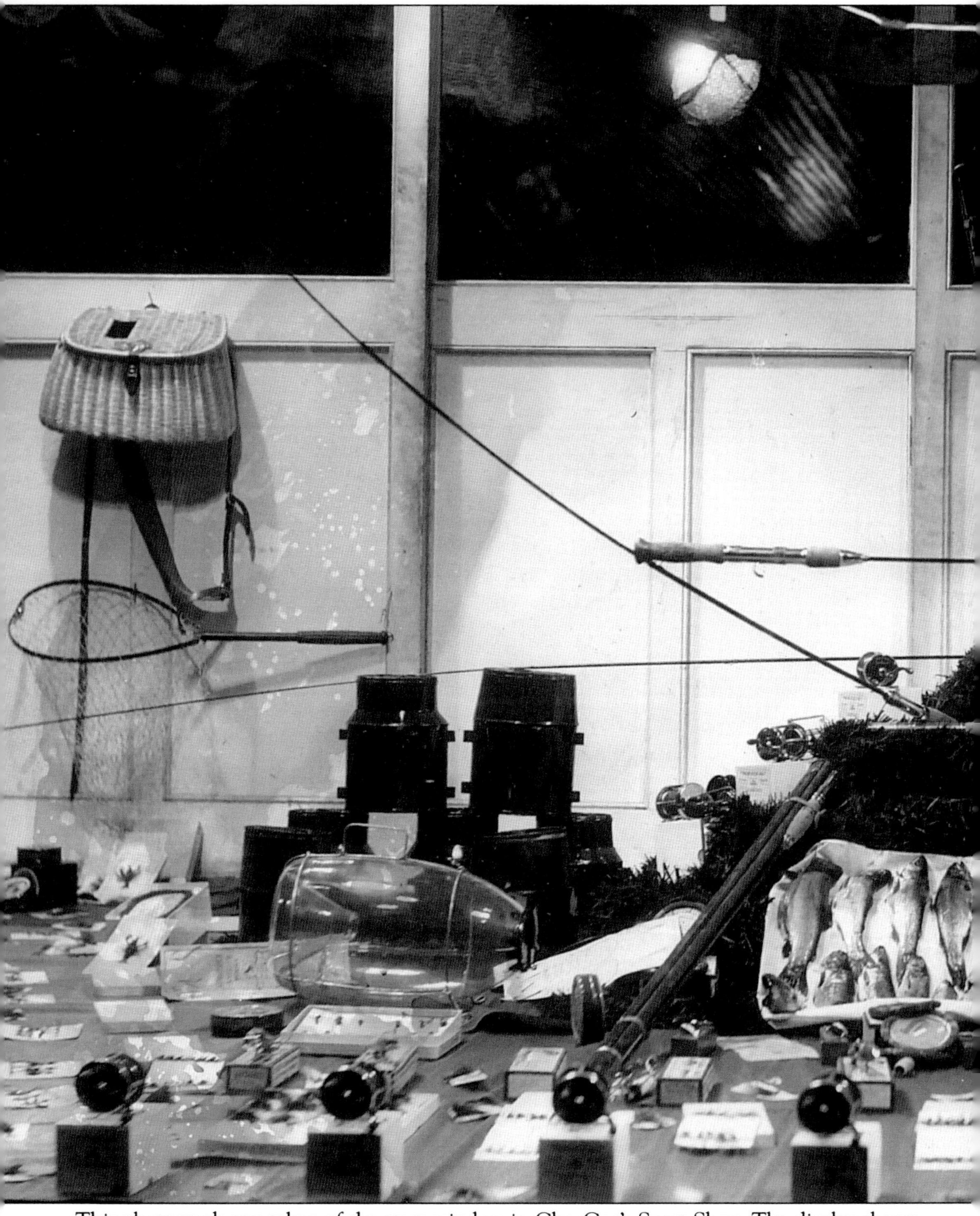

This photograph was taken of the store window in Clay Coe's Sport Shop. The display shows the culmination of his annual "Big Trout" contest, which was very popular among area fishermen. Mr. Coe has been recorded as saying that the success of his business was largely

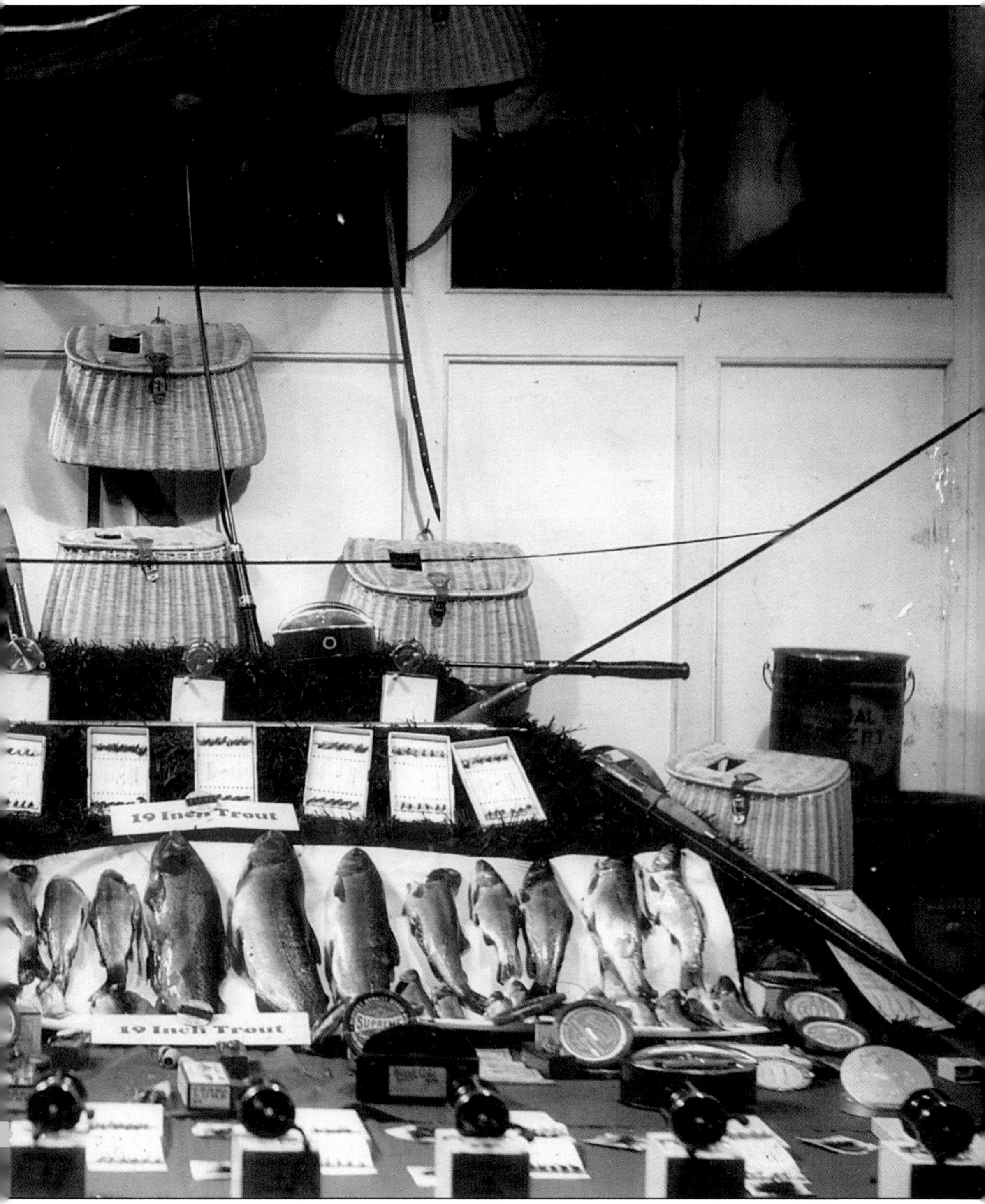


because of his personal honesty and the fact that he faithfully gave 10 percent of his profits to area churches.

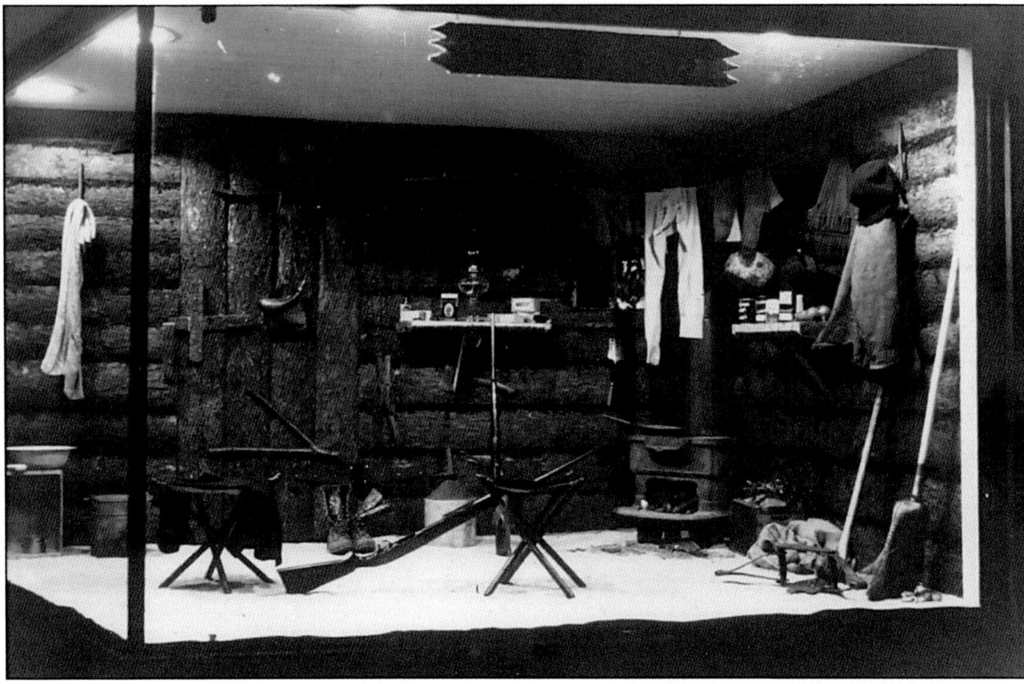

Here are two additional store window images Finley captured that catered to the hunters in the community. Large game became quite scarce in the 1920s and 1930s. Smaller creatures began to thin out in the area, too. One contributing factor could be explained by the newspaper announcement on page 104.

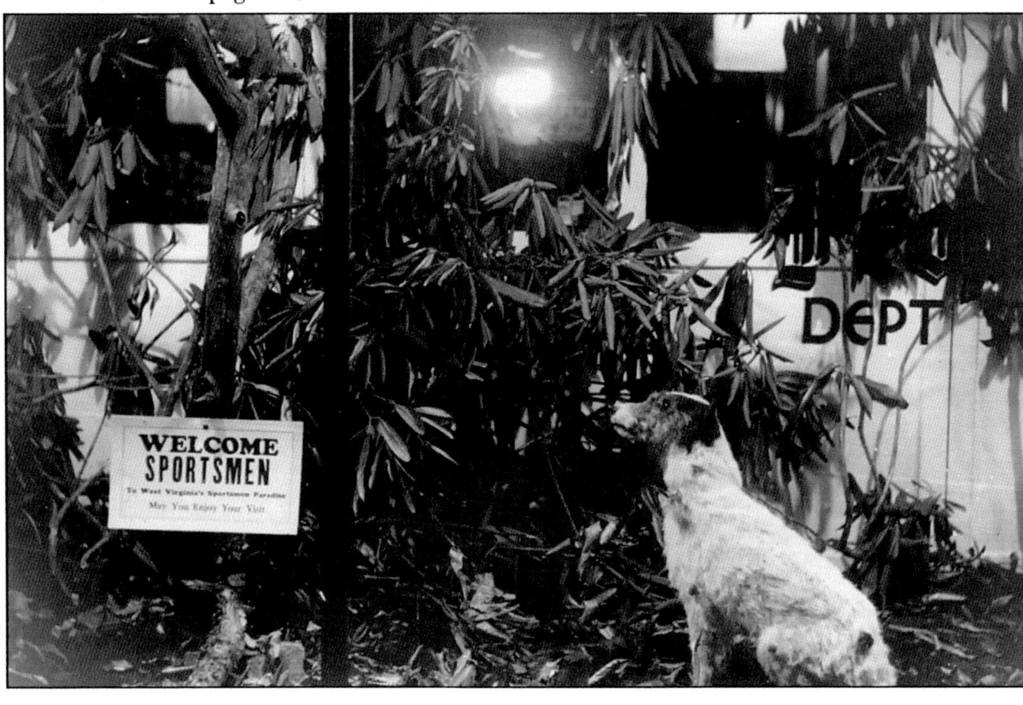

Richwood had a great deal of organized sports activity during its heyday. In addition to high school athletics, there was inter-league play between baseball teams from the mills and small businesses. There also was a boxing club with good coaching for its boxers and regular bouts with teams from the surrounding area. Pictured on this page are two brothers who were standouts for the town and later for their college. Pictured above is Beecher Hinkle, who was captain of the West Virginia University boxing team and twice the Eastern United States Intercollegiate Champion. He fought for the national championship and lost a decision he thought he should have won to a fellow from Penn State. The referee of the bout was former World Heavyweight Champion Gene Tunney. Beecher says Gene told him he had a better left hand than him. Below is Beecher's brother Clarence "Chink" Hinkle, who was undefeated his freshman year at WVU. He later transferred to Glenville State College where he graduated. Both of these men are retired, having served long careers as outstanding educators.

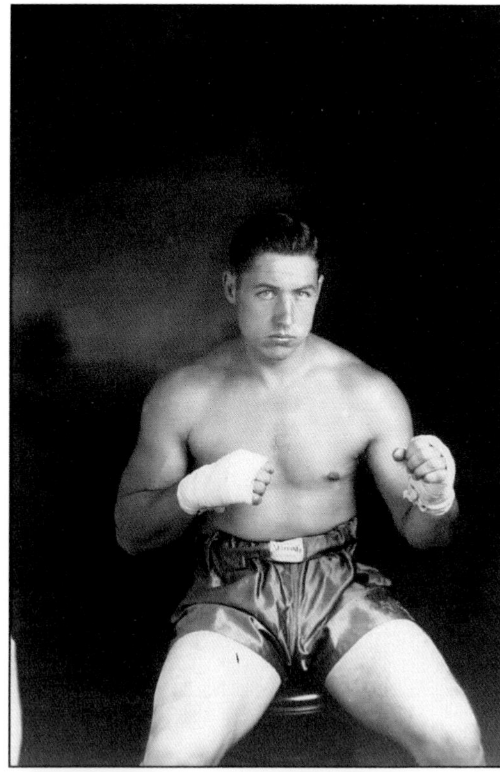

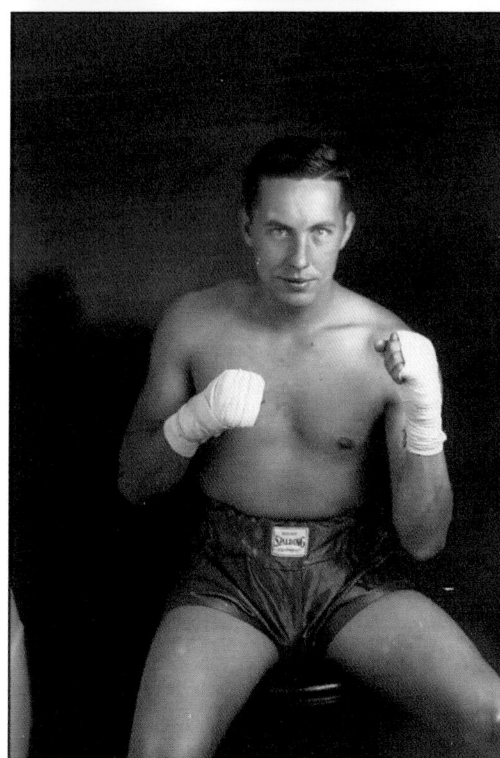

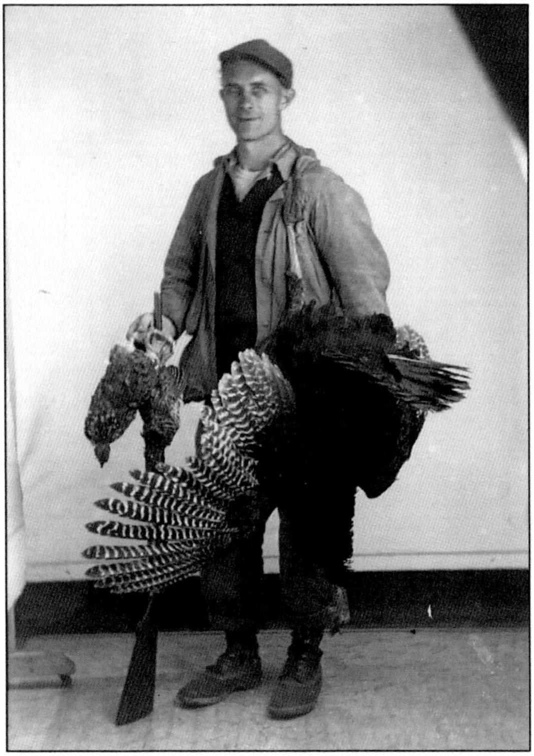

To the left is legendary outdoorsman, Richwood High School biology and Bible teacher, coach, and longtime fire chief Ed Buck. Probably no one knew the thousands of acres of forest comprising the watersheds of Cherry, Cranberry, and Williams Rivers better than Ed. He hunted, trapped, or fished almost every square foot of it. He caught trout on artificial flies and rattlesnakes with sticks. Here he holds one of the many turkeys he killed during his long life.

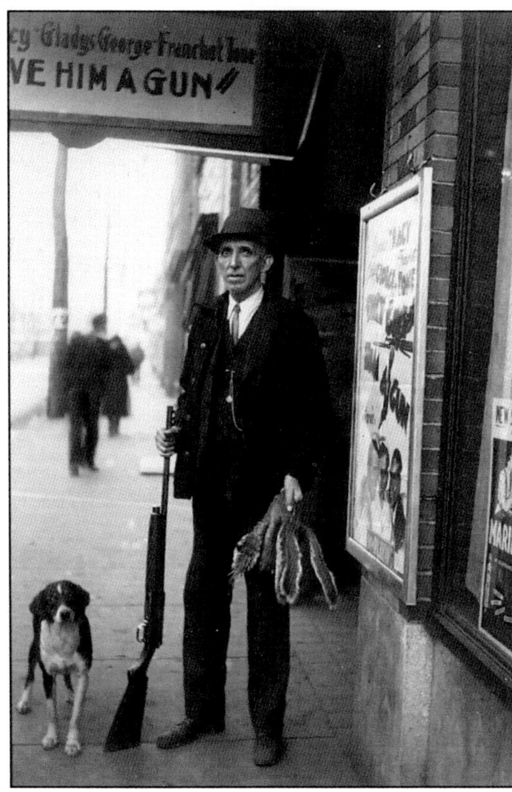


To the right is Charlie Holt, proprietor of the Star Theater, holding a "mess" of squirrels he killed with the help of his dog. It is doubtful that he wore a vested suit and tie while actually hunting. Finley Taylor reportedly said that often his subjects would insist on changing into their best clothes when approached for a photograph. The theater marquee seems appropriate for the pose: "Give him a gun!"

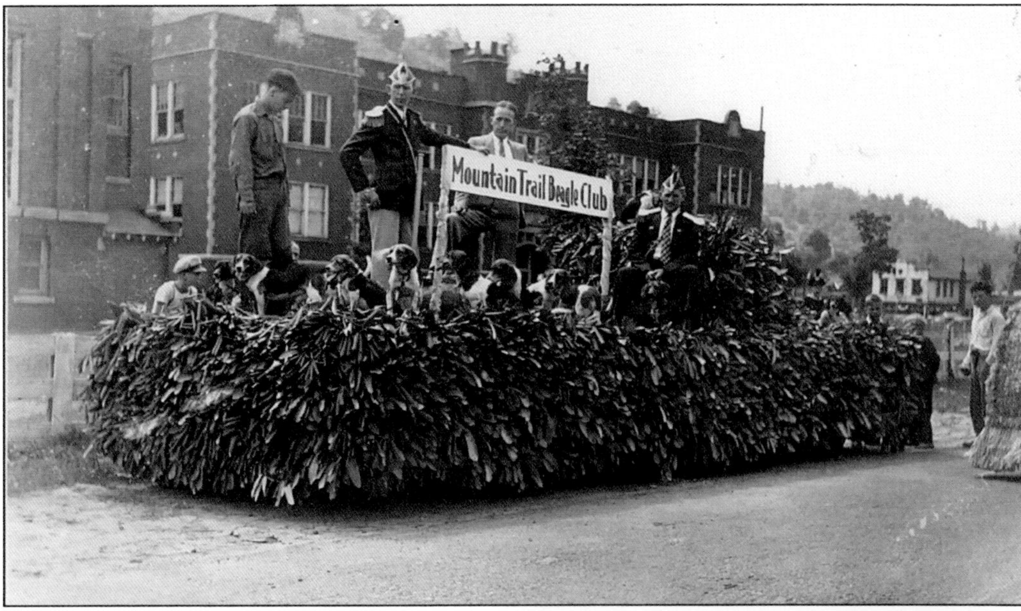


In addition to a boxing club, Richwood had a number of clubs relating to hunting. These included a National Rifle Association affiliate, a bear hunting club, a beagle club, and the notorious Nicholas County Rod and Gun Club. Above is the Spud and Splinter parade float sponsored by the Mountain Trail Beagle Club.
To the right is Jack Bennett and other unknown hunters with some of their dogs. Jack is seated in front on the left.

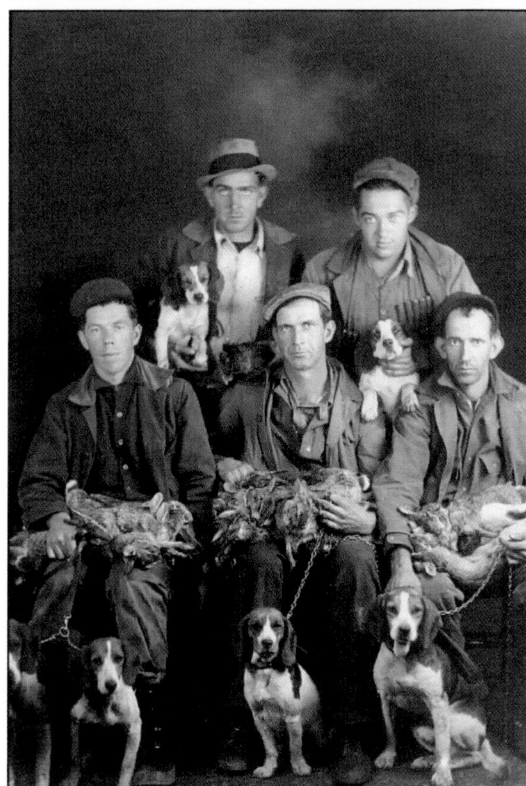

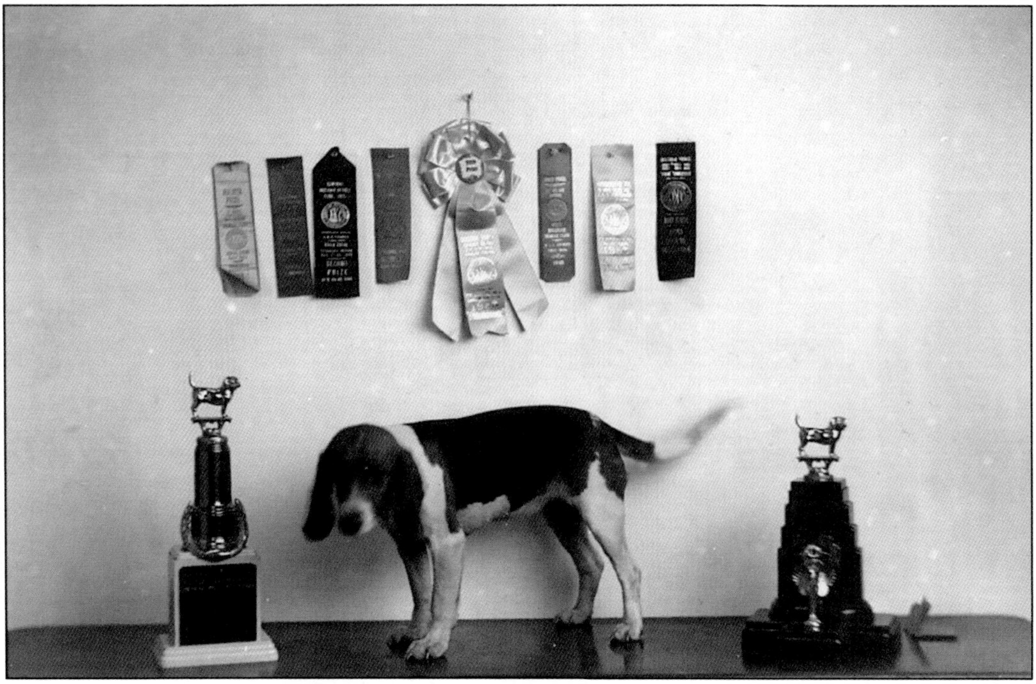

Jack Bennett, a Southside barber, trained prize-winning beagles. His dog, Mountain Trail Lawyer ("Lawyer" for short), became the first local dog to win a National Field Championship. Lawyer bested 86 other dogs in the Chicago Field Trials in September 1951.

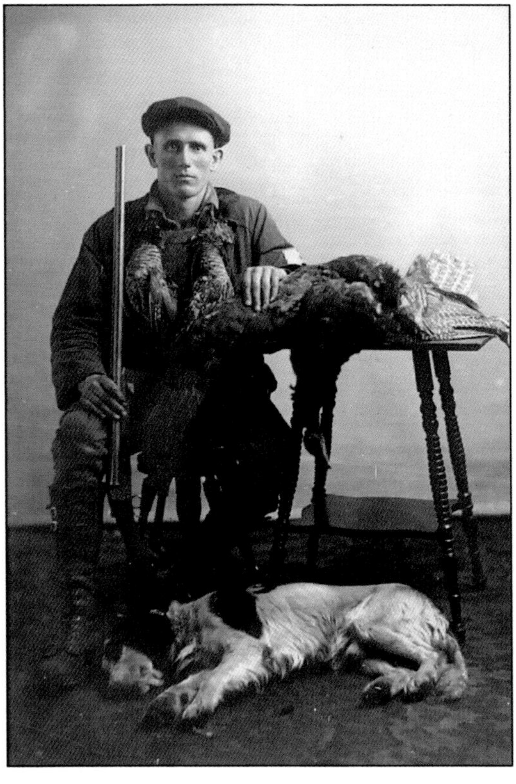

The man to the left with the double barrel shotgun is Wyatt McClung. He is reported to have been one of the very best hunters in the county.

Here is another one of Finley children's images. The raccoon seems to be saying, "Please, do anything to me you want—just don't tickle me!" All of these hunters are so serious, it was about time to interject a little humor into things.

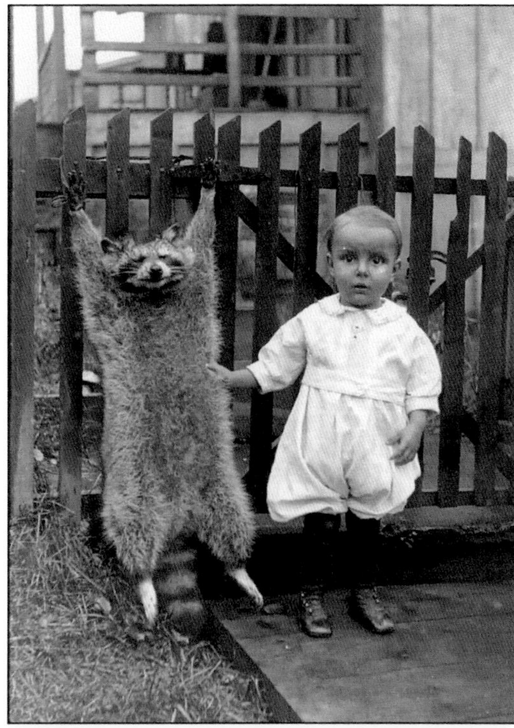

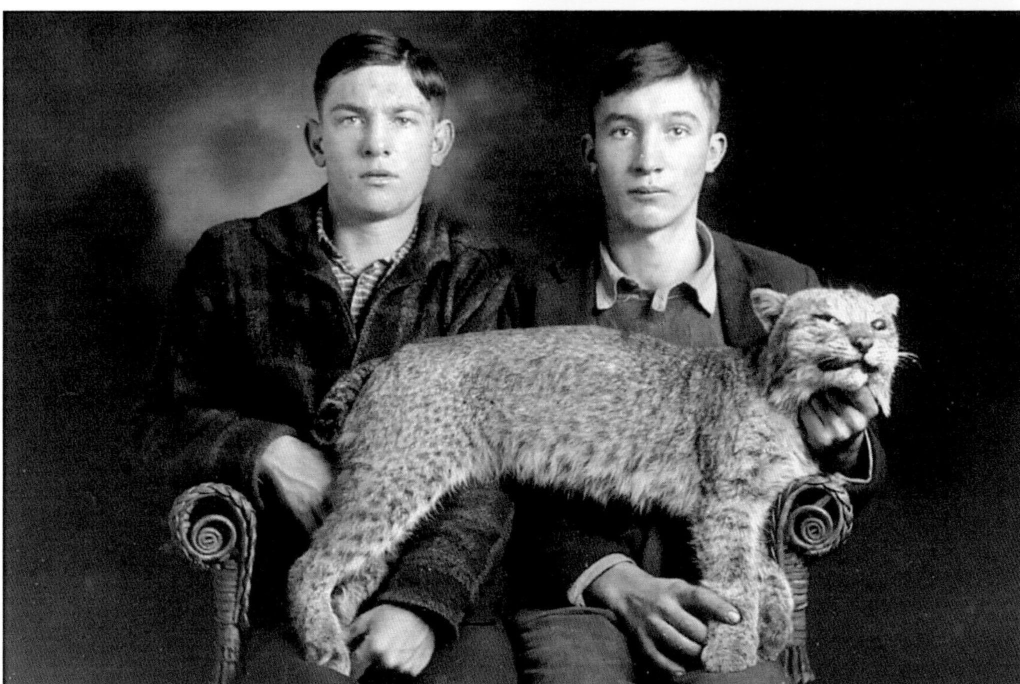

These two unidentified youngsters are holding the top point getter in the infamous contest whose announcement appears on the following page. The bobcat was viewed as a threat to wildlife so the state paid a bounty for their hides. Wild Cats were also worth 1,500 points in the great Nicholas County Rod and Gun Club Varmit Killing Contest.

# Varmit Killing Contest

TO BE HELD FROM

**March 15th to August 15th, 1934**

**Nicholas County Rod & Gun Club**

## POINTS ALLOWED FOR KILL

**Wild Cat..............................1,000**

**Gray Fox...............................500**

**Weasel..................................300**

**Mink.....................................300**

**Owls (except Screech)..............250**

**Hawks...................................200**

**Crows...................................200**

**King Fishers...........................100**

**Water Dogs.............................50**

**Red Squirrels..........................50**

**Mud Turtles............................25**

**Chipmunks.............................25**

**All Snakes..............................10**

**Rats or Mice...........................10**

Reproduced on this page is the announcement for the first annual Nicholas County Rod and Gun Club Varmit Killing Contest. It seems that the only animals not considered varmints were game birds like grouse, quail, and turkeys and big game animals such as deer and black bear. The quote in the introduction to this chapter focuses on the second big point-getter for the contest, the waterdog. Waterdogs are giant salamanders that live on the bottoms of rivers where they scavenge for food. Although they only had a value of 50 points in the contest, they were so numerous that they became the target for decimation by the local club members. Beecher Hinkle, author of the quote, reported that he and his brothers won the contest the first year because they were able to lay claim to several wild cats. As the quote alludes, they also did well catching waterdogs.

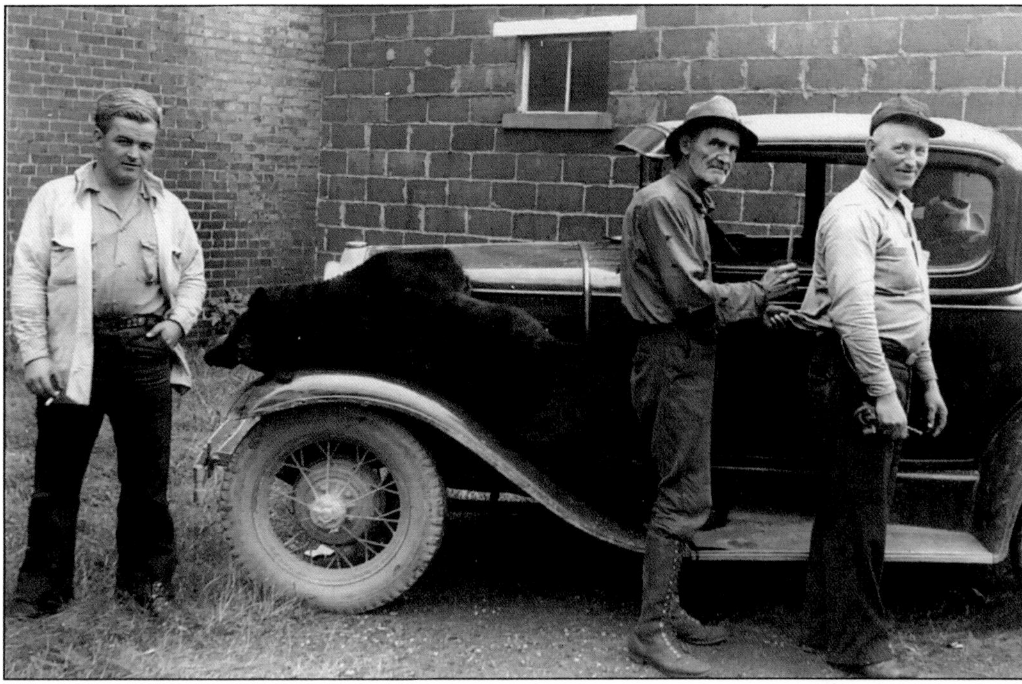

Above is an image of a time-honored tradition among hunters. If a hunter misses the animal he had an opportunity to bring down, his shirt tails are cut. Holding the knife in the middle is legendary bear hunter Felt Hanna. On the right is Luther Groves, of Nettie, who missed the bear. On the left is his son, Tom Groves, who killed the bear. Pictured below is probably the entire hunting party that helped in trailing and treeing the black bear.

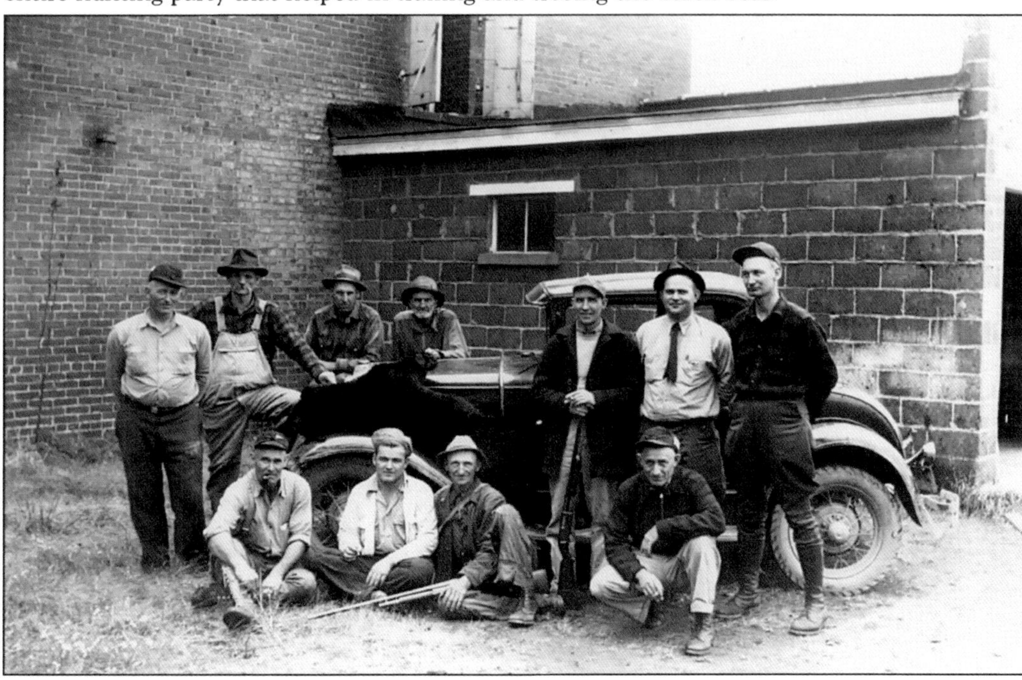

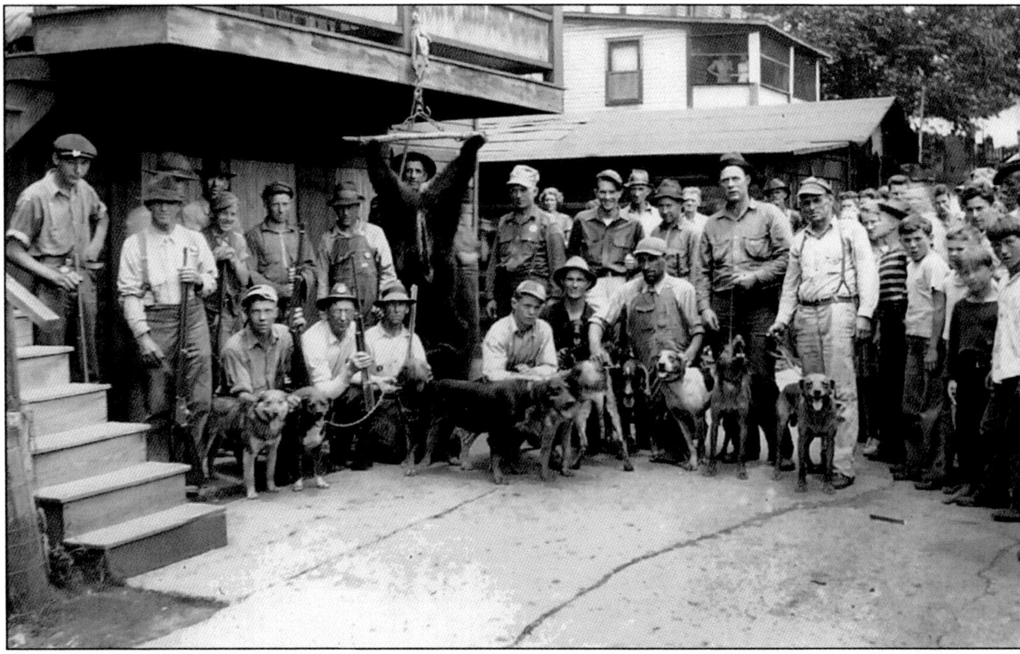

Above is probably the major portion of the Rod and Gun Club who have turned out to celebrate the killing of this big black bear. It could also be the Bear Hunter's Club.

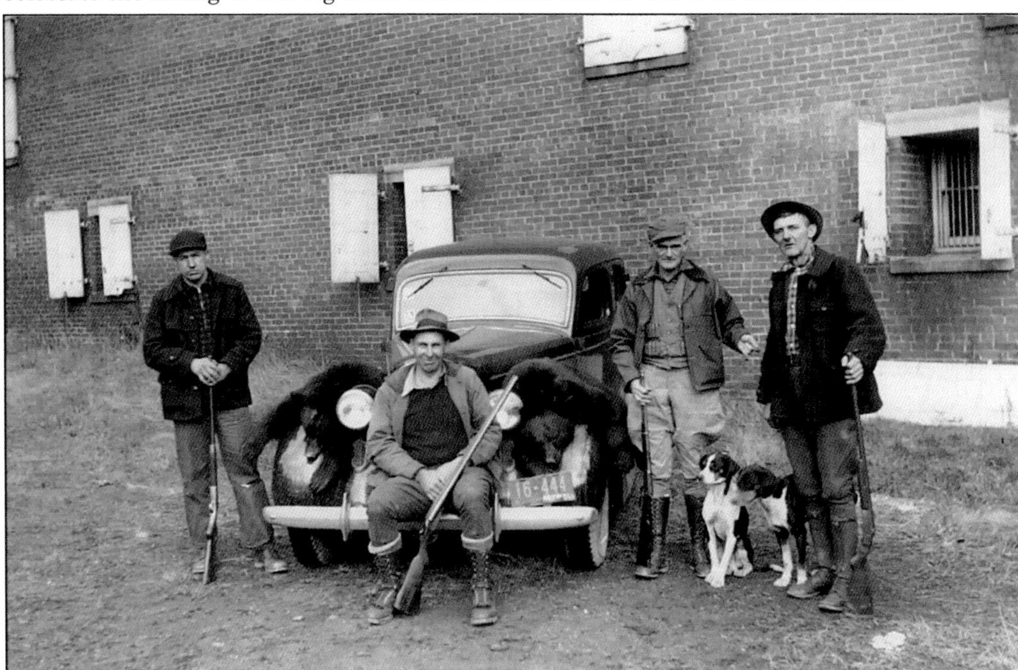

Above is another successful bear hunting party with two black bears. On the left is Beecher Hinkle. Seated on the car bumper between the bears is Beecher's brother Elbert Hinkle, probably the only smiling face in any of Finley's hunting pictures. Next is ? Frazier from out of town. On the extreme right is Herman Shaffer. The bears were killed in 1945 near Hunter's Run on the North Fork of Cherry River, just after Beecher was discharged from the army.

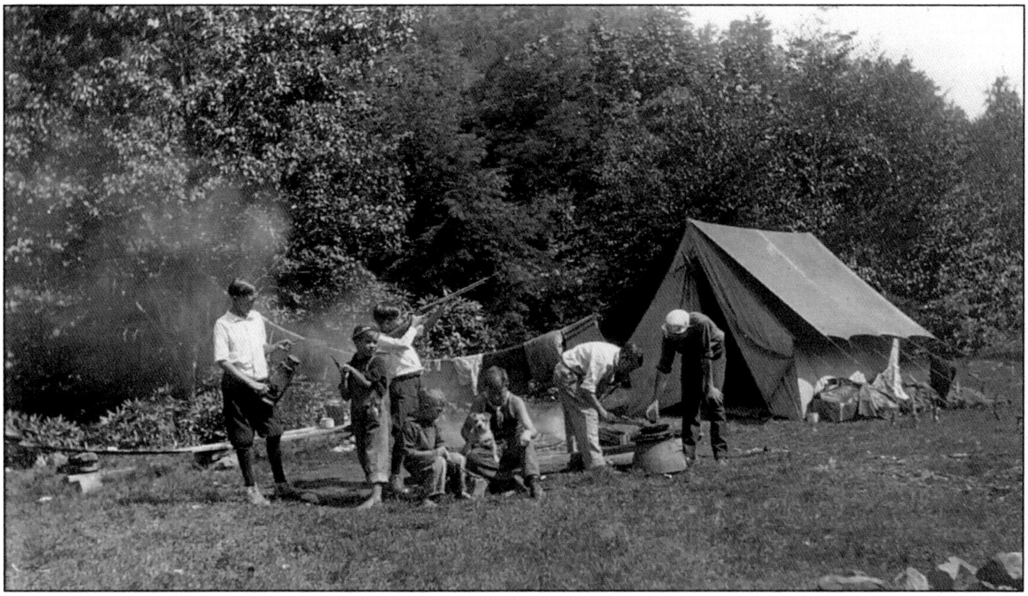

Here is a group of scouts enjoying an overnight camp-out at Organizational Camp Splinter on Cranberry River. This camp at the mouth of Jakeman Run was built on land donated by Cherry River Boom and Lumber Company. It has a fairly large building with a big fireplace, kitchen, tables, and bunk beds. It also has a number of smaller cabins, ball courts, and the famous swimming hole. The camp was managed by a collaboration of church and civic organizations in Richwood. In the 1930s two of the townspeople who helped coordinate activities at the camp were Father Fajal of the Holy Family Catholic Church and Ada Poling of the Calvary Methodist Church. The facility is still in operation today.

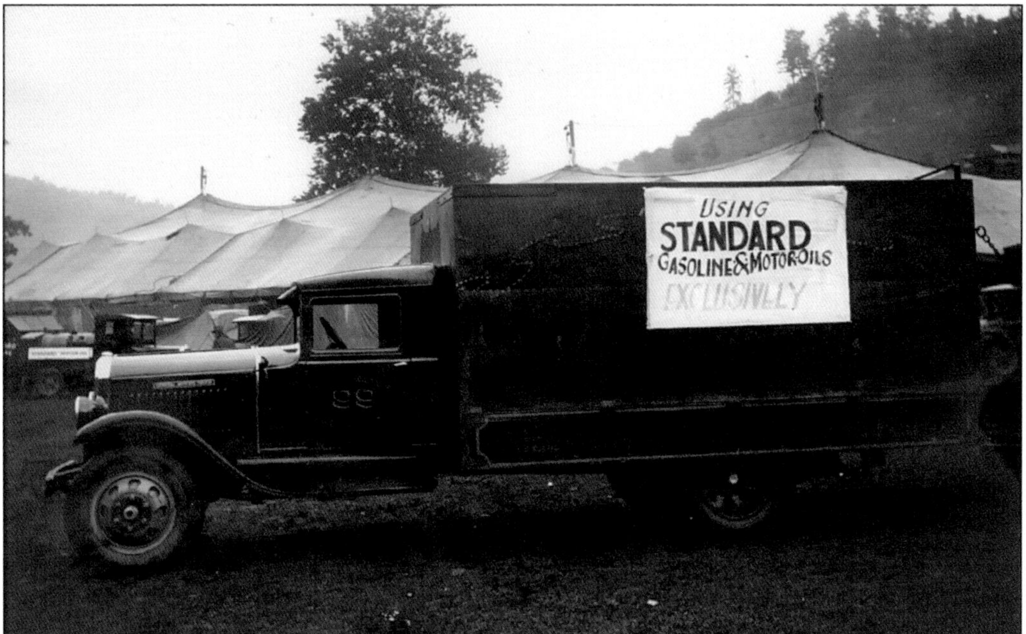


Behind the gasoline truck is a large circus tent. The railroad put Richwood on the map by bringing circuses, vaudeville shows, and other entertainment activities.

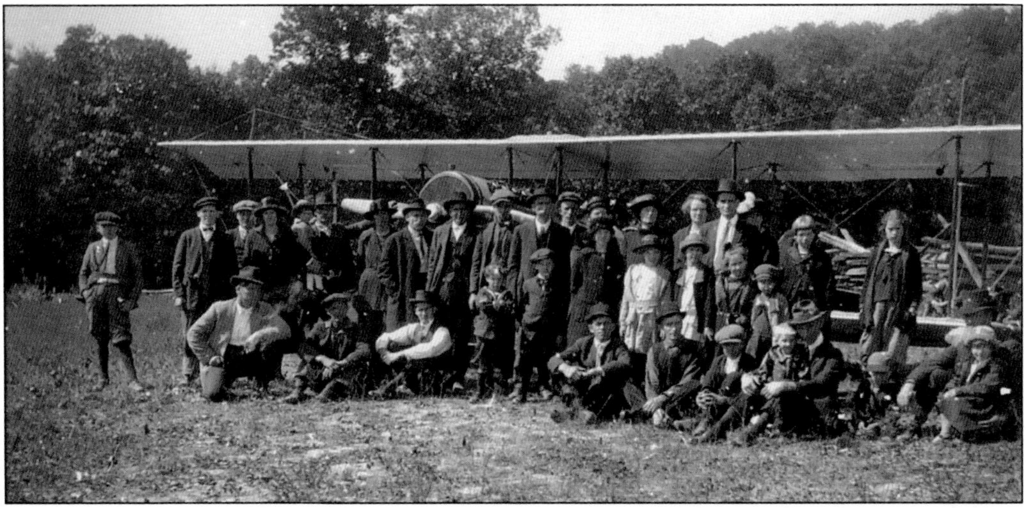

Here is another kind of outing. In the early years of aviation, the county's first airport was a field at Craigsville, presently the site of Craigsville Elementary School. Oakey Selman owned the field and invited barnstorming dare devils to come and thrill the fans with their aerobatics and rides in their planes.

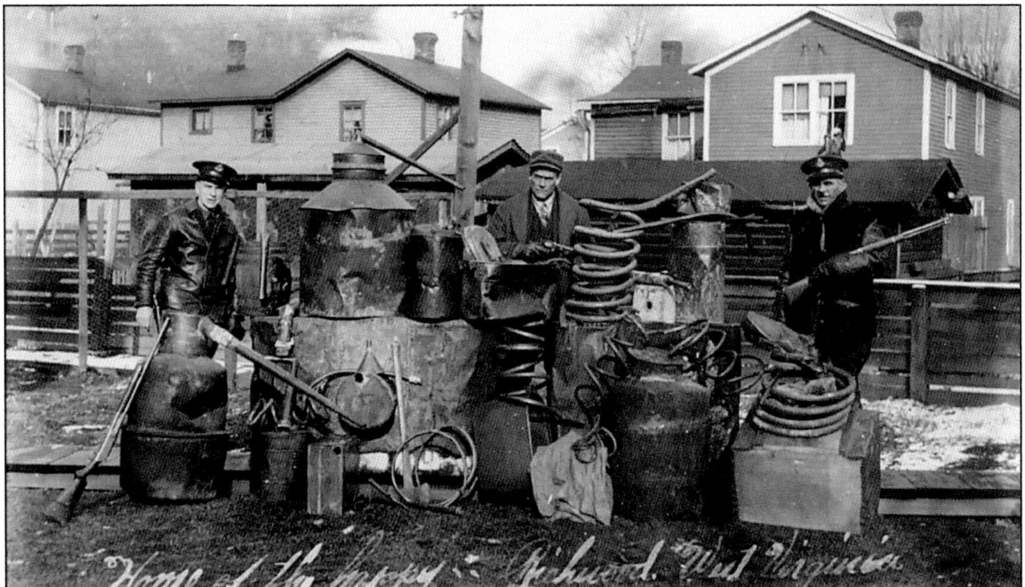


Above is a serious image that Finley postured into a happier note. These are several moonshine stills gathered up by the officers over a short period of time. The officer on the left is state policeman Corp. Charles Dick. In the center is Leonard Spencer, deputy sheriff and on the right is state policeman Tom Harman. Finley's handwritten caption for this photograph, with which he used to make postcards, is "Home of the Happy"—Richwood, West Virginia. This photograph was taken in 1929. Sadly, three years later, Trooper Dick died. Earlier in his career of hunting down illegal moonshine operations, he was involved in a gunfight in which his partner, Officer Lowe, was killed. Charles took three bullets to his body that could not be safely removed. His widow reported that the bullets were responsible for is death six years after the battle.

# AFTERWORD

*It had to be apparent when Richwood was incorporated in 1901 that its wood harvesting prosperity was destined to decline when the trees were gone. Cherry River Boom & Lumber Company's mills could process timber from 10,000 acres of land annually. With holdings of about 200,000 acres, the timeline for depleting their resource was approximately 20 years. The company's purchase of privately owned timber during these early years prolonged and slowed this march toward depletion but, when World War II approached, the timber was gone and so were the mills it fed. The exception was the Big Mill. Subsequent to several ownership changes and complete reconstruction, a modern mill still saws logs on the same site now owned by the Georgia Pacific Corporation. Beneath the surface of the deforested land lay large coal reserves. Mines had operated in the county since the beginning of the century. Even Cherry River Boom & Lumber Company had a mining operation with mines at Elk Lick Bottom on the South Fork of Cherry River and at Jerryville on Gauley River. After World War II, numerous companies operated coal mines in the county which revitalized Richwood's economy. However, by the early 1980s, a combination of factors including the depletion of the most easily recoverable coal and poor market conditions provided a blow to the town's economy from which it has yet to recover. Timber is a renewable resource and, to the town's great good fortune, Cherry River Boom & Lumber Company sold 175,000 acres of its holdings to the federal government in 1934 to expand the Monongahela National Forest. Although lumbering has continued on the government land, the forest has regrown to such an extent that Congress designated 25,000 acres as the Cranberry Wilderness Area under the Wilderness Act. Mining and lumbering continue to contribute to the area economy, but for Richwood, outdoor recreational opportunities resulting from the re-growth of its neighboring forestland seem to be the hope for the future. The book concludes in this chapter with images of the town's transition into the 21st century. By the early 1960s, the last remaining shay steam locomotives operating in the eastern United States were at the Ely-Thomas Lumber Company mill at Fenwick and at the Meadow River Lumber Company mill at Rainelle. Fortunately, the fact that they had become such a rarity resulted in these engines and some of Cherry River Boom & Lumber Company's engines to be preserved in museums instead of being scrapped. Pictured below is Ely's No. 2 shay, which resides in the Pennsylvania State Railroad Museum at Strasburg, Pennsylvania.*

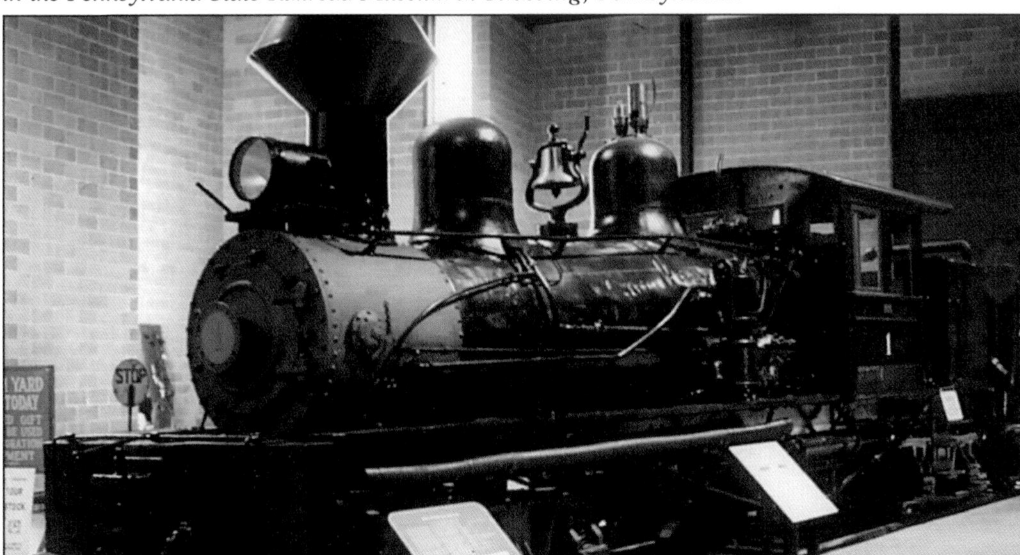

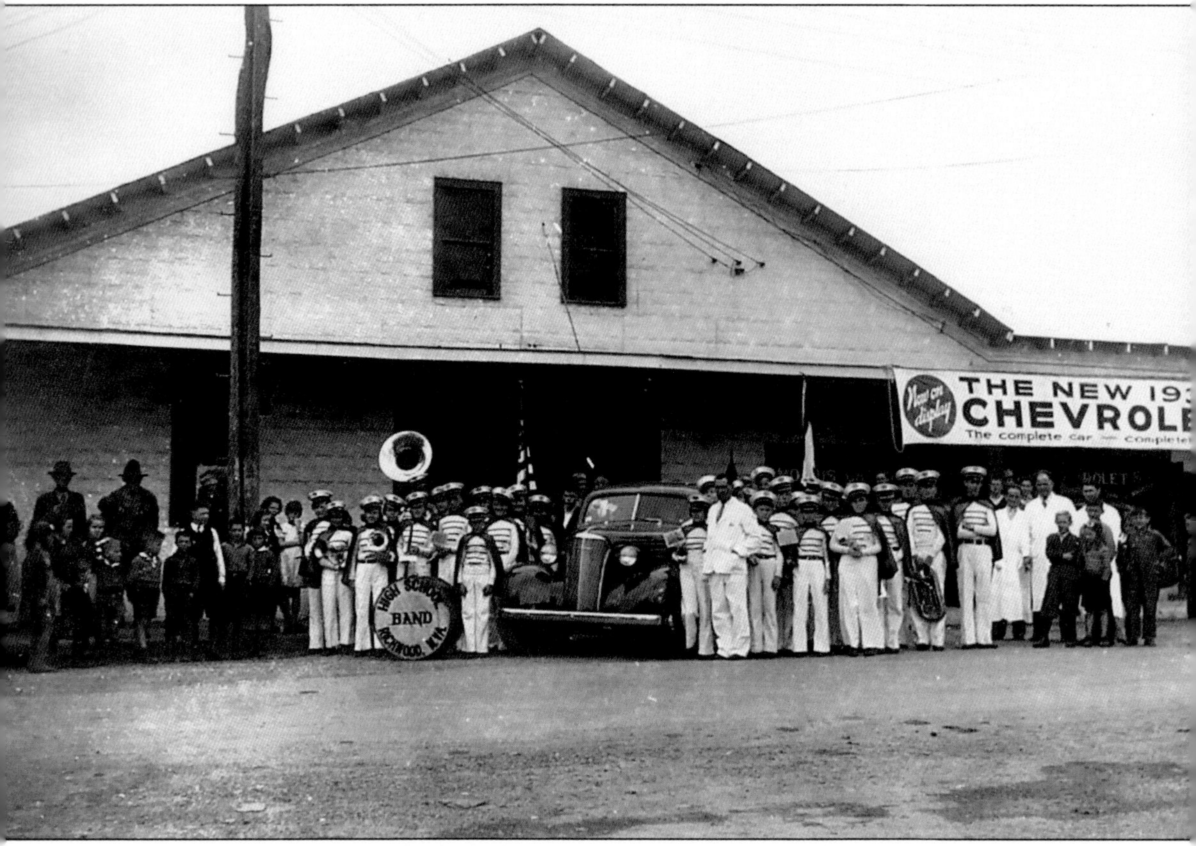


By the late 1930s, automobiles had almost totally eliminated the horse and wagon from the streets of Richwood. You might find a wagon being used on a farm, but they weren't seen on the streets in town. The town's doctors still made home visits but they had stopped traveling on horseback. The horse barns on Commercial Avenue behind city hall and behind McClung Hospital were torn down and replaced by small businesses. Shown below is the Richwood High School Band helping to promote sales of the 1937 Chevrolet at the dealership at the south end of Oakford Avenue.

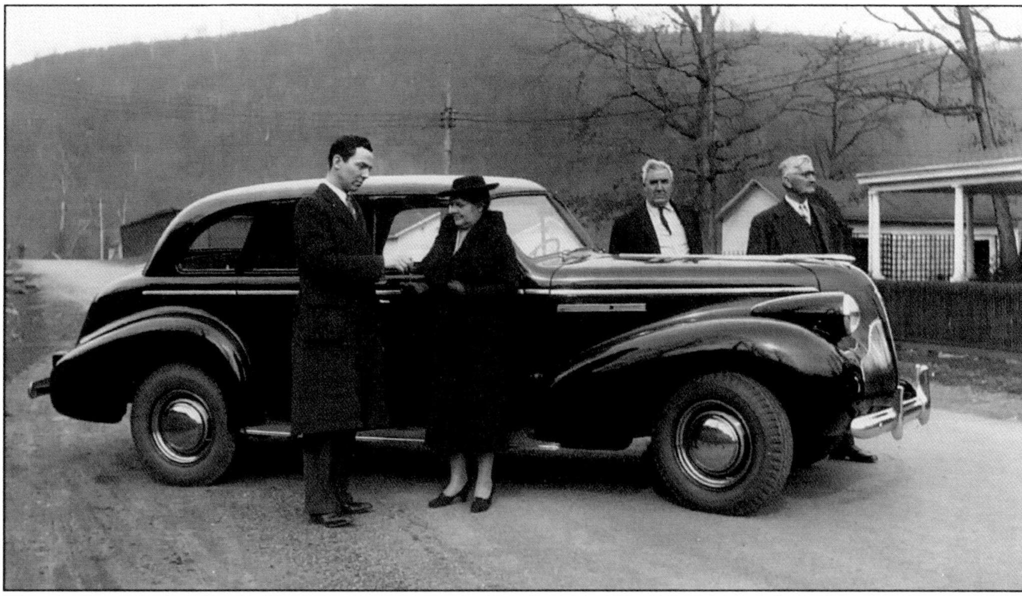

Here is an image of Madeline Roberts being presented with keys to a new Buick. Giving her the keys is Forrest Whitehouse, an Ivory Soap Company public relations man. Looking on is Bill Thomas, Buick dealer, and to his right is Dr. E.C. Bennette, town mayor.

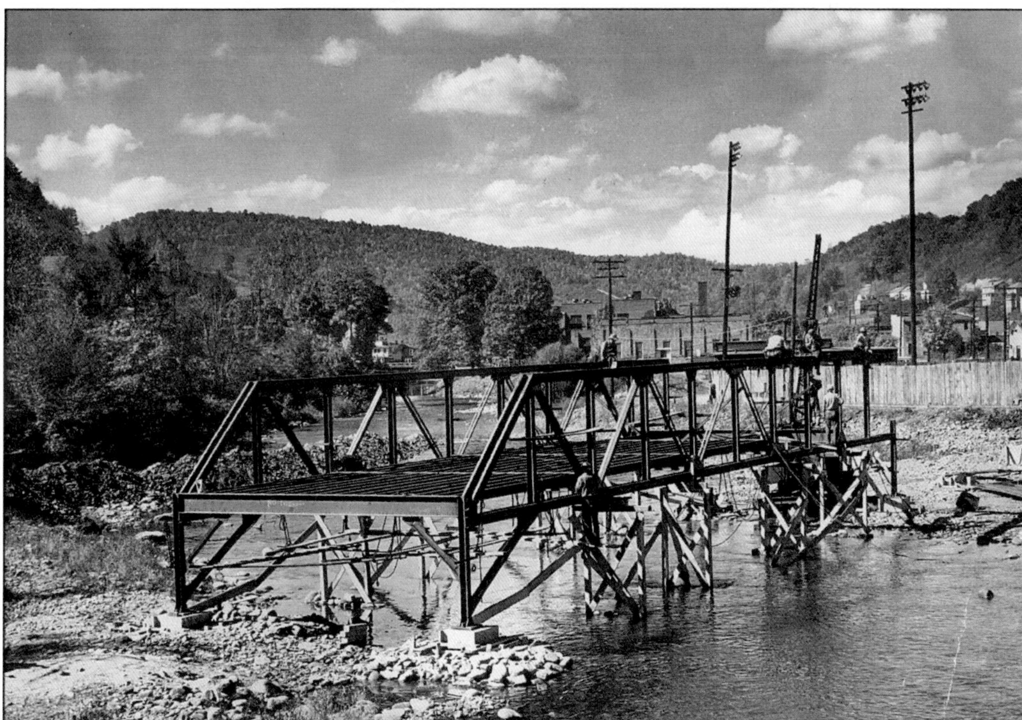

Road and bridge construction is a never ending endeavor. Here is the construction of a bridge across Cherry River to South Side in 1946. Prior to that time, only pedestrians could cross here via the swinging bridge visible in the picture. The bridge received extensive damage from the 1954 flood and was replaced in the 1970s. (Photograph by Richwood *News Leader*.)

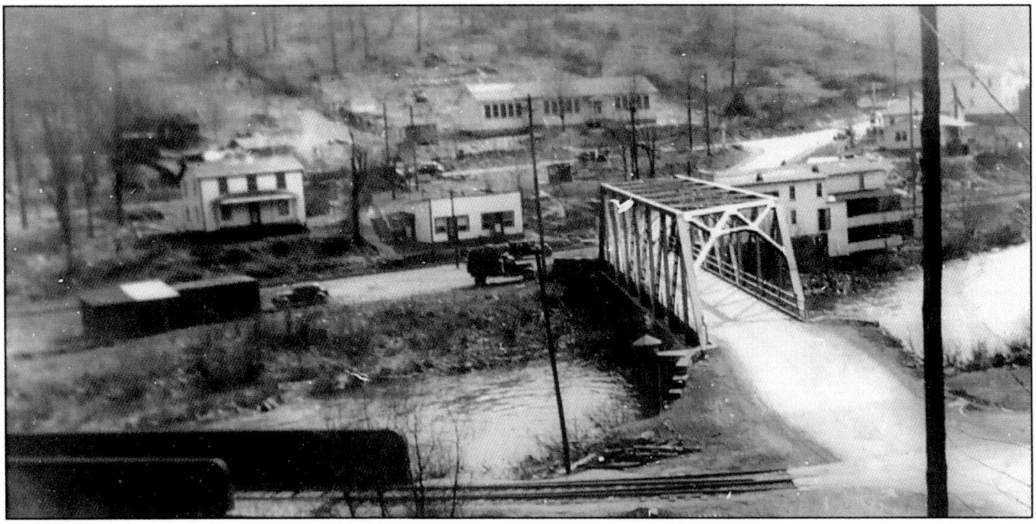

Pictured here is the first bridge built across Cherry River at Fenwick. In the decades ending the 20th century, bridges began to be replaced. Structures like the old Fenwick Bridge with their overhead trusses were not high enough to allow modern trucks to pass beneath them and so they had to be replaced. Other bridges like the South Side bridge, replaced in 1949, sustained repeated flood damage. Oakford Avenue bridge lasted until the 1970s when it was replaced. The Curtin and Holcomb bridges, completed in 1934, are still being used today. They continue to exist because Richwood can be approached by Route 39 crossing Cherry River on the new Fenwick bridge. (Photographer unknown.)

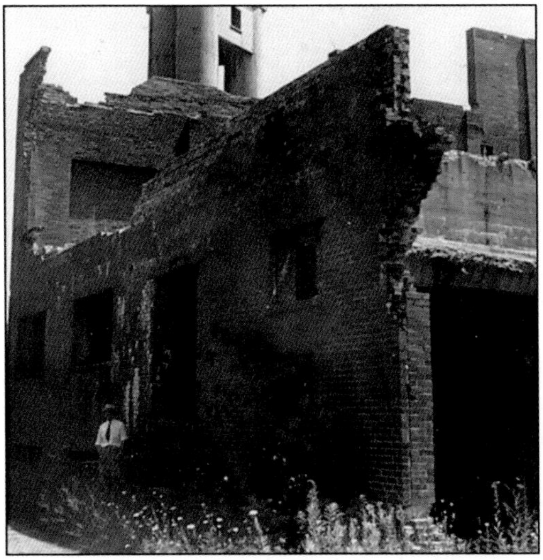

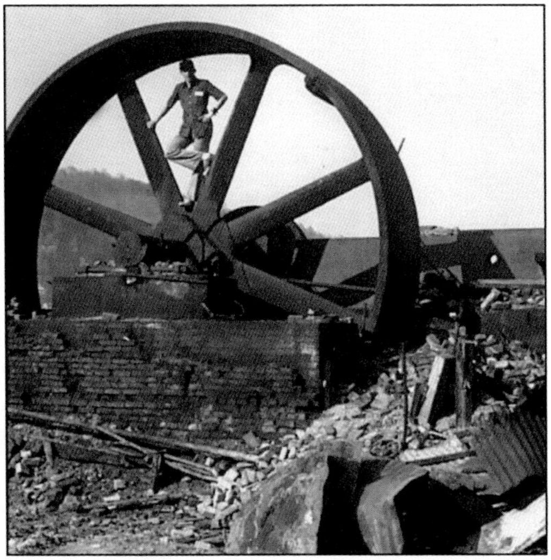

Old mills are a bigger problem than old bridges—especially large old mills such as the paper mill and tannery on the left. Reclaiming sites covered by massive concrete structures is difficult and expensive. Here is a picture of a small portion of the old paper mill. These old sites were not only eyesores, they were dangerous. A small child lost his life at this site when he fell 30 feet to the bottom of a pit while playing in the ruins. At great expense, this site was reclaimed in 1976 and is now the home Cherry River Elementary School. Pictured on the right is the main drive wheel from the Big Mill. The mill was torn down and replaced by a modern electric mill. The wheel still stands in this spot today as a monument to the steam-driven timber operations that were responsible for the birth of the town. (Photographs by Richwood *News Leader*.)

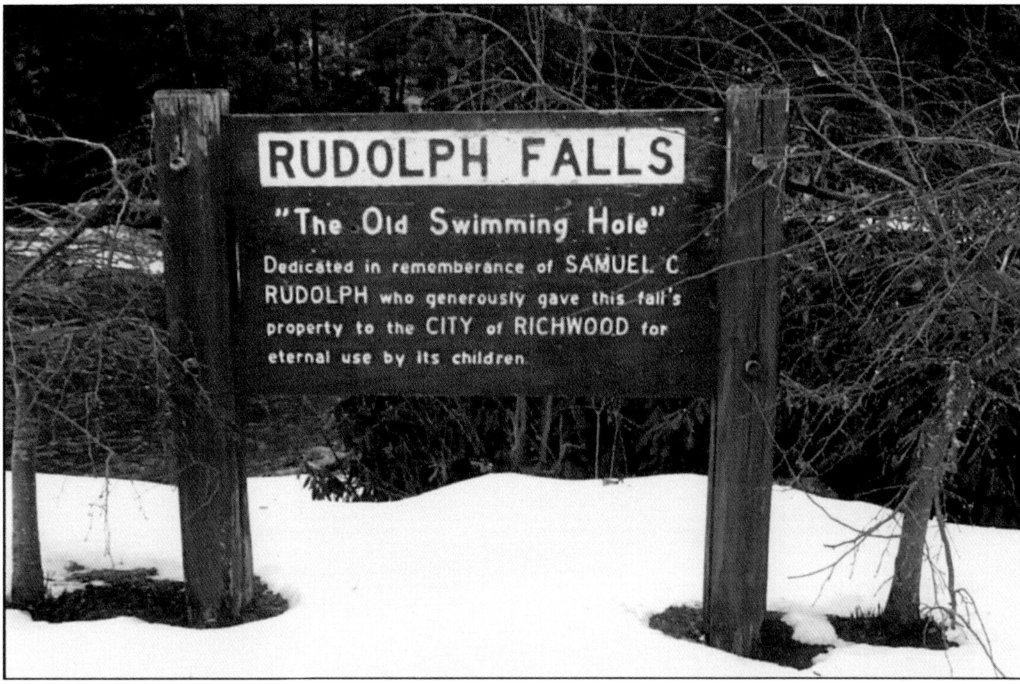


As stated earlier in the book, Cherry River Boom & Lumber Company was the patron saint of the town. Later owners could not afford to be so generous but the picture above attests to the fact that they did continue to give. The Rudolph family owned the mill for a time. The photograph of the swimming hole below shows that it has been filled in and is not what it used to be. While the water is as clean as ever, the rocks need to be cleaned. (Photographs by the author.)

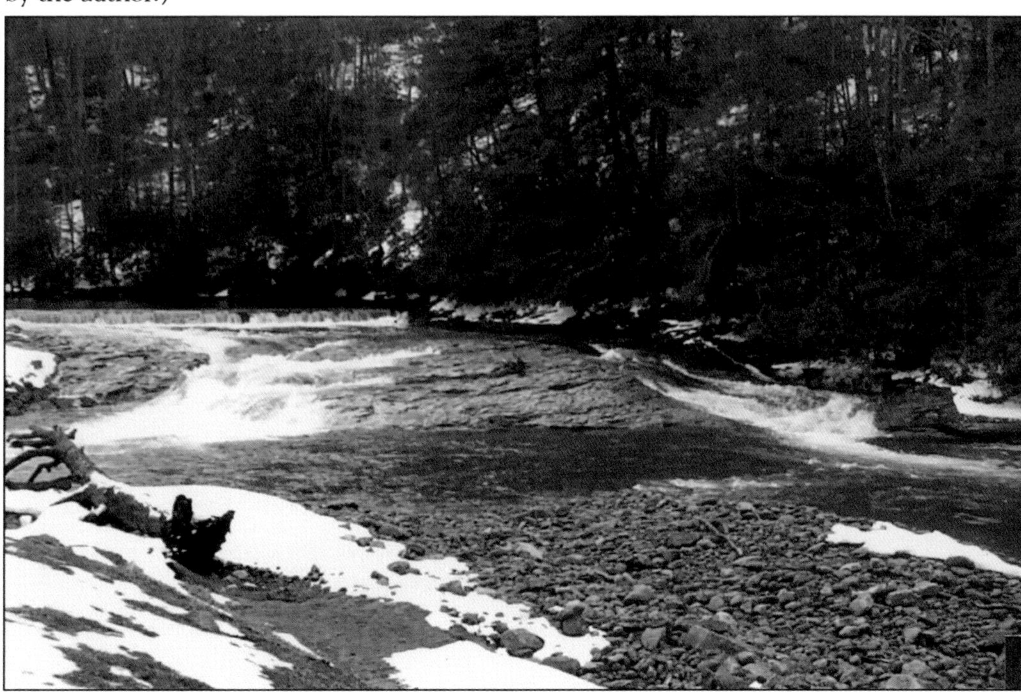

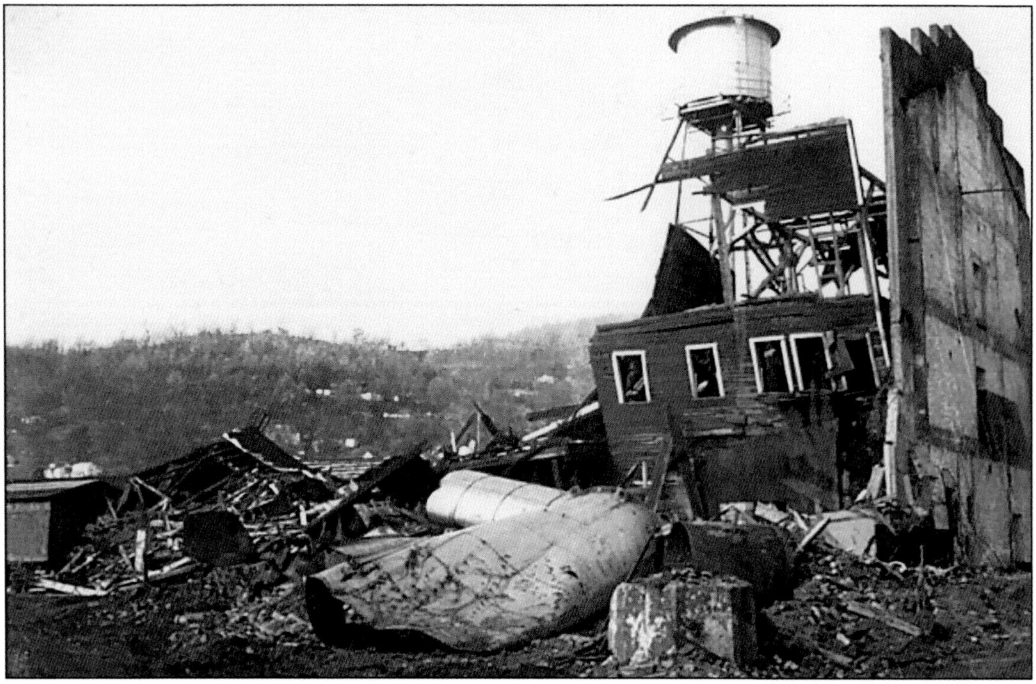

The last of the mills to close was the clothes pin factory. On a very limited basis, it continued to operate into the 1960s. The pictures above and below are from a sequence of photographs taken by the Richwood *News Leader* as the old mill was torn down to make way for construction of a strip plaza. Years earlier, the pin factory log pond had been filled in and utilized as the site for the junior high school. Not surprisingly, the building has been plagued with serious foundation problems.

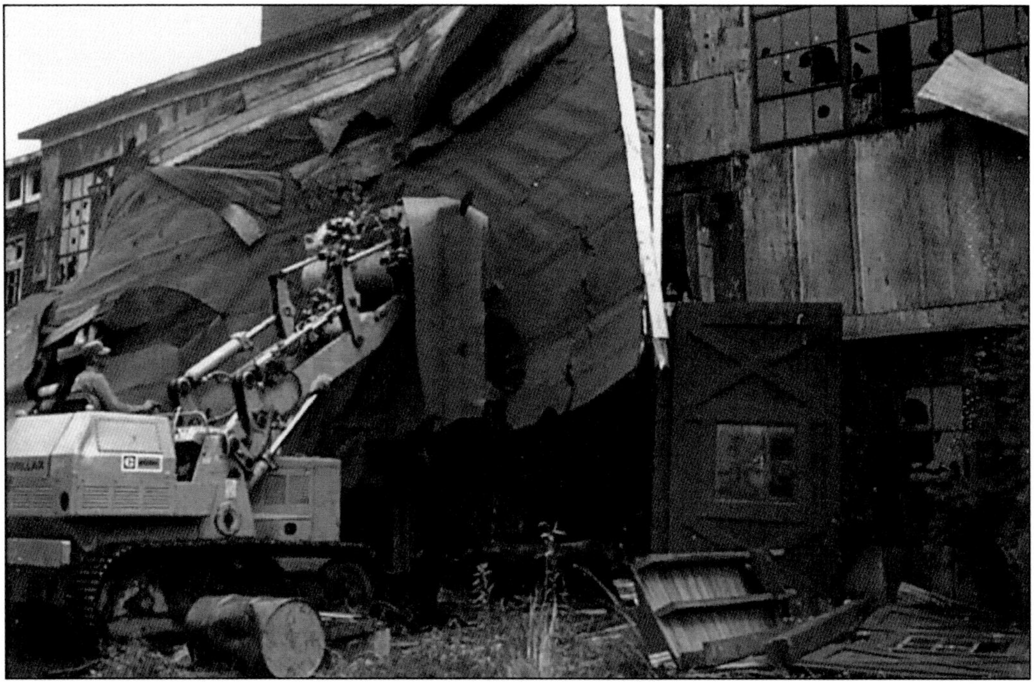

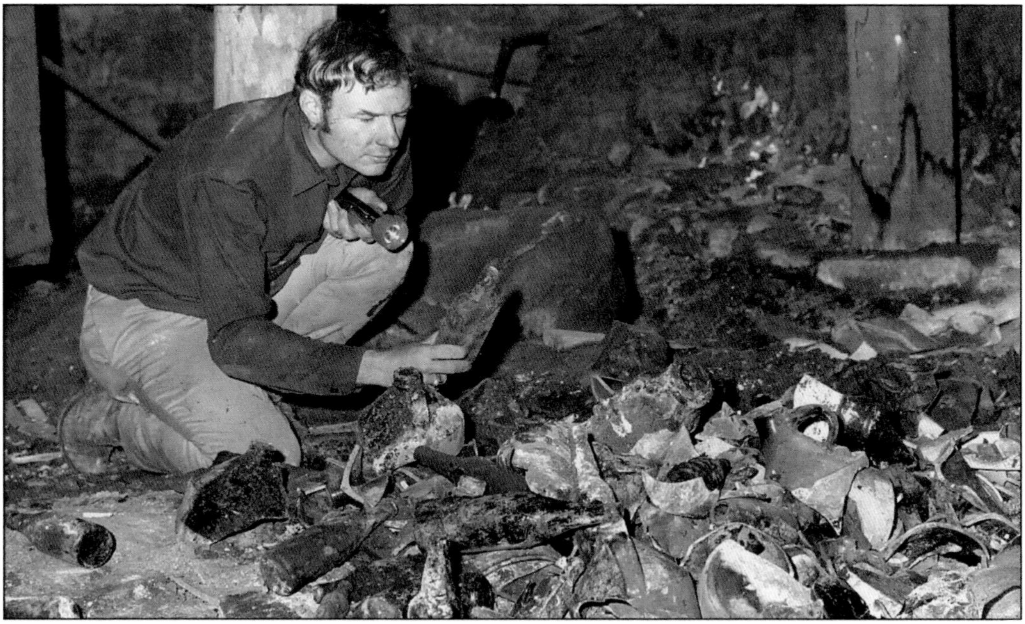

Richwood celebrated its centennial in 2001. A pleasant pastime for a number of Richwooders, including Walter Copley (shown above), was the search for relics from Richwood's past. In this picture, Walter is in the crawl space under the Snyder Building looking for old bottles. Walter and the author found over 100 old beer bottles on this dig. Unfortunately, every one of the scores of old whiskey jugs in the pile Walter is looking at were broken. (Photograph by the author.)

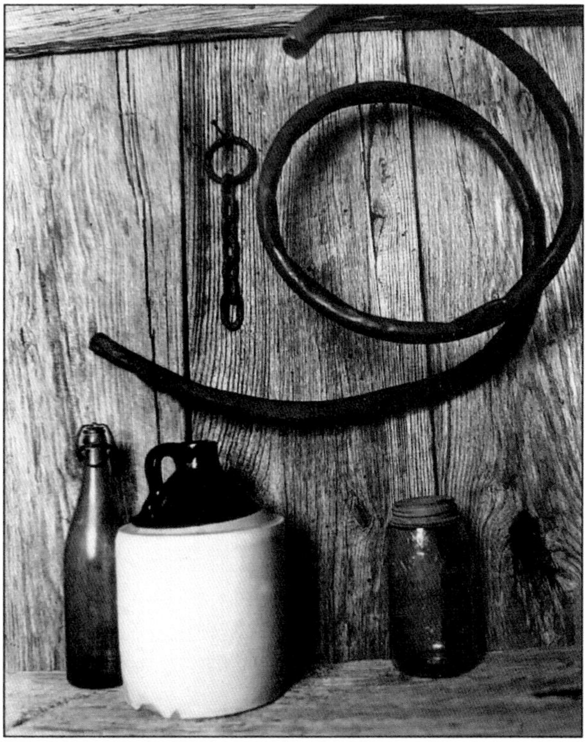

Pictured here are relics from some of the author's other adventures. These objects were found years ago along the North Fork of Cherry River. At the top is the coil from a still found lying beside Dessert Branch. The containers on the bottom are typical containers for moonshine. The first bottle on the left is what the local people call a "home brew bottle." Home brew includes wine as well as "corn licker." The next container is a stonewear jug found intact beside a railroad grade in the head of Hills Creek. The last container is a mason fruit jar, a favorite container for these entrepreneurs, probably because they were so readily available. (Photograph by the author.)

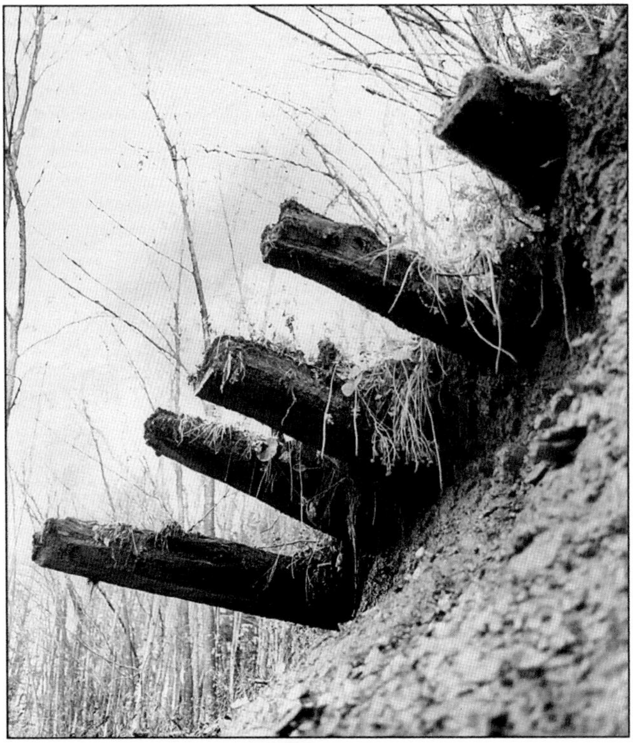

The logging railroads are gone from the forests and all that remains are their road beds and a few rotting wooden ties, like the one sticking out of the river bank in the photograph above. The stream bank has eroded away leaving these timbers precariously perched in the stream bank. It is not surprising that the more than 140 miles of Cherry River Boom & Lumber Company's timber access railroads are gone. However, it was quite a shock to find the Baltimore and Ohio mainline railroad and bridges had been taken away. Never again will we see a train of any kind pull up to the depot building that once was the focus of so much activity. On a positive note, the depot itself is still with us and has been well preserved by the townspeople. (Photograph by the author.)

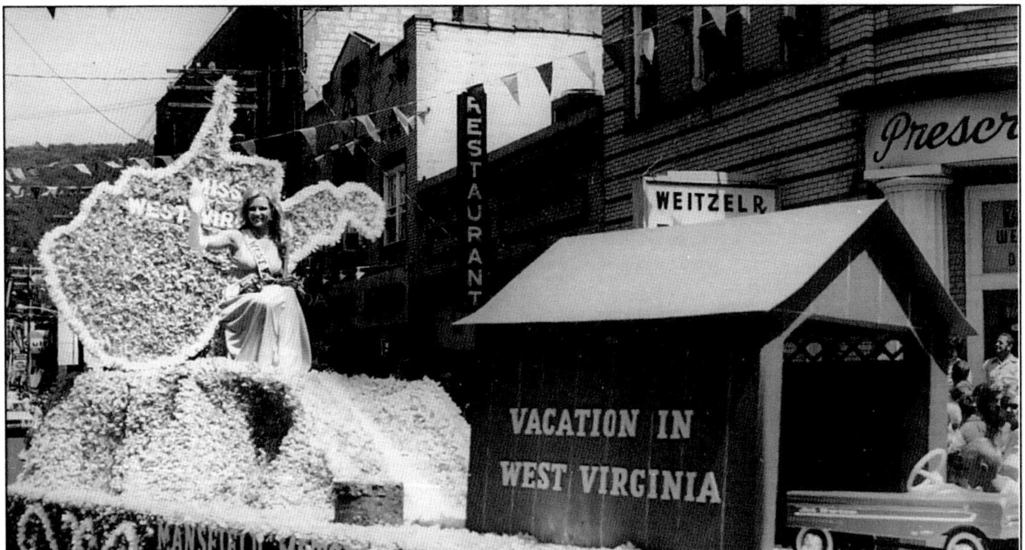


Many of Richwood's landmarks are gone, such as the railroad, the old high school building, the mills, the park in the center of town, and so on. However, the town has continued to maintain some of its longtime traditions that are people-centered, not material-centered. One of these is the annual Homecoming Festival (formerly Spud & Splinter Festival) and its accompanying Cherry River Navy maneuvers. Pictured above is Miss West Virginia waving to the crowd in the 1975 edition of the festival parade. The slogan on the float probably should have been "Vacation in West Virginia—preferably in or near Richwood." (Photograph by the author.)

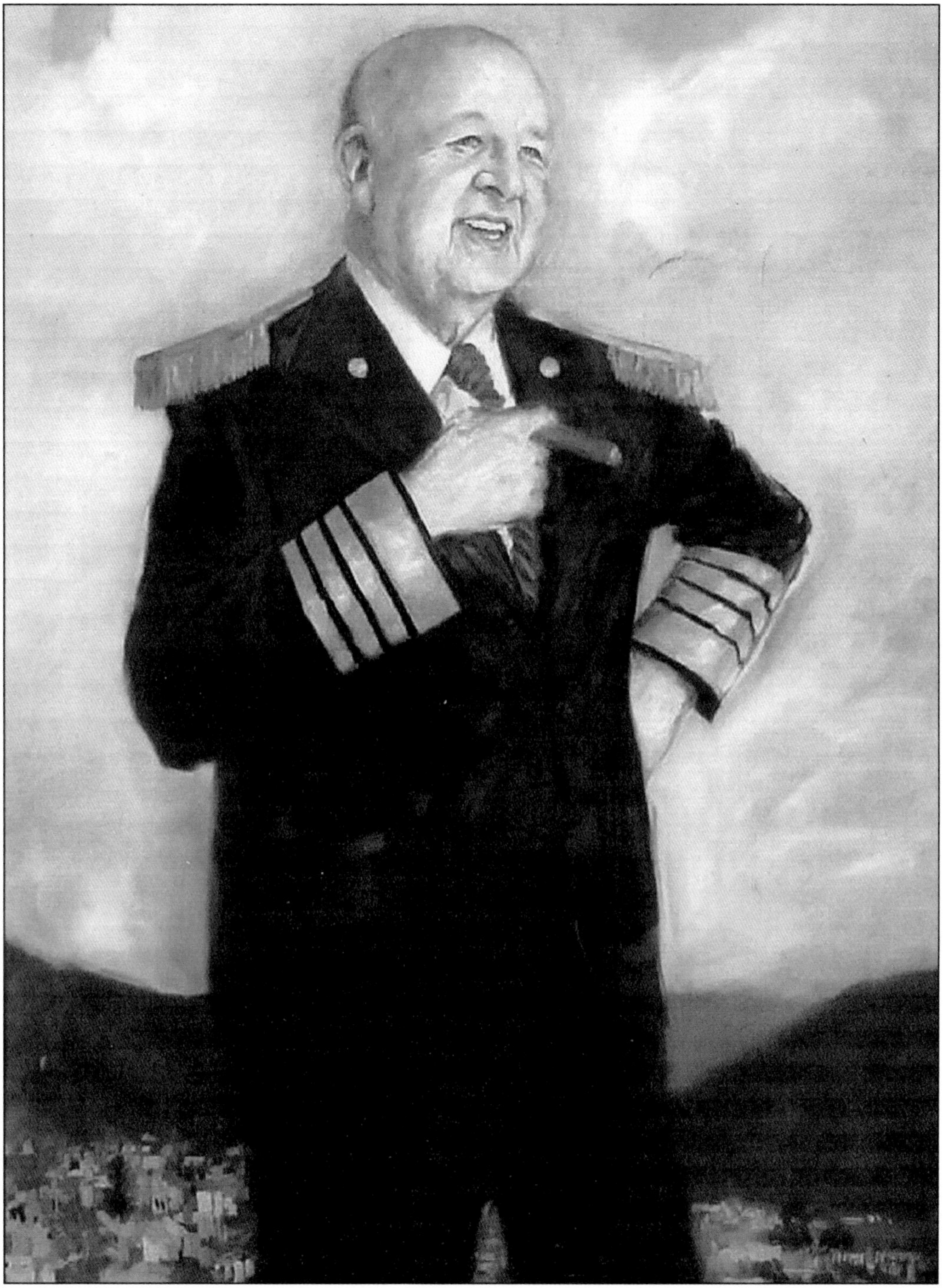

Pictured on this page is a photograph of a beautiful oil painting by Charles Erkwan portraying Bugs Teets, founder of the Cherry River Navy. He founded it as an editorial gimmick to help draw attention to the need for a road to Marlinton. There are scores of photographs of Bugs in the local papers but not one among Finley Taylor's negatives, other than long-distance shots. He was highly respected in the town—another institution that may be gone but not forgotten.

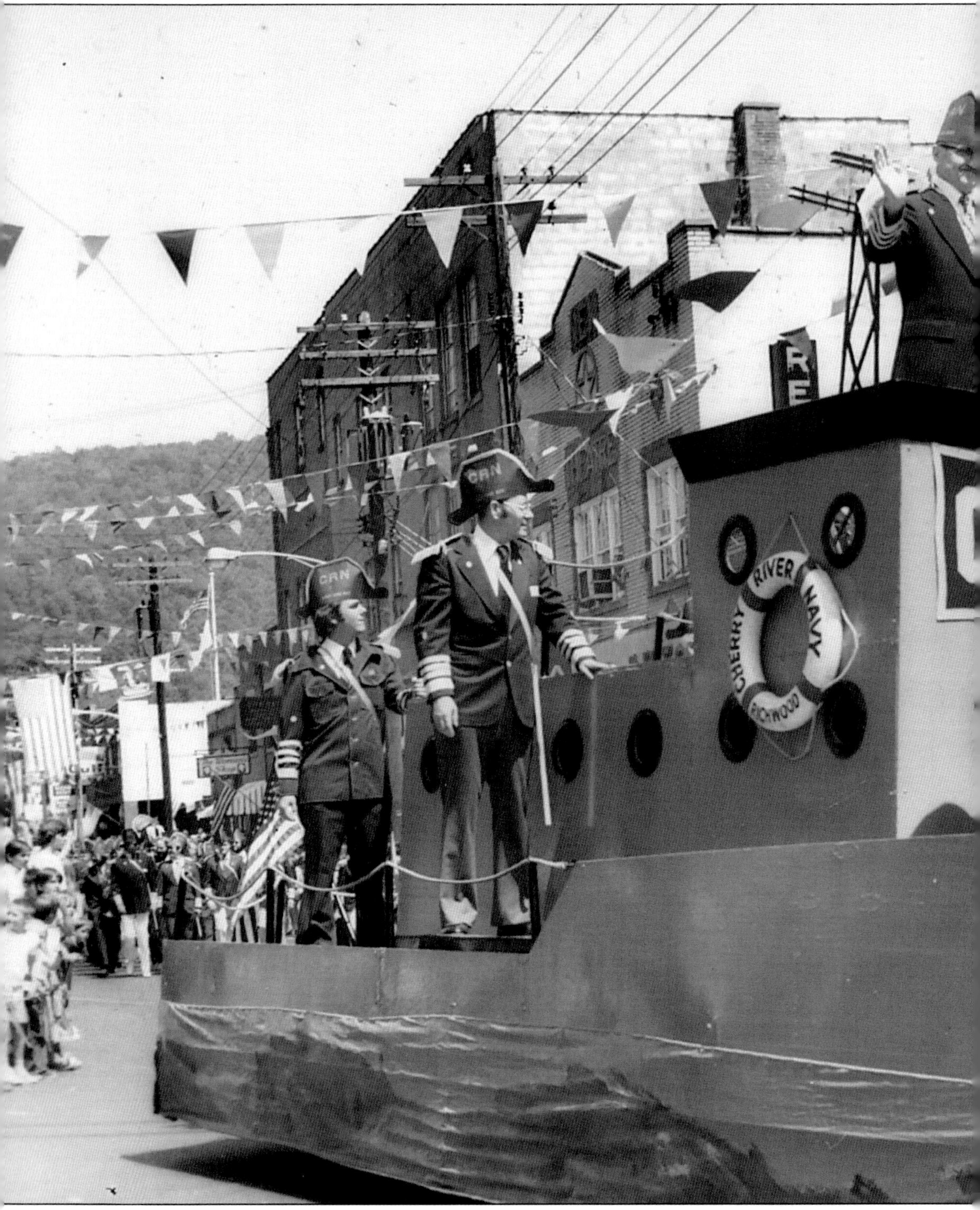


Pictured here is the CRN Mopswab in the 1975 Cherry River Navy maneuvers, part of the Homecoming Parade. Except for a brief drydocking during World War II, the Mopswab has sailed every year since the early 1930s, although it did undergo a name change. The Cherry

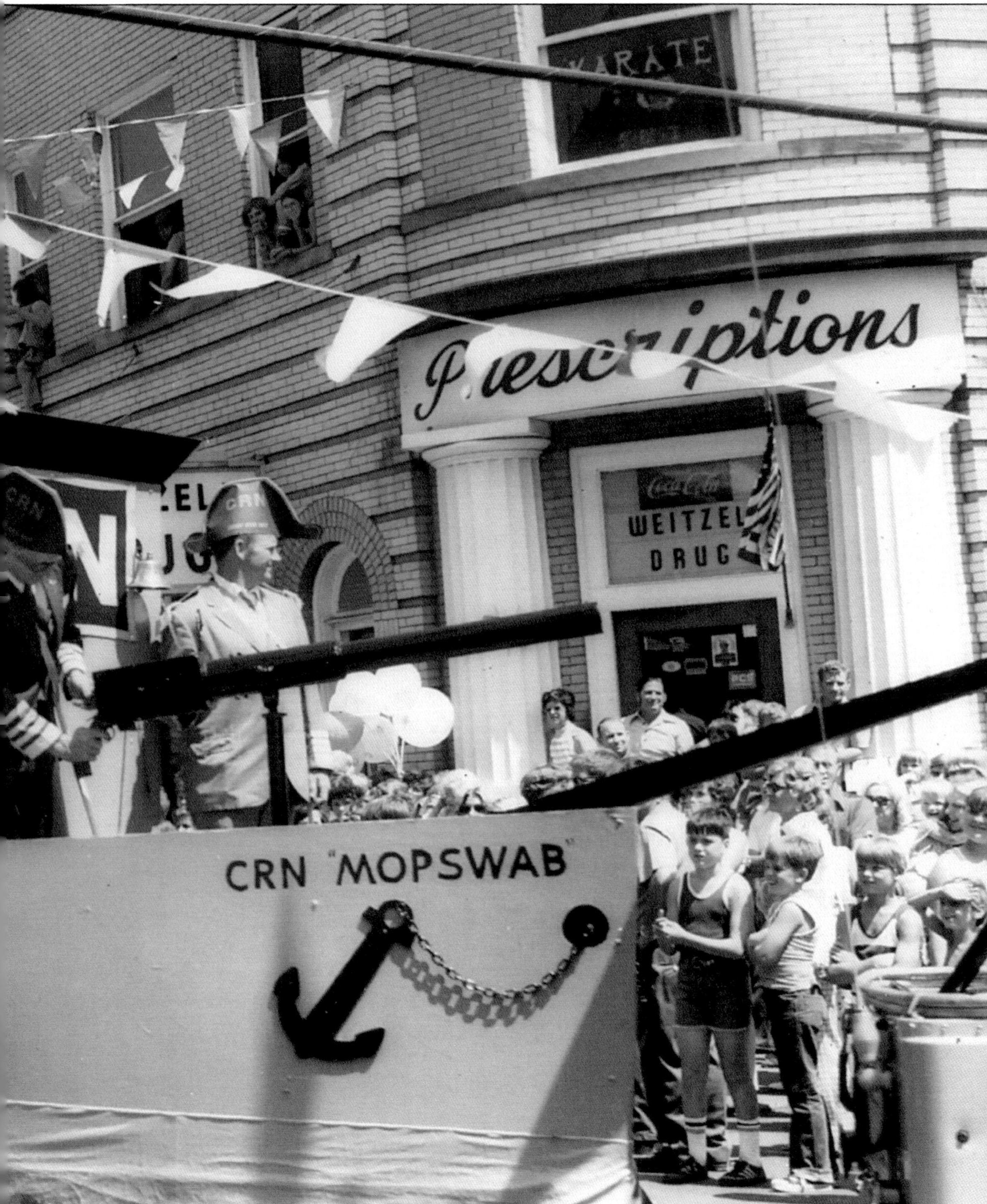


River Navy may have stayed in drydock had Bugs Teets not returned to live in Richwood and revived it. (Photograph by the author.)

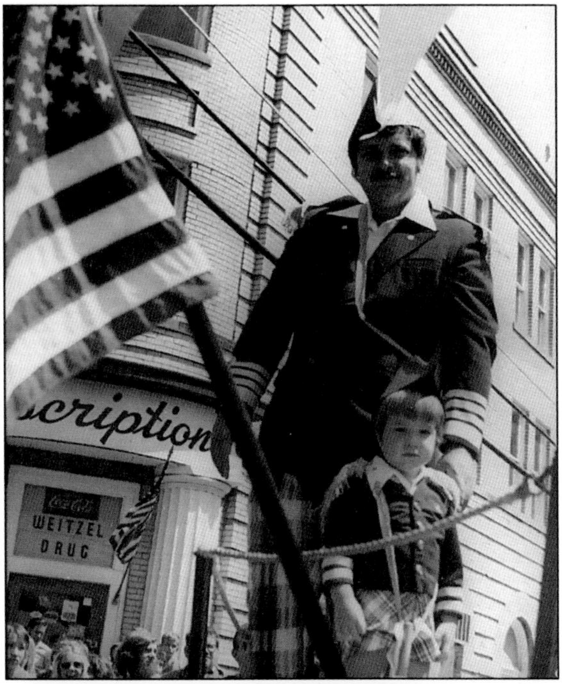


Here is another image of the 1975 Homecoming Parade. Pictured on the Mopswab is Adm. Bernard Lindsey and his son Andrew Scott, who represents the next generation of Cherry River Navy Admirals. You don't have to remain a town resident to become an admiral. Cherry River Navy Admirals and Ladies of the Admiralty have been commissioned across the nation. Many of them travel to the town in the first week of August and join the annual maneuvers. (Photograph by the author.)

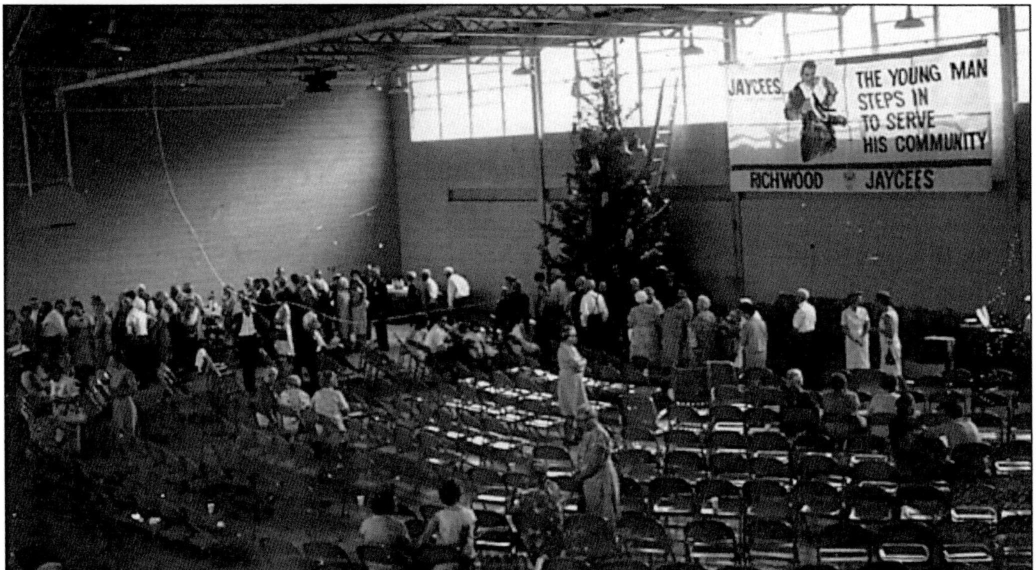


Pictured here is another Richwood tradition, the annual Past 80 Party. Before there was a party, the town's weekly papers frequently paid tribute to the oldest living members of the community and surrounding area. Bronson McClung and Jim Comstock, editors of the Richwood *News Leader*, established a party to which were invited every citizen in the state who was 80-years-old or older and could make it to Richwood with an attendant to help look after them. The basic theme for the party is Christmas in June. Entertainment is provided in the armory which is large enough to accommodate a huge Christmas tree. Attendees are given a turkey dinner with all the trimmings, special prizes, Christmas stockings stuffed with goodies, and a fruit basket. (Photograph by the author.)

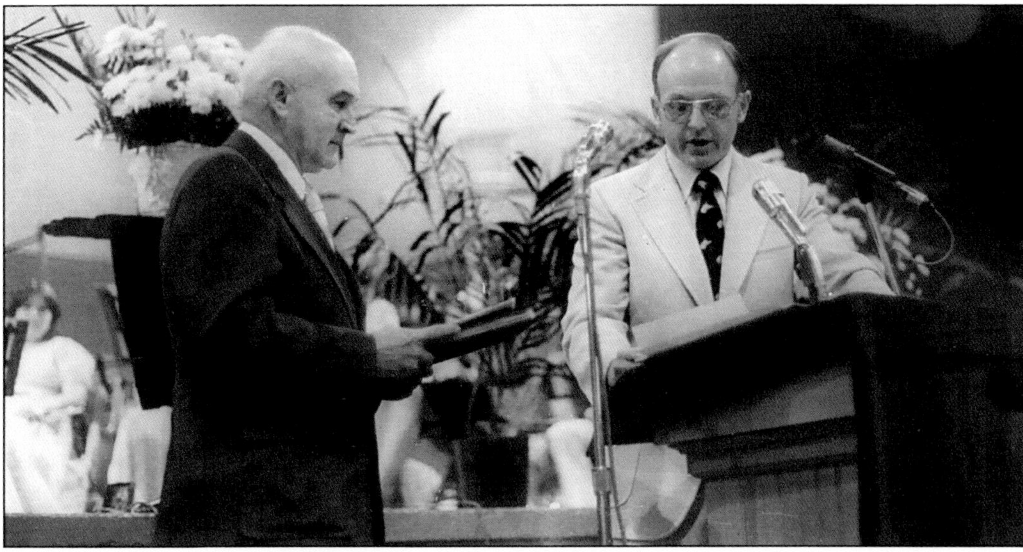

If you asked the people of Richwood to identify the town's most valuable human resource, they would probably say Edwin Pratt. Mr. Pratt was Richwood High School's longtime band leader until he retired many years ago. In addition to his school duties, every time the community had a function that needed a sound system or an emcee, Mr. Pratt was there for them. He helped out with other community affairs in ways too numerous to list here. When he retired, the town gave him a new car. Hundreds of citizens gathered in the school's gym to honor him. In the photograph above, he is being presented the keys to the car by Richwood attorney Dan Callahan. He has never stopped giving of his time and energy to the town. He must have earned at least three more cars since he was given this one! (Photograph by the author.)

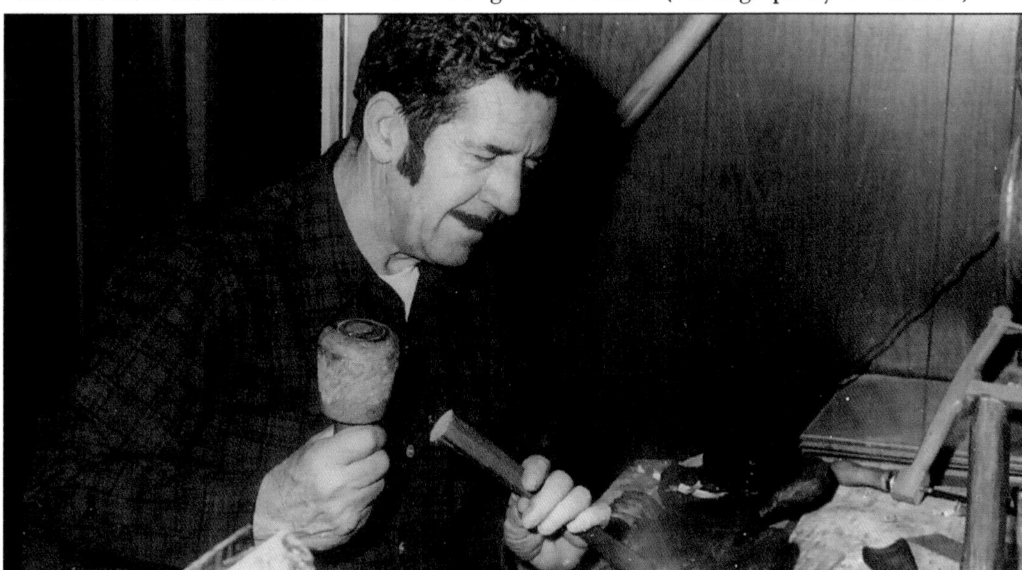

This is one of several talented Richwooders who carried craftsmanship into the last half of the town's first 100 years. Sterling Spencer, now deceased, was a sculptor of beautiful things from native woods. He was also one of the best hunters and outdoorsmen in the area. He had a vast knowledge of the forest and the things that live in the forests and he liked to share this knowledge with others. (Photograph by the author.)

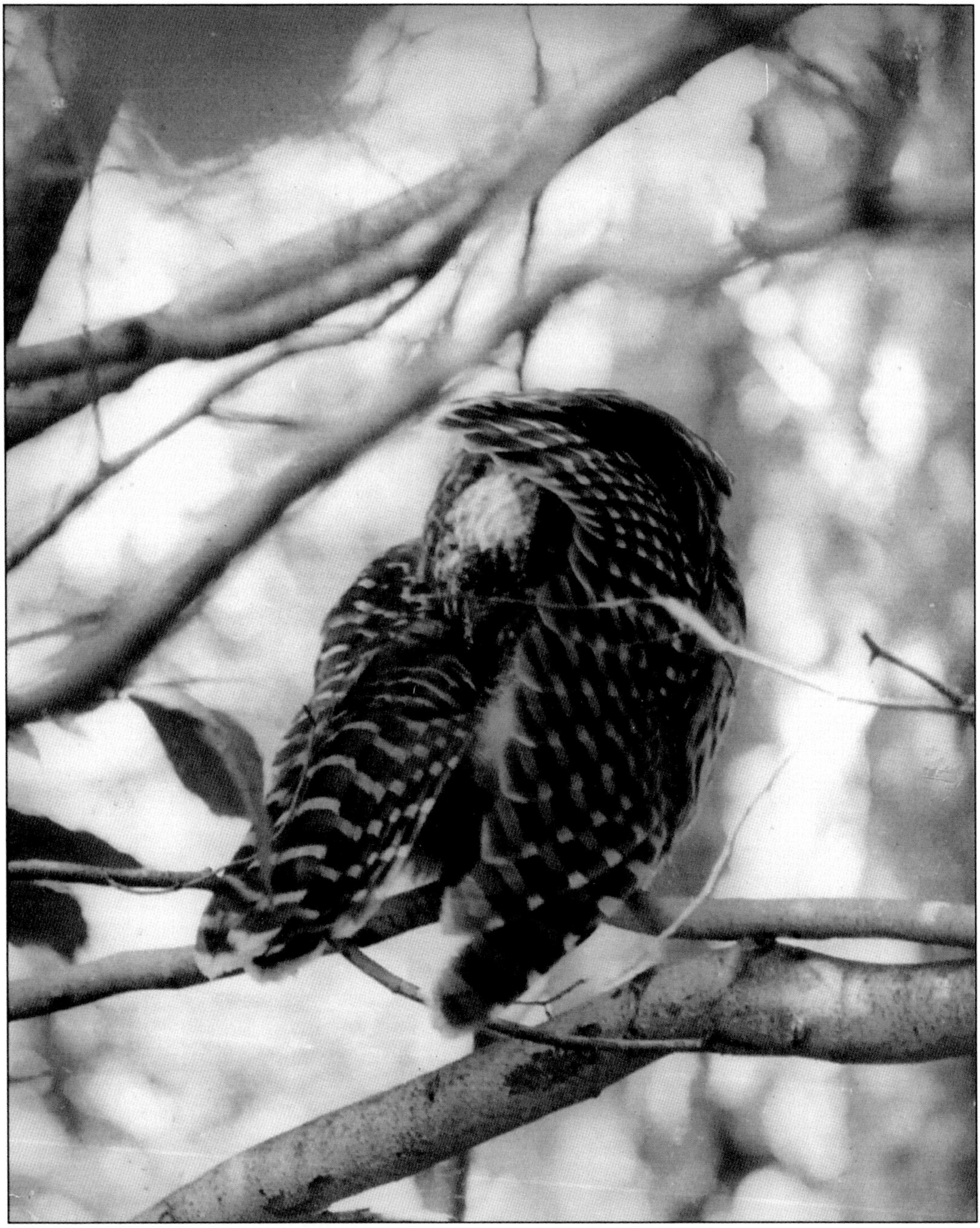

One of Richwood's annual traditions that was fortunately short-lived was the annual Varmit Killing Contest. Thank goodness it was stopped in time to allow people to enjoy creatures like the barred owl shown here. Wildlife is more plentiful in the national forest now than during the 1920s and 1930s, with a few exceptions. Waterdogs are very scarce as are native brook trout. Thanks to a very good state stocking program and organizations like Trout Unlimited, Richwood area streams have fish year-round. The best news of all is that the Cranberry River is recovering due to acid treatment stations at its head waters. (Photograph by the author.)

Richwood area streams provide great recreation to local enthusiasts as well as a growing number of out-of-county and out-of-state fishermen and women. The streams in the area are so beautiful that you cannot have a bad day fishing—even if you fail to catch fish. Pictured here is the author's father, Luther Sr., homing in on a native brook trout he spotted in the hole below the falls. (Photograph by the author.)

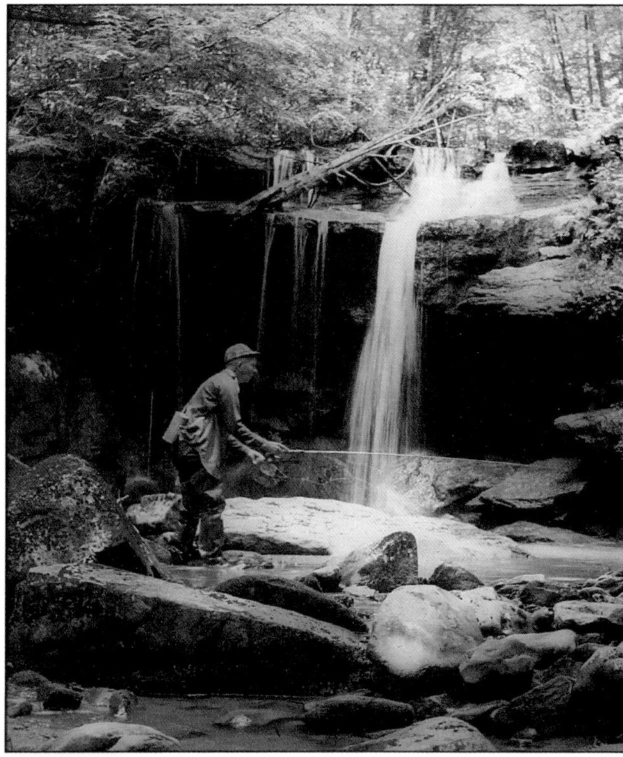

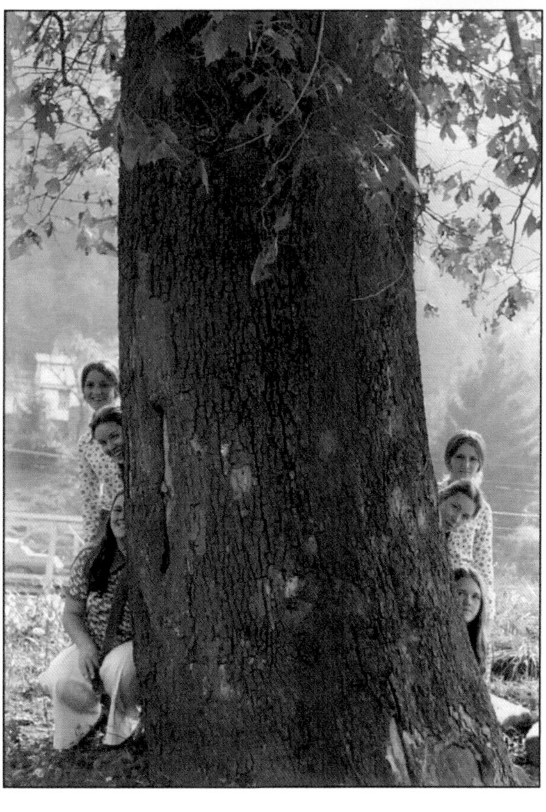

As stated earlier in the book, the national forest land in the area has regrown to the point that 25,000 acres were designated by Congress as a wilderness area. Huge trees once again populate the forest. The make-up of the forestland has been altered, however. For example, large stands of spruce no longer cover the high elevations. This big sycamore tree still stands above the river bank next to the South Side bridge near the high school. These former students are (from the top on the left) Rhonda Bayless, Cela Sawyer, and Debbie Cutright. The identity of the students on the right is unknown. (Photograph by the author.)

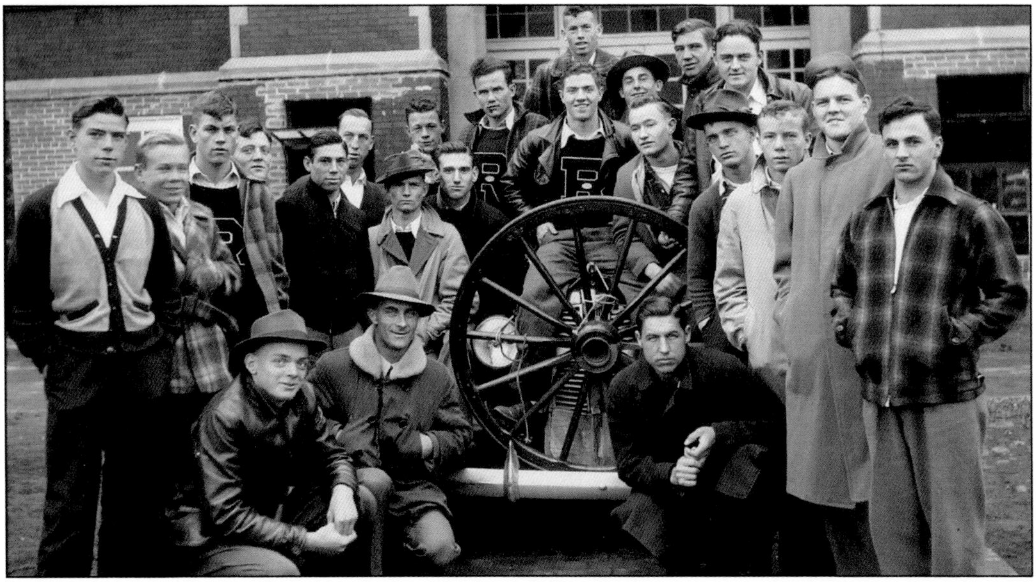

Finley Taylor's photograph above has been published many times. The Wagon Wheel was awarded to the victor in the Richwood High School versus Cowen High School annual football game. The tradition continued until Cowen High School closed its doors forever as a result of the consolidation of Cowen and Webster Springs High Schools. Starting on the left with the group standing are Wilson Crites, Eddie Prelaz, Pickle Spencer, Wendell Seabolt, Frank West, Lee Hinkle, Spike Meadows, Pete Smith, Sid Young, Frazier Humphreys, E.G. Lusk, Garmon Nichols, David McLaughlin, Ralph Newsome, David Groves, Olin Starkey, Ralph Johnson, Egg Meadows, and Tony Cerre. Up front are Keith Taylor, Ed Buck, and Beecher Hinkle.

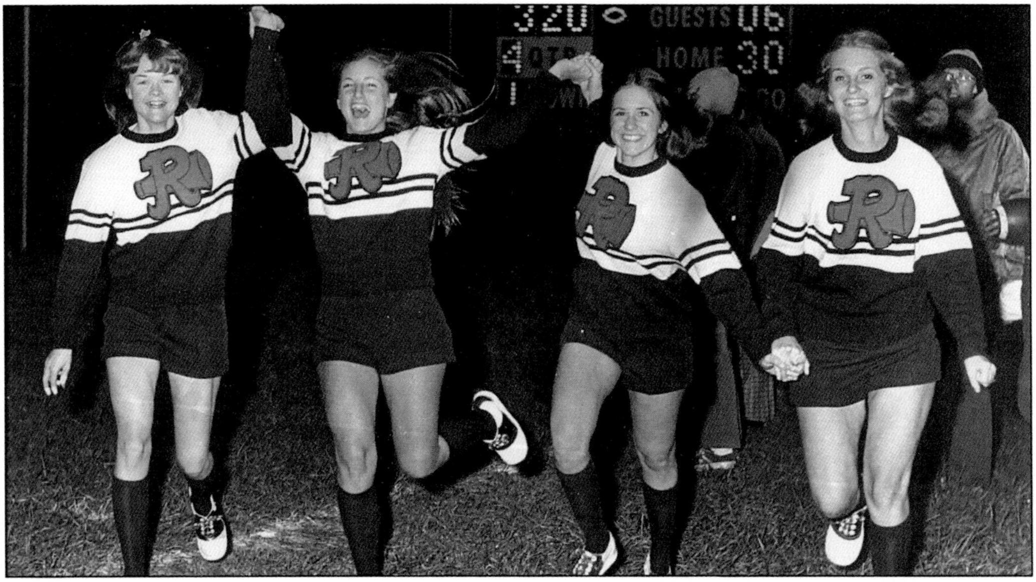


Happiness in the next generation is still found by winning football games. Pictured here are Richwood High School varsity cheerleaders after a home victory in October 1974 on Dean Memorial Field. From left to right are Diane Meadows, Tina Kirkland, Darlene Collins, and Rhonda Bayless. Diane's father Egg Meadows is in the happy group above. (Photograph by the author.)

On this page are three living connections with the past. It was an absolute delight to interview them and pull information from their amazing memories. Newman Whitman, top, was born in 1899. Newman has many connections to events presented in this book. He was a member of the jury that conducted the inquisition into the death of the young lady and young man who lost their lives at Curtin Ferry. Newman's father hosted Finly Taylor over night on some of his travels through the Canvas area. A shay engine owned by Pardee and Curtin Lumber Company caught his father's woods on fire at the farm and nearly burned down all of the fences. Newman worked on early county road construction between Nettie and Brock's Bridge. In Richwood, Newman worked at the paper mill, tannery, and on the construction of the road to Marlinton as a night watchman. He made 40¢ an hour at the tannery and on the Marlinton road project. Finally, when he returned to Richwood after working away for several years, he was admitted to the new hospital, which was the site of the tannery where he used to work. Pictured in the middle is Billy Hammonds. Billy was born in 1919 and worked in logging all of his life. He worked for several logging companies and contractors including Cherry River Boom & Lumber Company. He lived and worked for many years at the company's operation at Jerryville on Gauley River. He assisted the company doctor, Dr. Ellis Frame, in traveling to the company's patients in and around the town. When Dr. Frame left the company and set up private practice in Richwood, he often called on Billy to take him around to visit former patients. A younger Bill is pictured on page 82. Pictured on the bottom is another amazing individual. Anna Mary Woods was born in 1911 and lived in three of Cherry River Boom & Lumber Company's towns that were created as they logged in a westward direction. She lived at North Bend, eight miles above Richwood, at Dogway on Dogway Branch on the Cranberry River, and at Three Forks, at the mouth of the Middle Fork of Williams River. She said that when she lived at North Bend, the train went to town twice a day and she could travel to town every day if she wished. Ann Mary's father, James (Jimmy) Aken is pictured on pages 9 and 10.

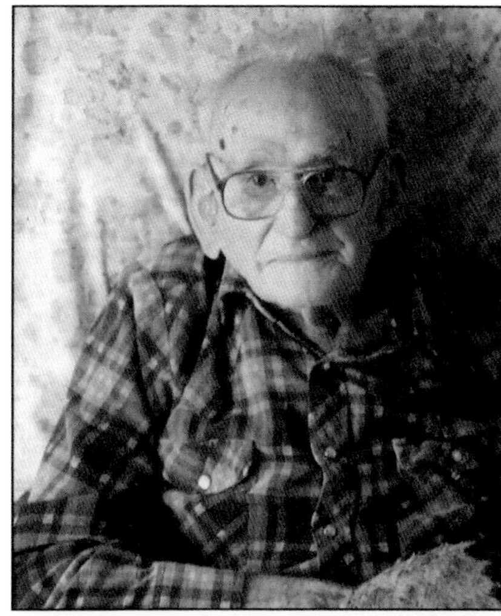

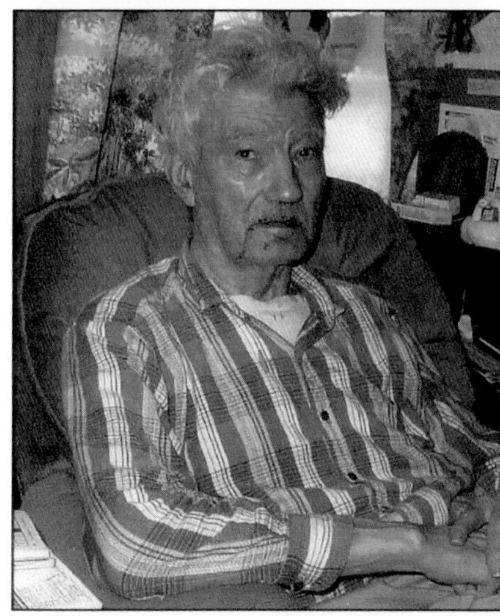

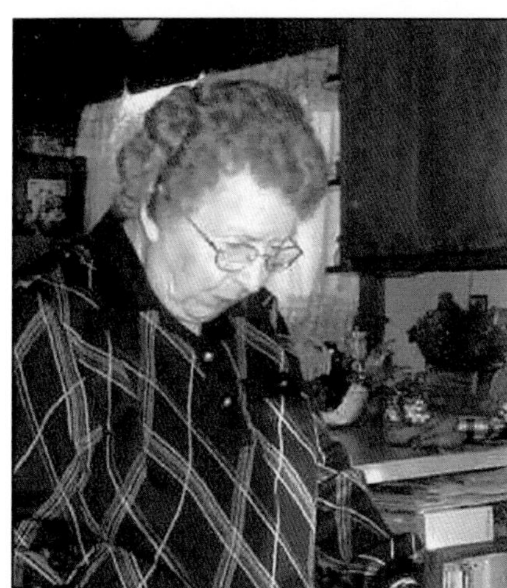

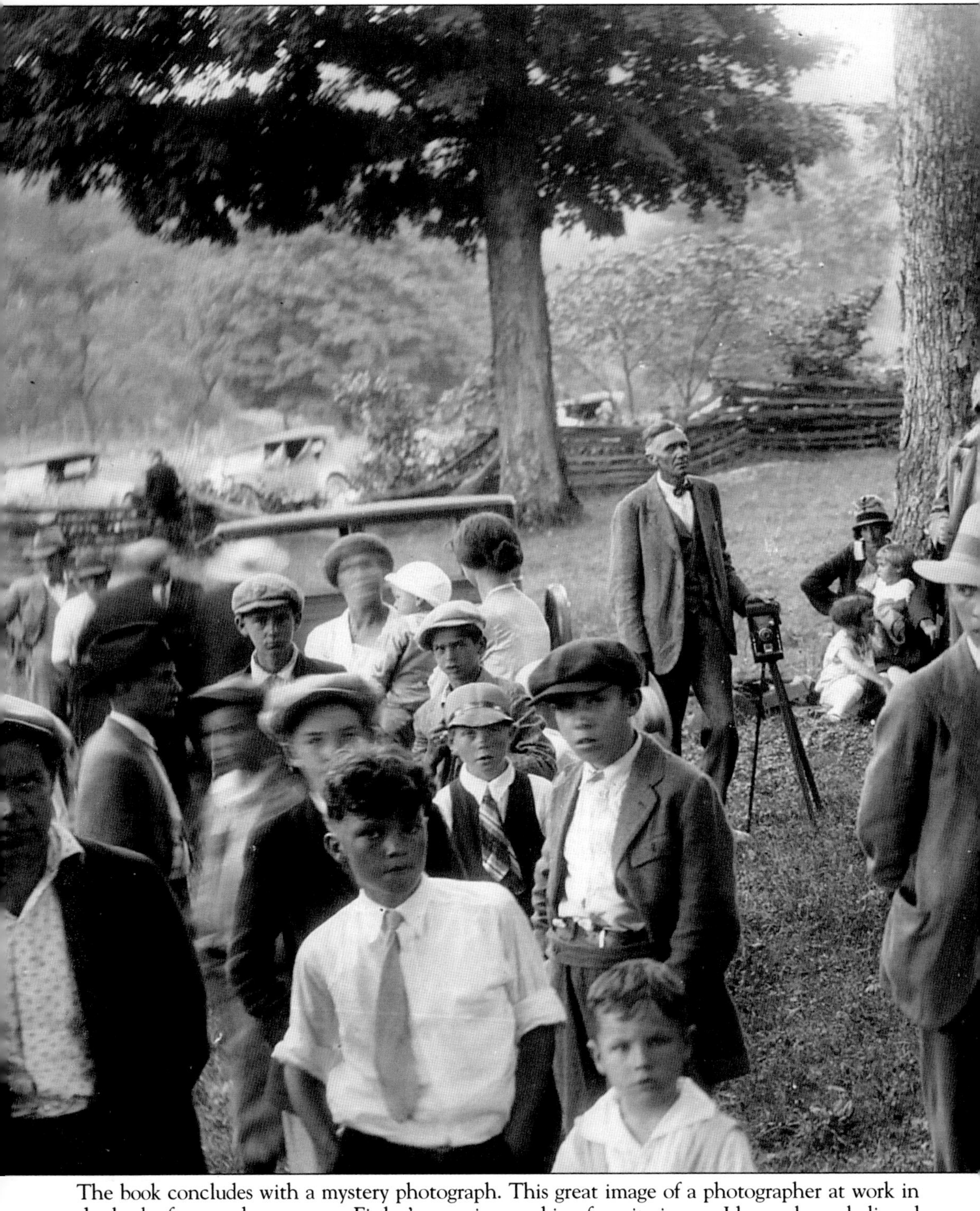

The book concludes with a mystery photograph. This great image of a photographer at work in the back of a crowd was among Finley's negatives and is a favorite image. I have always believed and hoped that the photographer was Finley himself. Newman Whitman told me that Finley had an assistant named Youdy, and it is possible that he may have taken this photograph of his

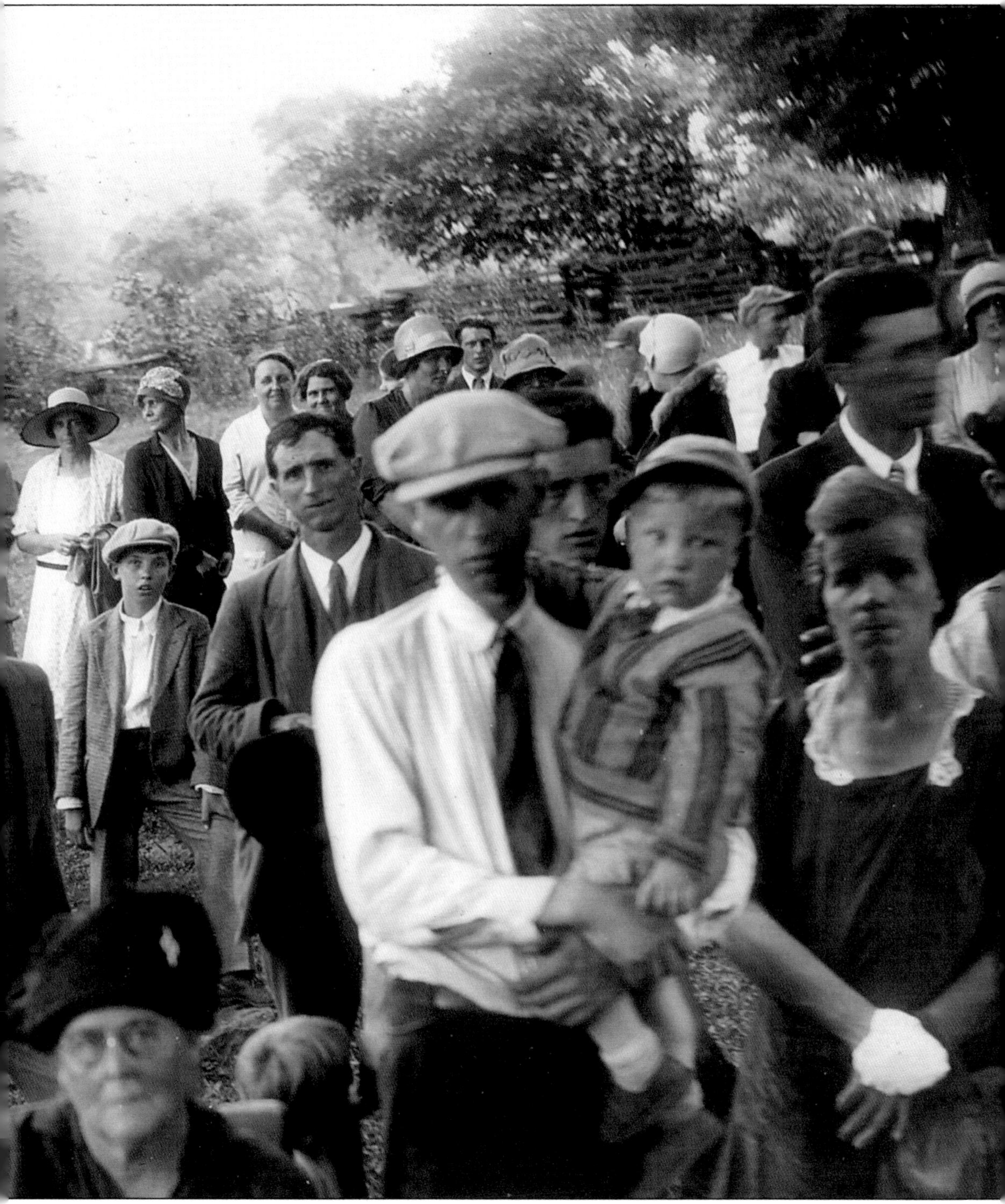

boss. The black-haired women and two young girls standing to his left could be his wife and daughters Maureen and Marie. As the image in this book makes its way out into the world, it is hopeful that someone will solve the mystery.

# ACKNOWLEDGMENTS

I will always be eternally grateful to Maureen Taylor Justice for allowing me the privilege of sharing Finley Taylor's work with the world. I will also be eternally regretful that I did not attempt to obtain information about the negatives when I first obtained them. Also, regretfully, I passed up an opportunity to meet and talk with Finley himself during my teaching years in Richwood. But I can say I worked for him. Through his daughter Maureen, I made a copy of a photograph for him which she said he pronounced as good work. The image was of the last public hanging in West Virginia.

I want to thank my daughter Amy Elizabeth Baker for her creative suggestions and for her help in proofreading the draft of the book before it went to the editor. She is a gifted writer that I expect to see write books of her own in the future. I want to thank Betty Lewis who introduced me to Arcadia Publishing and to Newman Whitman. I want to thank Newman Whitman, Billy Hammonds, Anna Mary Woods, Beecher Hinkle, Clorda Miller, and Olaf Lipscomb for allowing me to interview them. I hope they will allow me to interview them again for help in other works I have in progress.

I want to give a special thank you to Mark Romano, professional photographer of Mark Romano Studio, Summersville, West Virginia. Mark was very helpful and generous in sharing with me back-issues of local papers and pictures and memorabilia he obtained from the *News Leader* collection. He also introduced me to Anna Mary Woods and has given me the names of other contacts for future interviews.

Finally, I want to thank the staff at Richwood Public Library and the West Virginia Cultural Center Archives in Charleston for their assistance. Both facilities are to be congratulated for the quality of the resources they house and for the "user friendly" atmosphere provided for people to access these resources.